CLARRIE GRIMMETT

Ashley Mallett is a former spin bowler who played 38
Test matches for Australia from 1968 to 1980. He took
693 first class wickets at an average of 26, including 132
Test wickets, with an innings best of 8/59 versus Paki-
stan at Adelaide Oval in December, 1972. Biographer,
cricket writer, TV commentator and coach, Mallett has
worked tirelessly towards the resurgence of spin bowling in Australia. Since 1988 Mallett has run Spin Australia, a national program coaching the best and
emerging spinners throughout the country. He is recognised internationally as a coach, and conceived the first
All-Spin match ever played, in Alexandra, a black town-
ship on the outskirts of Johannesburg, South Africa.

Also by Ashley Mallett

Rowdy
Spin Out
100 Cricket Tips
Trumper, the Illustrated Biography
Master Sportsman Series

CLARRIE GRIMMETT

The Bradman of Spin

ASHLEY MALLETT

University of Queensland Press

First published 1993 by University of Queensland Press
Box 42, St Lucia, Queensland 4067 Australia

Typeset by University of Queensland Press
Printed in Australia by McPherson's Printing Group

Distributed in the USA and Canada by
International Specialized Book Services, Inc.,
5804 N.E. Hassalo Street, Portland, Oregon 97213-3640

Promotion of this title has been assisted by
the South Australian Government through
the Department for the Arts and Cultural Heritage.

Cataloguing in Publication Data
National Library of Australia

Mallett, Ashley, 1945-
  Clarrie Grimmett : the Bradman of spin.

  Includes index.

  1. Grimmett, C.V. (Clarence Victor), 1891-1980. 2. Cricket
  players — Australia — Biography. I. Title.

796.358092

ISBN 0 7022 2531 2

CONTENTS

Spin opens more batsmen's defence than pace. Learn to spin the ball. Practise 'til the ball obeys every whim of your fingers.

C.V. Grimmett

ACKNOWLEDGMENTS

The Malletts hail from Normandy. They settled in England after the "tour" of 1066. However, cricket was in the blood on my mother's side of the family.

I cherish the memory of my grandfather, Alexander Garnaut West, affectionately known as Pop. Scottish stock, although on my grandmother's side of the family there was a strong Norwegian connection, the Family Carlsson. Pop saw Trumper bat and he saw Grimmett bowl. He also introduced me to the game of cricket. Pop instilled in me a great and undying passion for the grand old game.

I am indebted to the many people who helped me with spin bowling. They included Alex Barrass, Wally Langdon, Neville Pratt, Les Favell, Jim Laker, Tony Lock, Don Bradman, Richie Benaud, Clarrie Grimmett, my mother Clarice Oline Mallett (nee West), my father Raymond Mallett and my brother Nicholas, who always batted so I could concentrate on my bowling in those inevitable backyard "Test" matches. And my eternal thanks to Bill O'Reilly, Clarrie's great bowling mate.

To my wife Christine Mallett, my best friend and partner and to my son, Benjamin Mallett, my right hand, and to all those aforementioned people, the quick and the dead, I dedicate this book.

FOREWORD

Clarence Victor Grimmett, my revered workmate, was the greatest leg-spin bowler I have ever seen — and that covers almost the full scope of leg-spin experts who have played cricket for Australia.

I met Ranji Hordern, the first Australian to master the wrong 'un, when, as a late model schoolboy, I played against I Zingari team which included the famous Hordern way back in 1923.

Arthur Mailey stayed long enough on the job to give me time to join him as a team-mate in the New South Wales Shield side in 1927, before the Education department sentenced me to three years' ostracism, far from the influence of first-class cricket.

That was long enough for me to make up my mind. I had seen Clarrie play for Victoria at Goulburn, my southern highlands schoolboy home, in 1919 when the Victorian side was returning from its first Sydney fixture after World War I, and I had seen him perform in the fifth Test against England in Sydney in 1924. From that spectacular entry he made to Test cricket he became my personal model.

His attitude towards the job of dismissing batting opposition was inspiring to watch. He embraced his job in a dedicated manner which would surely have suggested to trade union officials that the boss had him working on a piecework incentive system, and that he was therefore a man to be watched carefully.

Clarrie never had time to waste. He'd be halfway through an over in the time it takes some modern-day "quickies" to reach their marks down in the grey-blue distance. He sized a batsman up in a few deliveries, and concentrated on bowling straight at the stumps and landing the ball in the chosen awkward spot which demanded expert use of batting feet. He never resorted to "loop", as onlookers call it, but he was an expert in the overt change of pace, which was the very backbone of his undisputed claim to have been the greatest of his tribe.

"Grum" was an ideal team-mate. His motto was always "least said, soonest mended". Yet if something had to be said, he'd come out with it, looking you straight in the eyes as he did so. That sterling quality of his got him into serious trouble with selection committees late in his career. I was heartbroken when he was passed over for the 1938 tour of England and I had ample cause to regret his absence throughout the full course of that difficult campaign. I have always placed that dereliction of selection responsibilities on a par with the omission of Keith Miller from the team for South Africa in 1949.

Those misdemeanours will ultimately be forgotten if never forgiven, but we can all be quite certain that Clarrie Grimmett's amazing ability with the ball will live on as long as the game cricket is worth playing.

I'm delighted that the literary task of paying tribute to my grand old mate has fallen into the capable hands of Ashley Mallett, who himself won fame as one of the most talented Test off-spinners and who is therefore fully armed to handle the job knowledgeably, responsibly and with all the charm his subject deserves.

Bill O'Reilly
Blakehurst, NSW

PREFACE

Clarrie Grimmett's philosophy on the art of spin was simple: bowl until "the ball obeys every whim of your fingers". As Grimmett's story unfolds readers will gain an appreciation of Grimmett's extraordinary persistence and unfailing faith in his ability.

The little New Zealander moved to Sydney in 1914, then spent seven years in Melbourne, where he spun grandly for South Melbourne, and later Prahran. However there he suffered from the whims of the Victorian State selectors.

His habit of wearing a cap when bowling was taken as a sure sign that he was hiding his true age; a balding cricketer simply had to be an old cricketer.

Those who did not know Grimmett, but knew of him, thought it odd that this little man spent all of his leisure hours bowling leg-breaks, Boseys and top-spinners to an empty net in his Prahran yard, his only company a small black and white fox terrier called Joe who faithfully brought the balls back to his master's bowling mark.

Grimmett played only a few matches for Victoria in his years there. It was not until the last match of the 1923-24 season that Grimmett won his first Sheffield Shield cap. He took 1/12 and 8/86 for Victoria against South Australia at Adelaide Oval. Old hands Clem Hill and Vic Richardson learned from that Grimmett performance to believe what they had heard about the little leg-breaker; he was simply the best in the business.

Already moves had been made by the Adelaide club to secure his services. The Victorian selectors shrugged off the past and welcomed Grimmett back to Melbourne a hero, but the little man had already decided to make one final move to realise his dream to play Test cricket.

He chose to move to Adelaide, which Johnny Moyes described in his book *A Century of Cricketers* as "the haven for unwanted bowlers and the staging post on the road to England". I read Moyes' epic at the age of ten. The pages are filled with the heroes of yesteryear, including then budding champs such as Neil Harvey and Richie Benaud. A decade later and I too could identify with this "haven for unwanted bowlers".

In 1967 I travelled from Perth to Adelaide to see Grimmett at his Adelaide home. There was a faint chance I might stay in South Australia, but my main target was Grimmett: I wanted to see the coach, learn all I could and go home. On his backyard pitch Grimmett played two of my spinning deliveries. Each one met the middle of his Jack Hobbs' bat. The seventy-six-year-old spin wizard called out: "Give up bowling and become a batsman!"

He was a straight-shooter who didn't hold back. He was dead right, but he cushioned the blow by offering some hope. Grimmett explained my bowling was predictable and it was vitally important to trick the batsman in the air, with deliveries which followed a flight path just above the level of the batsman's eyes. Spinning hard was one thing, change of pace another, good rhythm another; yet all three combined to make the slow man a force in the game.

Clarrie had some bizarre ideas about batting, claiming that he taught the young Don Bradman how to play the late cut on the ship sailing to England in 1930, adding "The Don was a fast learner!" Yet his advice on spin was usually spot on.

Talking to Grimmett about bowling was very different to reading his books. His writing didn't explain his spinning strategy. However, anyone fortunate enough to talk to him could learn a great deal. He was forthright, willing, honest and relished the chance to talk spin.

Early in 1991 I decided to write the Grimmett biography, although I realised that a lot of young people might not identify with a cricketer who played long before their fathers took up the game. The year 1991 was significant, for 25 December was the centenary of Grimmett's birth. Grimmett played first-class cricket from 1911 until 1941, so even his playing era was lost to the new age. Something was needed to fuse the Grimmett skill to the modern era. This book is my way of providing that vital link.

Bill O'Reilly, who wrote the foreword, cherished Clarrie Grimmett, his "revered workmate". The Tiger's foreword was one of the last of his writings. It arrived written on lined airmail paper, the words flowing like a Bradman drive.

From my arrival in Adelaide in 1967 to play for South Australia and Australia, until Grimmett died in May 1980, we had many meetings. As this book neared completion, Bill O'Reilly died; Len Darling had died a month earlier. Both were teammates. I owe eternal thanks to both men.

I also owe a debt to the South Australian Cricket Association's David Johnston, former South Australian player Cec Starr, and the SACA medical officer and ex-State squad fast bowler Dr Donald Beard, who once was trapped lbw by a Grimmett topspinner which Clarrie told the Doc was "half as slow through the air and twice as fast off the pitch".

Clarrie was a veritable bowerbird; he kept everything. He kept all the letters written to him over the years by a *Wisden Cricketers' Almanack* of players such as Pelham Warner, Lord Hawke, Don Bradman, Frank Woolley, Wally Hammond, Bill O'Reilly, Jack Fingleton, Bill Bowes, Warwick Armstrong and Herbie Collins. There are even a few letters I wrote to him many years ago, newspaper cuttings, articles, books and tour pamphlets.

Clarrie's son, Vic, a professional photographer in Adelaide, and I waded through old negatives to find a good collection of pictures. Vic gave me access to all of his father's old papers, archival movie footage, newspaper cuttings and personal papers.

There's a letter from Herbert H. Fishwick, the *Sydney Mail* photographer who captured Clarrie's first Test wicket, when he clean bowled England left-hander Frank Woolley at the Sydney Cricket Ground in 1925. The photograph was enlarged, displayed in Kodak's windows in Adelaide, then presented to Clarrie as a memento. The original photograph still hangs on the study wall of Vic Grimmett's Adelaide home.

Among Grimmett's possessions are many sketches and paintings, done with the same hand that spun despair into the hearts of batsmen the world over. He sketched many of Adelaide's old buildings, with meticulous attention to detail. There are line drawings, pencil and charcoal sketches of pretty young women and there are the Grimmett oils, an enduring testimony to the little master's art. Grimmett at the wicket was universally known and acknowledged: Grimmett at the canvas was a well-hidden secret. Clarrie revelled in mystery.

During the writing of this biography I referred to books such as Moyes' *Century of Cricketers* (Angus & Robertson, 1949); Sir Pelham Warner's *Book of Cricket* (Sporting Handbooks Ltd, 1947); Jack Pollard's *Six and Out* (Pollard Publishing Company, 1971) and *Australian Cricket: The Game and the Players* (Hodder and Stoughton, 1982); Chris Harte's *The History of the Sheffield Shield* (Allen and Unwin, 1987) and his *History of the South Australian Cricket Association* (Sports Marketing, 1990); *Who's Who of Cricketers*, by Philip Bailey, Philip Thorn and Peter Wynne-Thomas (Newnes Books in association with the Association of Cricket Statisticians, 1984); *Bradman, the Illustrated Biography* by Michael Page (Macmillan, 1983); *The Game's The Thing* by M.A. Noble (Cassell and Company Ltd, 1926); *Adelaide Oval: Test Cricket 1884-1984*, by Bernard Whimpress and Nigel Hart (Wakefield Press and the SACA, 1984); *The Book of Cricket* by Denzil Batchelor (Collins, 1952); David Frith's *The Golden Age of Cricket 1890-1914* (Omega Books, 1978) and *The Slow Men* (Horwitz Grahame, 1984); *Tiger* by Bill O'Reilly (Collins, 1985); *An Illustrated History of Australian Cricket* by R.S. Whitington (Lansdowne Press, 1972); *The Phoenix History of Cricket* by Roy Webber (Phoenix Sports Books, 1960); *The Joy of Cricket* selected and edited by John Bright-Holmes (Secker and Warburg, 1984), various *Wisden Cricketers' Almanacks* and *The Wisden Book of Test Cricket, 1876-77 to 1977-78* by Bill Trindall (Macdonald and Jane's, London, 1979).

I received considerable help from Adelaide-based statistician Geoff Sando. I am grateful to Richie Benaud for his account of the first time he saw Grimmett bowl at the SCG in 1940, to Ian Chappell for a slice of the Grimmett humour passed down by his grandfather Vic Richardson and for his own recollections of

Clarrie explaining to him the pitfalls of running between wickets, to Sir Donald Bradman for his letter describing how he saw Grimmett the bowler, to Lindsay Hassett and Keith Miller; I thank them all.

Clarrie was a mystery this book may partially uncover. He was called a host of nicknames from Scarlet, to Grum, to the Gnome; yet he was universally known as the Fox.

There could be no worthier cricketing subject than Clarence Victor Grimmett.

1 GRIMMETT BOWLING TODAY

Little Clarrie Grimmett loved to trick people; he specialised in tricking batsmen. Grimmett spun more mystery into a cricket ball than any other man. If there was no mystery, Grimmett would say there was — ever plotting different ways to bemuse and defeat his opponents.

Grimmett was a leg-spinner, a master of deceit, fully armed with bowling tricks. He defeated some of the greatest batsmen to draw breath, and he could make the most fleet-footed of them appear to be wearing boots of lead when attempting to drive him.

Imagine a ball spun so hard that it hums, dipping away in a lovely curve with the trajectory of an archer's arrow. Don Bradman pounces with cat-like reflexes, his feet moving swiftly yet with silky smoothness, to reach the ball as it strikes the turf. Bradman hammers the ball to the cover fence. But the game has only just begun. Grimmett's face shows no emotion. It takes the Wicket Fox an hour. He has patience. Again the spinning Grimmett delivery dips in that lovely curve, but this time with a slight, almost imperceptible, change in pace. The onlooker is fooled. So is Bradman. Although his footwork is swift and sure, the ball drops short of where the Don expects. Too far into his stroke to check it, his lofted drive is caught at cover point. The Wicket Fox wins.

Known as the sly old Fox of cricket, Clarence Victor Grimmett spun his way into the game's folklore with his incomparable ability to control the leg-break. His career spanned thirty years, from 1911 to 1940; during that time he collected 1424 wickets in 248 first-class matches, bagging 5 wickets or more in an innings no less than 127 times. He played first-class cricket for Wellington, New Zealand, Victoria, Western Australia, South Australia and, of course, Australia.

Grimmett was special. His name will live forever in cricket history. Conversations with great cricketers such as Don Bradman, Keith Miller, Bill O'Reilly, Les Hutton and Frank Woolley confirmed that Grimmett's bowling was magnificent; his accuracy uncanny. Sadly, as Grimmett played his last big match more than fifty years ago, there are many today who have never seen this genius of spin bowl.

In every era cricketers tend to think the players of their day are the best of all time. For instance, was Trumper a better bat than Bradman? Statistics weigh so heavily in favour of Bradman that the question appears an absurdity, yet there is a doubt. Grimmett bowled only a few balls to Trumper, but the great stylist of the Golden Age of Cricket (1890–1914) was his boyhood hero. Trumper made a lasting impression upon Grimmett; he would always argue for Trumper ahead of Bradman.

Those who argue for Trumper, whose Test average of 39.04 in 48 matches pales into relative insignificance against Bradman's average of 99.94 in 52 matches, speak of Trumper's grace and style as being superior to Bradman's ruthlessness and efficiency. Few, however, dispute who was the greatest slow leg-breaker of them all; it was Clarrie Grimmett.

Bradman and Grimmett were alike in that they believed in results and were relentless in their pursuit of success. Grimmett, the Fox, was the veritable Bradman of spin.

Grimmett schemed incessantly, searching for the mystery delivery which would help to confound his opponents further. He was known by a variety of names including "Grum", the name Bill O'Reilly always used for him (dealt with thoroughly in the chapter "The Tiger and The Fox"), "Scarlet" (after the Scarlet Pimpernel), and "the Gnome", the latter perhaps a reference to Clarrie's slight stature and sharp features.

Whatever the nickname of the season, he was universally known as the Fox; batsmen were his prey. Grimmett loved to hear a team-mate such as Len Darling or Jack Fingleton sidle up to him after a Grimmett top-spinner had skipped off the pitch to trap an unwary batsman lbw with, "Why Grum, you sly old Fox, he thought it was your leg-break". Clarrie would hug himself with convulsive delight. The greater the batsman, the better he bowled.

To bring the genius of Grimmett to life for the modern reader, I have indulged in a brief interlude of fantasy.

Imagine Clarrie Grimmett bowling today, against the cream of Australia's modern batsmen. The scene is Adelaide Oval, the venue where Grimmett spun his magic for sixteen years.

* * *

He was there, in front of the crowd, then suddenly he was gone; he simply melted into the people around him. There was always mystery about this tiny genius of spin. Clarrie had surreptitiously slipped into the ground, silently merging with the sea of faces in and about the members' stand. He was changed, ready for battle before his captain walked into the dressingroom.

Allan Border's men were about to take on a Rest of Australia XI, led by Ian Chappell. Clarrie wore his trusty thick faded red woollen singlet under his shirt, the garment which kept him away from the chill zone. He had prepared himself well, ensuring the studs in his boots were secure and the right length, that his toenails were trimmed and his socks clean and well-fitting. He was sitting and sipping tea when in breezed the captain.

"Vic [Richardson, Chappell's grandfather and Clarrie's South Australian captain for a decade from the 1924–25 summer] tells me you are a good captain," Clarrie said, his face beaming as he stood to shake Chappell's hand.

"Still bowling those straight breaks, Clarrie?"

"You'll see soon enough. They'll come to you at first slip. I hope you can catch!"

Advance publicity had been immense. Grimmett's appearance would surely test Border's men. For years they had dined lavishly on well-done medium pace. There was not a spinner in the land who could command the sort of accuracy the Fox attained in his first-class career.

Chappell and the Fox discussed, at length, the field placing Clarrie wanted for each of Border's men. Clarrie liked to have a man deep at mid-on and sometimes two out.

"I don't rely on breadth of turn. That might beat the ordinary players, but to get good men out you need to flight the ball. Flight is

the answer," Clarrie insisted. "And a spin bowler cannot flight the ball properly without a man or two in the deep." He roughed out a field placing for Dean Jones on a bit of paper, then said firmly:

"I want my point right on square, cutting off the single. Don't have him deep. They won't cut me."

"Two short covers for Geoff Marsh?"

"He's very much a bottom-hand player, Ian. He won't get one single ball from me to cut, but I might get him to attempt to drive…"

Chappell found the little leg-spinning legend possessed incredible confidence.

Imagine all the people. They were swarming into the ground, eager to witness this modern miracle — Grimmett once again bowling at Adelaide Oval. Border won the toss and decided to bat on the typically good Adelaide Oval wicket. The crowd didn't have to wait long for some excitement, although Geoff Marsh disagreed. He was struck on the chin, a nasty blow, and was forced to leave the field for attention. David Boon waddled to the crease and Grimmett, at cover, ran his tongue over his top lip. He couldn't wait to have a crack at Boon.

All eyes were on the little man at cover. He flexed his gnarled spinning digits, interlocked his fingers, then stretched hard; hold, release; hold, release. The exercise, a routine he used all his bowling life, was repeated between deliveries. He rolled his arm over in the hope that it caught the skipper's eye. Chappell was aware; so too was the prying eye of television. In the good old days cricketers played without this intrusion. Television heightens a player's tension, if he allows it to worry him. Clarrie Grimmett's philosophy did not allow such outside influences to become a factor.

Suddenly the animated crowd grew strangely silent; a hush fell over the ground like a cloak. Grimmett was about to bowl his first ball.

The old men in the crowd found themselves smiling. They knew that if the Fox bowled at his best he would sweep through Border's batting line-up.

Those too young to have seen Grimmett bowl and those unfamiliar with the man and his deeds sat in fascination. What could this tiny slip of a man accomplish against Mark Taylor and David Boon? Clarrie bowled first to Taylor, the solid left-hander.

In his first Test match, Clarrie came up against the great Kent left-hander, Frank Woolley. Woolley had been expecting a wrong 'un early on, but Clarrie never served up what was expected. He always kept batsmen guessing. As with Don Bradman, Clarrie Grimmett was the man for the big occasion. The better the opposition, the better he bowled. The Fox loved the heat of battle. This was his two hundred and forty-ninth first-class match.

He dearly wanted a bag of five wickets (or more!) not merely to add to his impressive career figures, but also to prove to the moderns that he was a genius with the ball in any company and at any time.

Confident that he would land the ball exactly where he wanted, Grimmett moved in. He wore his 1930 green baggy cap for sentimental reasons. Luck played no part. (The Fox reckoned if he bowled well enough for long enough luck would take care of itself.)

He swung into action. Just a few paces to the crease. On the upswing of his bowling arm his left hand met his right, perhaps to steady it, but more likely to help conceal his grip. His arm came through fairly low, although by no means round arm.

Grimmett crouched; this made it appear that his arm was lower than it actually was, yet he had a vigorous follow through. The ball pitched a few centimetres outside the line of off-stump. Taylor pushed well forward and smothered the spin.

Chappell had mentioned Taylor's penchant to sweep, but Clarrie insisted he knew an easier and less costly way to send Taylor packing.

"Mark [Taylor] is a good, solid player. He reminds me of Maurice Leyland, compact and able to hit anything loose," Clarrie said. "However, when he comes forward there is a chance to open up a gap between bat and pad. That's what I hope to do. It worked with Woolley at the SCG in '25."

The skipper roared.

Grimmett was confident he could swerve the ball away from Taylor, thus creating a gap between bat and pad, given that Taylor's front foot came straight down the pitch, as it did that first ball. Clarrie's eyes never left his intended victim. He walked backwards to his mark, watching and scheming. Another perfectly pitched leg-break and Taylor played forward, his bat and pad again working in close harmony. Clarrie noticed a slight gap between bat and pad, but not wide enough to allow the passage of a cricket ball. It was a hot Adelaide day; mid-February. The searing heat hardly worried sad-faced Grimmett. Under that old peaked cap, Grimmett's eyes were shaded. He regarded wearing a cap when bowling to be as essential to his craft as a lens cap is to the camera. Grimmett reckoned his cap helped "regulate" the size of his pupils and was vital to his success.

(Throughout his fabulous career Clarrie endured constant barbs over the wearing of his cap when bowling. Clarrie's receding hairline provided most of the ammunition: it was claimed he was hiding his near-baldness, in case it gave the selectors the excuse they wanted to drop the man many thought to be older than he, in fact, admitted. Grimmett always rejected such claims.)

Greg Matthews warmed up at extra cover. Chappell indicated that Matthews would bowl the next over.

Ball three of Grimmett's over and Taylor moved forward again, turning the ball with the spin on the on-side. Michael Bevan, a champion in the making, fielded at a straightish mid-wicket. Clarrie waved to Chappell at slip; just a little wave to catch the skipper's attention: it meant "Watch this one!"

Grimmett came in. Any jerkiness in the approach was forgotten as his arm swung over; pure rhythm, the arm, wrist and finger working in perfect harmony with the brain.

Chappell, at first slip, watched the flight of the ball all the way. It appeared to have exactly the same pace as the previous ball, but as Taylor moved forward to meet it, the ball suddenly swerved away. The away swing was late and alarming.

Remember, this is fantasy, but it is just how Grimmett in top form could bowl, anywhere at any time in an innings.

The ball whipped off the pitch, through the "gate", and crashed into Taylor's middle and off-stumps. The Fox had struck. Players rushed to Grimmett's side, but the tiny man raised his right arm in mock protest; he wanted nothing to do with back slapping or hugging. Any fiendish delight he felt was reflected in his sparkling blue eyes. (Perhaps a glance into those blue eyes would have shown a Rumpelstiltskin-like figure dancing a little jig about the flames of ambition.)

Bill O'Reilly, the great bowler who partnered Grimmett in many successful Test campaigns, had told Clarrie before the match began, "I'd give my right arm to get a crack at [Dean] Jones." A gifted strokemaker, Dean Jones had never come up against Grimmett's nagging accuracy and bowling strategy. Clarrie had noticed, in watching Jones at the nets, that the tall Victorian often committed himself too early against the spinner; he was a batsman who telegraphed his intentions.

Then Allan Border strode to the crease. Like Taylor, Border liked to sweep and often hit the ball in the air, but Grimmett didn't want a man in the deep on the leg-side. He reckoned he could work on Border in much the same manner as he had attacked Taylor. Late swerve would test these players. Border survived the final two deliveries. Both pitched on a good length outside off spinning in. Grimmett gave Border no respite. A wicket maiden and Grimmett moved to his spot at cover.

Wearing his cap, Matthews discussed his field with Chappell, then proceeded to bowl, a modern folk hero bowling in tandem with a legend. The Fox watched the entire over, which cost Matthews four runs (a short ball outside off-stump which Boon cut to the fence), before offering some advice.

"Your action is fine and your follow through is good, but you must bowl to a plan. I get the feeling that you are bowling mechanically, with no particular strategy. Bring Boon forward driving to mid-off for three or four balls, then change your pace, a slower one. It might deceive him in flight and the spin will take the ball to the onside of the wicket. Maybe a catch to short mid-wicket."

"I'd rather bowl to Border. Can you give him a single?" Matthews asked.

"Who do you think I am, Arthur Mailey? I've never been in the habit of giving runs away. I won't give Border the hint of chance, let alone a run. This is war, my boy!"

Grimmett preferred to bowl at Boon, his leg-breaks spinning away from the right-hander, but he reasoned that Boon would wait, and left-hander Border was a better challenge. It took Grimmett three balls to get Border; it was all too easy. Border left a huge gap between bat and pad to the Grimmett swerving leg-break. It moved away late, spun back and hit the off-stump.

There was urgency in Dean Jones' stride as he hurried to the crease. Clarrie had two men stationed at short cover; one about six paces to Clarrie's left, another five or six paces further away to that fieldsman's left.

Between these two fieldsmen and fairly deep a man was set to cut off any ball hit too hard for either of the short covers to intercept.

There was no fieldsman at mid-off straight. Jones reckoned that here was the chance to use his feet, get to the pitch of the ball and belt

Grimmett straight down the ground for four. In theory Jones was correct. Grimmett moved in, with his rhythmic little jaunt, the left hand covering the right until up and over it went, the ball humming in the air as it curved its way down the track towards the confident Jones. Jones started towards the ball, but again the curve perplexed him, and he found he almost overran the delivery. Jones slammed his bat down hard and the ball cannoned into his pads, then spun madly on the track. Not even "Roadrunner" Jones could turn the mishit into a quick single.

The over ended; Clarrie was calling the tune. Jones was a nervous starter, but today he was hungry for a good score. Another couple of overs were played; Matthews bowled a maiden, then Grimmett tied the eager Jones down. There seemed to be no gaps. For the first time in his life Jones was confronted with a leg-spinner who simply did not bowl a bad ball. It was daunting.

Jones thought Grimmett planned to have him caught at one of the two short covers. He noted a fair gap between mid-on and mid-wicket. If Grimmett strayed onto the line of the pads he would hit him through the on-side, fairly straight. Another tight Matthews over ended, with the last ball beating Boon in flight. The ball spun, catching a thick inside edge; luckily for Boon it scuttled away for two runs forward of square. That Matthews delivery brought applause from the tiny man at cover.

Before the start of his next over, Grimmett joined two members of the team at the wicket. Darren Lehmann, the talented Victorian left-hand bat, and Michael Bevan (New South Wales) listened intently.

"I'll get him [Jones] with the third ball of my third over, from right now," Grimmett said. Lehmann and Bevan stared in disbelief. Clarrie gave each player instructions. Bevan was fielding at mid-on, Lehmann at mid-wicket.

After each of Grimmett's deliveries they were to move slightly to their right. "Now the idea is for Jones to keep hitting me on the on-side. Gradually I will bowl further and further towards his pads and his strokes will be more and more against the leg-spin. He will find himself having to drive progressively wider and wider. If you two move gradually to your right, he [Jones] might not wake to the ploy. Let's see…"

Bevan and Lehmann found themselves grinning at each other. They admired the Fox's obvious genius with the ball, but this plan stretched strategy to the point of madness.

Jones scored a couple of twos the next over or two, but many of his power-laden strokes were cut off. Dean Jones had taken the bait, but would he be hooked? Tension was high for that inner circle when Grimmett began the critical third over. Max Walker told an enraptured television audience: "Jones has begun to get the old Fox's measure. He's starting to stray onto Jones' legs and that can be fatal."

The gap between Bevan and Lehmann had not changed at all, but their positioning in relation to the pitch had widened greatly. The trap was set. Grimmett's first two deliveries were not far enough to the leg-side for Jones to drive for any runs, but he hit them firmly, straight to Bevan at mid-on. Good shots for none, every time. Bevan eyed Lehmann. They smiled. Here it came; the fatal ball.

Grimmett looked innocence itself. He came in to bowl with that familiar hop, skip and over. A no-ball would be a dampener, but then he had never bowled a no-ball. His third ball appeared the same as the others. Bevan detected it as moving slightly slower in the air but it looked as though it would pitch about middle and leg. Jones was of the same opinion. He reckoned it was fair game and dived down the track to drive. This ball, however, was the famous Grimmett swerver. It literally took off in flight, swinging late towards and outside leg-stump. Before pitching it had beaten Jones completely.

He was stranded and looked back as the keeper, Tasmanian Mark Aitkinson, whipped off the bails. It was a case of being stumped round his legs. The Fox's extraordinary plan worked perfectly.

Lehmann nodded knowingly in the direction of Bevan and the pair burst into laughter. They knew what their skipper didn't see. Chappell figured Clarrie "saw Jones on the move". Few bowlers could have put such a plan into action, let alone have executed it perfectly.

The same plan had worked against the great Englishman Wally Hammond in the second innings of the first Test at Nottingham in 1934.

"Not all my plans work," Clarrie laughed. "But even a bad plan is better than no plan. There is no need to watch the television replay when a plan works, for you have already seen it happen in your mind's eye."

Cricket, spin bowling in particular, was Clarrie's life…

2 THE BOY GRIMMETT

The Grimmett family hail from Faringdon, England. Clarrie's great-grandfather, Thomas Grimmett, owned a quarry. He was a mason and worked the stone, ideal for building, which abounded near Burford, Oxfordshire. Stone for St Paul's Cathedral came from that area. Clarrie's grandfather, Richard Grimmett, was born at Burford, which is about fifteen kilometres north of Faringdon, on 16 November 1839, while Clarrie's grandmother, Charlotte Rachel Grimmett (nee Hunt), known as "CR", was born on 15 June, 1835. Clarrie's father, Richard James (Dick) Grimmett was born on 4 April, 1867. Richard and his six brothers, Jack, Ezra, William, Thomas, Ernest and Rowland, were all born in Coxwell Street, Faringdon. (Two more children, Fred and Lily, swelled numbers later in New Zealand.)

Richard and CR, decided to make a new life in Dunedin, New Zealand. The "assisted passage" scheme provided them with the incentive to leave their native England. It was to cost them not one penny. Had they been forced to pay, the entire Grimmett family could have sailed for a fare of seventy-two pounds ten shillings. At that time, the Grimmetts' eldest child, Jack, was 11, Ezra, 9, William, 8, Dick, 6, Thomas, 5, Ernest, 2 and Rowland, 4 months. The assisted passage scheme had come into being in 1870. The Grimmetts were not the sort to look a gift horse in the mouth, and they arranged to depart in 1873.

On Christmas Eve the Grimmett family boarded the *Scimitar*, which flew the house flag of the New Zealand Shipping Company. She carried a company of 357 passengers and crew. The *Scimitar* was a sturdy craft and well-handled, but the voyage was a gruelling one. There were outbreaks of diseases, including scarlet fever and measles; twenty-six people died. On the other side of the scale, there were four recorded births, two baptisms and one marriage during the voyage; all in sixty-seven days from land to land, plus another three to the final berth in Dunedin.

The *Scimitar* made twenty-five voyages to New Zealand, most of them under the name of *Rangitchi*. She was rigged as a barque and later became a hulk in Noumea. During World War I when Clarrie Grimmett was making his name in Sydney grade cricket, the vessel was brought to Sydney. During a gale she broke her tow and was adrift for forty hours, later returning to Noumea and a lasting anonymity.

Grandfather Richard Grimmett was a kind and gentle man. He toiled long and hard at his building trade. The church was his great spiritual comfort and his only interest outside his family. Although quiet and unobtrusive, Richard was a lay preacher. He was slight and fair, with sparkling blue eyes. Charlotte (CR) was small and nuggety. She was decidedly tight-fisted and mean. No wonder Clarrie was miserly with the ball, never giving anything away.

All the boys attended Caversham School, Dunedin, except Jack, and Fred; the latter died when he was six years old. Most of the boys followed their father into the family business of building. Their contracting business operated throughout Otago and the name of Grimmett was prominent in the area. They built the Hampden Catholic Church in 1895, which was a curious departure from their usual line of business, given their later attitude towards Catholicism. It was during 1874 that the Grimmetts joined forces with the Salvation Army — a break-away movement from the Methodist church. Both Richard and CR were devoted to the Salvation Army. They spent every available moment attending meetings, the benevolent institute and charities.

CR sold copies of the famous Salvation Army magazine, the *War Cry*, and she wore her army uniform every day after her husband died in 1906. Charlotte Grimmett was to suffer a stroke in a Dunedin street while selling the magazine; she died three days later at the age of eighty-five.

The inevitable religious clash had come years earlier for the Grimmett family. On 15 February, 1891, Richard and Charlotte were profoundly shocked when their son, Richard, known always as Dick, carried out his threat to marry a Catholic girl, Mary McDermott, who had come from County Roscommon, Ireland. Initially Richard and CR put on a brave face, mainly for Dick's sake. He had found his true love and even their distaste for Catholicism was not going to cloud their judgment.

The little town of Caversham might well have erupted with an extra cheer or two and perhaps one more champagne in every household on Christmas night, 1891, for then a baby was born who was destined to become the "king of spin". Clarrie Grimmett's birth did not rate a notice in the *Otago Daily Times*, for such luxuries were reserved for the "quality" who lived in the hills suburbs. When Clarrie was born, Mary Grimmett was twenty-eight, four years her husband's senior. She could neither read nor write, but made her mark on the birth certificate. Richard and Mary Grimmett had wasted little time in producing a child. They had been married in South Dunedin that same year. Soon Clarrie was joined by a sister, Eva, born on 29 January, 1893.

Clarrie's grandfather had built his last home in South Street, Caversham, in 1882. This distinctive, two-storey brick house was a real fashion piece of the day. It sported a semicircular arch from the front room down to the sunroom. It is now 29 Fitzroy Street, the road name having been changed. The house name, "Faringdon Villa", is clearly visible, set in cement, on the front wall. Dick and Mary Grimmett set up house nearby, in David Street. Clarrie was probably born in that David Street residence, but there is no evidence to show whether he was born at home or in a nursing home.

Friction between CR and Mary, Methodist versus Catholic, quickly came to a head and Dick and Mary moved to Wellington. A Richard (Dick) Grimmett, bricklayer, appears in the Wellington directories of the late 1890s and after the turn of the century. The Grimmetts lived in Dock Street and later in Roxburgh Street, close to Basin Reserve, home of Wellington cricket.

Clarrie Grimmett's grandparents were unable to accept Dick's Catholic wife. Three years after Dick and Mary married (1894) CR visited her eldest son, Jack, at Nelson. On her return to Dunedin, she called in to Wellington to see Dick. Richard and

CR had cut themselves off from Dick and Mary to such an extent that she had no idea where Dick lived. She hunted everywhere for her son, finally placing a peremptory notice in the personal column of the *Evening Post*:

> Richard Grimmett to come to his
> Mother at Mrs Frosts, immediately.

Religion divided the family as it has sadly divided the Irish in their own land. Clarrie Grimmett was brought up a Roman Catholic. He would eventually drift away from religion: he instead became totally enraptured, indeed obsessed, with the joy and mystery of leg-spin bowling. He devoted his body and soul to cricket.

Clarrie's mother, Mary, was to die in 1930 while he was en route to England, bound for his most successful tour of England with an Australian XI. His father was to end his days in relative obscurity. There is great mystery about Dick Grimmett. Clarrie did not speak much about his parents, especially his father; Clarrie believed he changed his name in the late 1920s so people could not identify him with the famous Australian cricketer. Dick Grimmett had by then fallen on hard times and he wanted to save his son from any embarrassment.

Clarrie revealed a love of ball games early in life. Next door to the Grimmetts' Roxburgh Street house lived the sporting-mad Harris family. George Harris was a cripple. He was not wheelchair-bound, but required crutches to move about. He was an avid cricket fan and scorer for the local team. Clarrie would later enthuse over George Harris' scorecards, saying they were works of art. All the Harris boys were keen on their cricket and they all loved bowling leg-breaks. If they couldn't find a cricket ball, they would spin a tennis ball, or an orange. Arthur Mailey always considered a well-spun orange tasted all the juicier for its spinning.

Clarrie was aged six when he began to follow the older Harris kids as they tripped happily down to Wellington's famous Basin Reserve to have a hit. George Harris was fifteen, Charles, ten and Arthur, eight. The boys would play impromptu cricket matches in the street, with an asphalt pitch and a telegraph pole for stumps. The flint-hard track proved a true surface. It provided bounce and ample breadth of turn. These cricket-mad urchins of Wellington would scatter in all directions at the sudden appearance of uniformed Constable Thirsk, who would seem to materialise out of the gloom. He was huge. A good-natured fellow, he was never able to win the boys' confidence. They were too busy hiding.

He was a cartoonist's dream. *Punch* would be proud to promote him in its well-read pages. Constable Thirsk would give a little chuckle to himself and hurriedly leave the scene, for he knew the light was fading fast. There could be time for five more overs. He duly noted the arms and legs protruding at odd and ungainly angles from behind the roadside hedge. However, he also knew that there was danger for the boys at dusk, though traffic was not the hectic stream of today when Clarrie was a boy. There were no motor vehicles, but a bolting horse, with a dray in tow, presented real danger to any child in its path.

The cricket was of the spartan kind: no gloves or pads (Clarrie would later learn that his hero, Victor Trumper, preferred not to wear batting gloves). The inevitable bruise was worn with pride — a battle scar; the painful reminder of combat. Players simply had to watch the ball all the way, and miss it at their own peril! Cricket was very much a labour of love for Clarrie, who always tried to emulate his hero Trumper. He would charge down the track to a Harris leg-break and smite it with all his power, imagining that he was the great Victor Trumper, who had advanced down the wicket with quick and sure footwork to meet the Bosanquet delivery and caress the half-volley to the mid-off boundary. The crowd erupted! Trumper settled down once more — then Clarrie was brought back to earth with a resounding thump, as a Harris leg-break clean-bowled him and almost simultaneously Mary Grimmett declared: "Clarrie! Dinner's on the table!"

Mary and Richard Grimmett gave Clarrie plenty of love and encouragement; however, they knew little of the game. They always provided their son with creams and the equipment he needed to give of his best. They applauded his successes and helped to ease the hurt of failure.

Basin Reserve became a sort of Mecca for Clarrie and the Harris boys. Most of Basin Reserve was in excellent order in those days, a few years before the Boer War and Trumper's triumphant tour of England in 1902. However, a portion of this famous ground was rather neglected. As rough as any Australian cow paddock, this was the area open for use by anyone — usually most of the kids in the neighbourhood. Often Clarrie was the one entrusted to carry the spade George Harris (junior) would use to smooth out the rough spots on their pitch. It was an unwritten law: first in, first served. The youngsters had to get to the ground early to grab the best batting strip. The very idea of having to use a spade to help "smooth" the wicket indicates that the pitches must have been particularly helpful to the fielding team. All the boys loved to bowl out of the back of the hand and their well-spun offerings rewarded them with exaggerated turn on those uneven surfaces. Clarrie's expertise in bowling leg-breaks greatly impressed the Harris brothers. He needed to be good to keep up with his older spin mates, for all the Harris boys could make the ball curve in flight, turn and bounce.

Ever the small one, Clarrie's very name seemed to suit him. He was slight, but wiry and seemingly tireless. He revelled in not merely dismissing a batsman, but in making the ball fizz, spinning it in such a controlled and calculated manner that it often humbled his opponent. He enjoyed the ecstasy of bowling. He toiled to deceive. From the early days, Clarrie found that it was the combination of flight and breadth of turn that would defeat a batsman. It was not good enough simply to turn the ball, nor was it sufficient to toss it up without spinning hard. He tried that method and found that the only scientific reason for the ball to fall to earth was gravity. He decided to give gravity a helping hand. By spinning the ball hard and over the top, Clarrie found that the ball dipped; the harder he spun it, the more acute was the dip. It also would make a humming sound. The sound of that humming ball heralded the demise of many a fine batsman; the victim's funeral march was music to Clarrie's ears.

The humming song of spin, however, was not the real danger for batsmen. It was the imparted over-spin which caused the ball to dip and land slightly shorter than the batsman calculated. This deceived him in flight. Clarrie realised the importance of the position of the wrist and how the wrist position could dictate the various angles of turn. The more over-spin the bowler gained, the more dip and bounce; the less over-spin, or bowling the leg-break with the seam "square on" to the batsman, the greater the breadth of turn, the slighter the bounce.

Clarrie began to study and question why a ball behaved in a particular way. Not yet in his teens, Clarrie developed an investigative curiosity. He found that commonsense must prevail. There was always an explanation for the manner in which a ball, held in a certain way, would react in relation to the forces applied to it. His approach to cricket was never clouded by theory. Spin always held its fascination. It served Clarrie well in those encounters with and against the Harris brothers.

Yet when it came to the all-important showpiece, school cricket, Clarrie was not entirely convinced about the value of spin bowling. In those games, Clarrie rushed in and bowled as fast as he could. Any ball bowled at a pace less than flat out and he reckoned it would invite heavy and severe punishment. Spin bowling was the thing furthest from Clarrie's mind when he ran in to bowl at the Mount Cook Boys' School nets. At the age of fourteen, Clarrie was so slight that he could have passed for a boy much younger. He was, however, strong and wiry and he could bowl at a remarkable speed. Good judges in junior cricket had already marked Grimmett down as likely to develop into a fine fast bowler. There was one proviso. Clarrie would need to fill out and grow. But Clarrie never did grow very tall, nor did he become very robust. He remained spare, but he lacked neither resolve nor stamina. Mount Cook Boys' School nets became the place to learn the art of cricket.

The school sportsmaster, F.A. "Dimp" Hempelmann, was something of a demon to the boys. They admired and respected him, for his love of sport was evident. More importantly, he cared for his young charges. He was tough, but fair. Under Hempelmann's keen eye it was general practice for each of the bowlers to finish their stint in the nets by bowling six balls in succession. Hempelmann was wise enough to know that great effort was required to finish the session in this manner. He watched intently. This was the test of character. There was never a harsh word. Hempelmann had the knack of putting a boy in his place by raising his eyebrows. This rebuff would follow a long-hop or a similar poor delivery. The boys expected it, just as they rejected any praise for anything less than a stroke right out of the top drawer or a brilliant delivery. False praise was a rare commodity at Mount Cook.

One afternoon, Clarrie was letting fly with his six quick deliveries. He put every effort into his work, but by the end of the over, after a heavy workload on that warm day, Clarrie was nearly spent. Hempelmann observed Grimmett's six deliveries. He was impressed, but not quite satisfied.

"Clarrie, would you please send me down another six balls?" he asked.

Young Grimmett could hardly stand, let alone rush in and bowl again. Wearily he meandered back to his mark, careful to take his normal full run, and began his approach.

The boys had been bowling for a good hour before Hempelmann called for the final six deliveries. Now Clarrie was being called upon to bowl yet another six balls. He was exhausted. Another six balls? The request might just as well have been to run up to the top of Mount Cook wearing army boots. Despite all his efforts to maintain a good rhythm, Clarrie stumbled up to the wicket. Lost to fatigue, his usual rhythm deserted him. He felt limp and lethargic, at the point of collapse. It may have been a combination of fatigue and mischief in Clarrie which caused him suddenly to grip the ball differently and send down what the Harris brothers already knew to be Grimmett's special and most gifted trademark — a perfectly pitched leg-break.

The ball curved in slightly and upon pitching, it gripped on the responsive, soft and yielding turf and spun prodigiously across the unsuspecting batsman. He missed the ball by a mile and Hempelmann could hardly contain his glee.

"Ah, Mr Grimmett, that is better. From now on, my young man, you shall bowl only leg-breaks. Yes, Mr Grimmett, it is leg-breaks from now on."

Clarrie wasn't sure about such a change. Bowling leg-breaks with and against the Harris brothers on the broken turf on the poor section of Basin Reserve was one thing. Bowling leg-breaks to good school batsmen on true wickets was quite another matter. But Mr Hempelmann's request outweighed mere personal considerations. Clarrie was stumped.

He began to dread the next school match. As it turned out, Hempelmann was called away from the game to meet his brother at the docks; he had arrived from England a day earlier than expected. Dimp Hempelmann left the ground just before Clarrie was brought on to bowl. Clarrie seized his chance. With his sportsmaster out of sight, Clarrie lengthened his length of run to its former glory and charged in to bowl as fast as he possibly could. Grimmett the demon fast bowler fairly terrorised the opposition batsmen. He scythed through the batting, taking seven wickets for three runs.

News of Grimmett's fast bowling spread throughout the island. Two weeks later, he was selected to play for the Combined Wellington Schools against Wairarapa Schools, an important fixture. Elated at his selection, Clarrie dreamt all week of opening the bowling and charging in to send the stumps flying with his express deliveries. Then came that fateful day, the big game. Who should be standing as one of the umpires, but the Mount Cook School sportsmaster, Dimp Hempelmann. The boys took the field and Clarrie used all sorts of ridiculous ruses to avoid the skipper's eye. Nothing worked. Eventually the captain said: "You're opening, Grimmett!" This would have been no surprise, for Grimmett's fast bowling feats had become legendary. Yet he knew that he must bowl his leg-breaks. Hempelmann would frown if he bowled fast and in those days it was not unusual for a fast bowler and a spinner to open the bowling.

Fear gripped Grimmett. He was afraid his leg-breaks would come in for unmerciful punishment. It might well spell the end for his promising cricket future. The skipper's announcement brought Clarrie to his senses. He must show his worth.

"C'mon Grimmett. Let's see how fast you can bowl," the captain enthused.

A regulation fast bowler's field was set. Hempelmann was tempted to intervene when Clarrie gingerly handed him his cap. Clarrie, of course, later always wore his cap when he bowled. It became a trademark, adding to the aura of mystery which surrounded him. Mr Hempelmann noted the deep fine leg and third man, as Clarrie, after thanking God that it wasn't Trumper facing what he believed would turn out to be quite innocuous fare, sauntered in to bowl. To the amazement of all, Clarrie's first

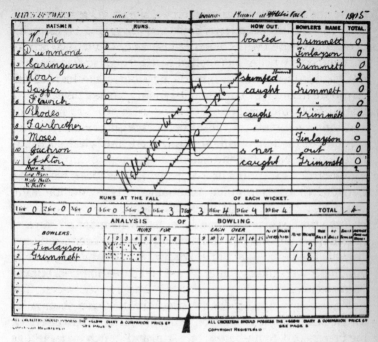

BATSMEN	RUNS.		HOW OUT.	BOWLER'S NAME	TOTAL.
1 Walden	0		bowled	Grimmett	0
2 Drummond	0		"	Finlayson	0
3 Scrimgeour	0		"	Grimmett	0
4 Hoar	II		stumped		2
5 Gayfer	0		caught	Grimmett	0
6 Fenwick	0		"		0
7 Rhodes	0		caught	Grimmett	0
8 Fairbrother	0		"		0
9 Moses	0		"	Finlayson	0
10 Jackson	0		not out		0
11 Ashton	0		caught	Grimmett	0
Byes 2					2
Leg Byes					
Wide Balls					
N. Balls					

RUNS AT THE FALL							OF EACH WICKET.				TOTAL	4
1 for 0	2 for 0	3 for 0	4 for 0	5 for 2	6 for 3	7 for 3	8 for 4	9 for 4	10 for 4			

BOWLERS.	RUNS FOR								EACH OVER															
	1	2	3	4	5	6	7	8	9	10	11	12	13	14	15	Overs	Maidens	Runs	Wkts	Wides	No Balls	Average	
1 Finlayson																1		2					
2 Grimmett																1		8					

Scorecard for schools match, 1905 at which Grimmett bowled leg-breaks

ball was a highly tossed leg-break, which pitched on a perfect length and beat the batsman's forward defensive prod. Clarrie's team-mates hardly had time to recover when the innings was over; Grimmett 6/5. He fared even better in the Wairarapa Schools second innings, taking an incredible 8/1. The scorecard of that match, played on a mild January day in Wellington, back in 1905, is today in the possession of Clarrie's only son, Victor, who lives in Adelaide. Never again did Clarrie need Mr Hempelmann to prompt him to bowl leg-breaks.

Grimmett was sold on the art. A young fast bowler, Finlayson, opened the bowling with Grimmett in the second innings. He took 2/1, and Wairarapa Schools were all out for four runs! Clarrie's strike rate was marvellous; he bowled just twenty-four deliveries, making it a wicket every three balls. A keen cricket enthusiast, Dimp Hempelmann played both cricket and rugby, but his greatest attribute was in teaching the games, their technique and etiquette. In cricket, especially, there were the MCC laws and the unwritten laws. Both were important. Mr Hempelmann was blessed with commonsense. The Mount Cook School cricketers were never overloaded with theory. He also coached the boys in rifle shooting, made popular at the turn of the century by Lord Kitchener and his men, who had defeated the Boers a few summers before.

Young Grimmett proved to be a crack shot. He was a key member of the school rifle shooting team and was selected to represent the New Zealand schools in the Empire Cup. Clarrie's shooters did exceptionally well; they ran a close second to Canada. Clarrie Grimmett maintained his reputation as a straight shooter throughout his long life.

From the age of ten Clarrie devoured every magazine article, newspaper story or book on anything remotely connected with cricket. The cricketers' Bible, *Wisden*, was an obvious source, but there were many other books available for cricket-mad youngsters.

He also developed about that time what he called "sympathy for the ball". Before coming on to bowl, Clarrie would interlock the fingers of both his hands, then pull and stretch his fingers as hard as he could. He would also tense and flex his fingers. By the time he gripped the ball, it tended to nestle into his hand naturally and seemed smaller and easier to control.

Sunny Saturday, 17 March, 1905, proved a great day in the life of Clarrie Grimmett. It was the second day of a three-day match between Monty Noble's Australian team and a New Zealand XI. The day had begun well for Clarrie, because he heard people in the streets of Wellington enthusing over the prospect of Trumper batting that very afternoon on Clarrie's beloved Basin Reserve. Trumper usually opened, but the word was that he would bat number six. New Zealand had been bundled out the previous day for an inglorious total of 94. Today was destined to be Trumper's day. Clarrie raced down to the ground, having taken time to don his new blue suit. If it was to be Trumper's day, then it would also be, most assuredly, Clarrie Grimmett's day. He wanted to look the part. There were no worries about entrance money.

The Wellington-based cricket-mad urchins were well-versed

with the challenge presented by barbed wire. It stretched in razor-sharp spirals atop the thick brick wall which extended right around the ground. For a small boy, who could hardly see over the top of a full-sized pair of pads, and wearing a new blue suit, the challenge was awesome. Yet for Clarrie nothing would stand in the way of watching Trumper face that first ball. The thrill was, of course, twofold. The challenge of getting into the ground to see the Australians play, especially Trumper, was the overriding factor. It was a bonus to do so without having to fork out the threepenny entrance fee.

Clarrie wasn't aware that tall, slim Warwick Armstrong (later to fall victim to an expanded waistline) and Clem Hill were batting together. Clarrie need not have scrambled quite so desperately, for Trumper was still padded up in the pavilion. Inevitably Clarrie became snagged on a barb, and his frantic efforts to wrench himself clear of the wire caused him to tear an ugly hole in his new suit trousers. His mother would never forgive him. But that was a problem he would address later. The previous day New Zealand had batted in the drizzle. Their sensational collapse didn't help matters for few people turned up and only fifty-seven pounds found their way into the cricket coffers. Clarrie wondered whether the figures might have been better were the barbed wire atop the perimeter wall stretched a couple of metres higher.

Armstrong went almost as soon as Clarrie sat down, as if the gods had decreed that Trumper should make an appearance. Trumper's batting excited everyone, especially the impressionable youngsters. Runs fairly flowed from his magic bat. With Clem Hill as a partner, Trumper demolished the bowling, but there was nothing vicious in his onslaught. The runs came with delightful leg-glances and late cuts, artful off and cover drives and lofted shots which hardly made a sound as they met the middle of the master's blade, sending the ball careering over mid-wicket or wide mid-on, one bounce and over the fence. Trumper hit 20 majestic fours and 4 huge sixes in his innings of 172, the Hill-Trumper partnership realising 269 runs in just 117 minutes. It was extraordinary batting. Australia finished the day at 9/593.

Clarrie left the ground with wings on his feet; he never forgot that day. He had missed seeing "Farmer" Bill Howell bowl the previous day. Howell took 4/20. Some twenty years later Clarrie was to play in Howell's Benefit Match at the Sydney Cricket Ground (SCG). However, after watching Trumper in full flight, Clarrie believed he had seen the greatest batsman of them all. He never changed that opinion.

In schools cricket, Clarrie bowled his spinners, although occasionally he resorted to bowling the odd quick delivery, by bringing his arm up in much the same manner as his stock leg-break, then suddenly whipping his arm through at speed.

The ruse often worked in schools cricket, but later in senior ranks Clarrie found such obvious changes of pace were a waste of time, often proving costly. He discarded the fast, straight ball and replaced it with the top-spinner. It was a winning delivery. Clarrie reckoned it got him many wickets. When used sparingly in disguise with his stock leg-break, the Grimmett top- or over-spinner was deadly.

As a youngster, Clarrie was reading an English magazine about a fellow who was bowling leg-breaks on the beach. The man gradually wore a hole in the sand, for he consistently landed his front foot on the same spot. Nothing unusual in that; however, when the hole became deeper, the fellow's shoulder dropped and instead of leg-breaks developing, the ball turned in the opposite direction, spinning from the off. His shoulder had dropped to such an extent, because of his front foot landing in the deep hole, that the ball was delivered out of the back of his hand. This beach cricket buff had inadvertently "invented" the Bosey, or wrong 'un. This inspired Clarrie to experiment. He learned to make the ball break in other ways than those the bowling action indicated. With most of his experiments, Clarrie would first try with a tennis ball, delivering underarm. Later he would adapt the principle to bowling overarm. When Clarrie was eleven, a fine exponent of "lobs", Simpson Hayward, toured New Zealand with the MCC and he greatly impressed Clarrie with the amount of spin he managed to impart on the ball.

Hayward spun the ball so viciously, Clarrie felt he might be applying a different principle. Had Clarrie summoned enough courage to ask Hayward to explain his spin methods, Clarrie's famous mystery ball, the flipper, might not have taken so long to evolve. When Hayward was at Basin Reserve, young Grimmett held back. He later regretted being too timid to ask questions of the veteran English lob bowler. Through years of experimenting with different grips and seam position in relation to his fingers, Clarrie found he could apply more pressure to the ball by holding it between the thumb and second finger.

"I put in hours of practice and experimented with this method," he told me. "Only after much hard work was I satisfied that I could control the mystery delivery. It was a matter of then fitting the ball into my match plans."

Clarrie worked for twelve years in perfecting his flipper. He had the patience of Job, the skill to match and the cunning of a fox.

"The reason why I waited so long before trying it [the flipper] in a match was my pride in my bowling methods wouldn't allow me to bowl a ball that didn't perfectly fit my strategy. I never regretted it."

Grimmett used the Bosey or wrong 'un sparingly before he introduced his flipper to his bowling repertoire.

Clarrie was continually trying to improve every ball he bowled. The Grimmett pruning knife was a finishing tool, polishing a fine piece of art. "I used the Bosey on rare occasions; usually it came more into play against the left-hander. I realised that the new ball [flipper] had great possibilities. And it was sound in principle to concentrate on my leg-break and straight ball [top spinner and flipper], since the fewer other balls I bowled, the less risk I ran of losing control."

Clarrie revered the players who turned out to play for Wellington at Basin Reserve. One of the leading players was "Pup" Hutchings, so nicknamed because of his prominent eyes. One day he saw Clarrie standing near a net. Young Grimmett, still in knickerbockers, was invited to bowl. Clarrie jumped at the opportunity; he soon had quite an audience as he began to wheel down a succession of deadly accurate leg-breaks. Hutchings struggled to survive. It surprised everyone but Clarrie when his evil dipping top-spinner completely beat Hutchings, uprooting the right-hander's middle stump. Pup's eyes stuck out like organ stops.

"He did not say a word," Clarrie said, "but I could tell he didn't pick the top-spinner. His eyes gave him away. I settled for a series of four leg-breaks, all pitching off-stump, spinning further away, then the fifth would be the searing top-spinner aimed to take off-stump."

Again the straight one defeated the New Zealand batting representative. He was greatly impressed with Clarrie.

"Did you try to bowl those straight ones, son?" Pup asked Clarrie.

"Yessir!" the young man enthused, his blue eyes sparkling.

"Well, young Grimmett, whatever you do, stick to your leg-breaks and the occasional straight one — that top-spinner will be your greatest wicket-taker."

Hutchings offered wise advice. Many of Grimmett's wickets came via the top-spinner. He set the batsmen up with his leg-breaks; then came the fatal ball, clean bowled or lbw, either way another wicket to the Fox.

While Clarrie's bowling strategy always contained plans to dismiss a batsman caught in the covers and at slip or at cover off well-flighted leg-breaks, he told me he had always "taken fiendish delight in getting a player out bowled or lbw with the top-spinner". At practice and from an early age, Clarrie always worked to a plan. He aimed to get a player out in a certain manner. Practice became a great challenge, never a drudgery for him.

When Clarrie left school he went to a technical college where he became engrossed in another art: drawing. He loved to sketch and was destined to become a brilliant artist. At the age of fifteen, the art of drawing superseded the art of cricket for Grimmett.

Strangely, cricket had become low on Clarrie's list of priorities. During the season of 1905-6, Clarrie didn't pick up a bat or a ball all summer; quite extraordinary with the memory of Trumper's artistry in March, 1905 at Basin Reserve still fresh in his mind. These early years proved tough. Study seemed all-consuming. Perhaps the artist's pen could not find a harmonious blend with the science of spin. Round the age of fifteen, the young Don Bradman quit cricket for one full season, concentrating on tennis. Happily, both cricketers returned to cricket after only a season out of action.

Clarrie's apparent lack of interest in cricket seeped into the winter of 1906, even after YMCA officials pleaded with him to play for their Boys' League Team. The team manager continued to pester young Grimmett, but Clarrie resisted and refused to play. It took a couple of Clarrie's old team-mates at Mount Cook School to talk him round. They pleaded with him. He listened, but did not commit himself. Reluctantly, he followed them down to the ground and when he saw his mates in the nets, the old urge to bowl came back with a rush. He could not resist joining in. He played the whole of that 1906-7 summer for YMCA, winning both the batting and bowling trophies.

Immediately the cricket ended that season, Clarrie was taken on as an apprentice signwriter at Smith and Smith Ltd, Cuba and Victoria Streets, Wellington. The oil, coloured glass and wallpaper merchants were delighted with young Grimmett. He enjoyed a long and enjoyable partnership with Smith and Smith. Clarrie was to leave the firm in 1914, when he packed his signwriting tools and his bag of bowling tricks and set off for Sydney to make a name for himself in the game of cricket. Smith and Smith provided Grimmett with a reference, which reads:

> Clarence Grimmett served his apprenticeship with Smith and Smith Ltd as a signwriter, commencing in April 1907 and has been with us continuously ever since. He has proved to be a good tradesman, and we are well satisfied with his work and conduct.
>
> He is leaving of his own accord with a view to extending his experience in Sydney and we can confidently recommend him as being thoroughly reliable.
>
> [Signed] Smith and Smith Ltd, 1 May, 1914.

The reluctant YMCA all-rounder enjoyed his second Boys' League Team season in 1907-8, as the team comprised mostly youngsters, but with four seniors. Clarrie believed that those senior players brought the best out of the others, to such an extent that many went on to play for Wellington Province, for New Zealand and one even played Test cricket for Australia. The team of 1907-8 included Edgar Phillips (captain), W. Hughes, Herb McGirr, W. Warne, Teddy Roberts, Clarrie Grimmett, W. Smith (killed in action during World War I), E. Loader,

H. Scott, M. Baker, Harold Wilson, William Wilson and Robert Parton. McGirr represented New Zealand.

The team won thirteen of its fourteen matches, losing one game to Thorndon A, for whom well-known New Zealand cricketers Doug Binnie and Harold Murphy played. Clarrie performed brilliantly with the ball, taking 63 wickets for 282 runs, at an average of 4.4 runs apiece. Clarrie averaged 16.3 with the bat. He went to the crease nineteen times. But it was with the ball that Grimmett excelled, taking 8/6 against St Andrews; 4/0 against Diamonds; 4/11 and 6/30 against the only team that beat YMCA, Thorndon A and 6/9 against St Peters. Grimmett hit an unconquered 48 in partnership with Teddy Roberts (64 not out), the pair hitting an unbroken partnership of 114 against Marist Brothers. While Clarrie took most wickets, his average of 4.4 was too high to win over W. Warne, whose 53 wickets at 3.6 runs apiece claimed the trophy. When district cricket was introduced into Wellington, Clarrie made the switch from YMCA to Wellington East. There were many good players in Wellington, enough to field an A and a B side. Clarrie noted that while the sides were supposed to be of equal strength, whenever the A team was a man short, there was no hesitation in poaching a man from the B team.

"I played several matches with the Bs before being promoted, but I neither batted or bowled in the first few games I played with the As," Clarrie once told me. He went on:

> In Hickey and Gibbs they had two bowlers who could be relied upon to dismiss the opposing side without having to call upon me and our batsmen were so good that five or six of them would make enough runs to enable our captain to declare before I got a chance with the bat.
>
> I spent my time in the outfield and when I asked for a transfer back to the Bs so I could get some batting or bowling, the authorities refused my request. I threatened to join a junior club to get some pleasure out of the game but they talked me into remaining with the As.

Clarrie recalled how the season was almost at an end before he finally got a decent bowl. "We were playing Wellington Centrals, our rivals for the premiership and, fortunately for me, their opening batsmen gave Hickey and Gibbs such a rough time that the captain, in desperation, at last threw the ball to me. To everyone's surprise I took the only five wickets which fell that afternoon, and at very reasonable cost." That day Clarrie tried out his Bosey for the first time in a match. Clarrie always preferred to call the delivery a Bosey, rather than the wrong 'un or googly. The Bosey was named after its inventor, Bernard James Tindal Bosanquet, who, round the turn of the century, had great fun with the ball with the seeming leg-break action which spun from the off. In 1930 the Maharaja of Nawangar (better known as the brilliant Indian-born England batsman Duleepsinhji) gave a dinner during the Australians' match against Sussex at Brighton.

Coincidentally Grimmett found himself sitting next to Bosanquet. They spoke of spin generally and the Bosey specifically. Clarrie told Bosanquet of the magazine article he once read of the leg-spinner wheeling them down at the beach.

Bosanquet acknowledged having once read the same article. He also confessed to Clarrie that when he stumbled across the new mystery ball, the Bosey, he had no idea that the delivery was the cricketing equivalent of inventing the wheel.

"Like me, Bosanquet was an intense enthusiast, and our talk on spin and other types of bowling lasted until well after midnight," Clarrie recalled. "When the dinner ended, we walked the esplanade, strolling for hours, the length of Brighton Beach and back. Eventually we went home with the milk."

As the seasons wore on, Clarrie's bowling steadily improved, his accuracy nearing the pinpoint control which would remain his hallmark in later years.

The day after his eighteenth birthday, 26 December, 1909, was a red-letter day in the Grimmett household. That day the slim leg-spinner played his first representative match for Wellington B team against Marlborough at Blenheim. The names suggest a vastly different battle and young Grimmett, after falling for only six runs with the bat, helped rout the "enemy" by taking 8/58 in the two Marlborough innings. Two long and frustrating years passed before Clarrie was called into the Wellington XI to play his first Plunket Shield match.

He had come under the experienced gaze of Jack Saunders, the old Australian left-armer, who delivered swing or spin at

1911-1912 — AUCKLAND v. WELLINGTON.

At Basin Reserve, Wellington, Feb. 23, 1912. Auckland won by 1 wicket.

WELLINGTON.

First Innings.		Second Innings.	
Blamires, E. O., lbw b Somervell	46	b Thompson	8
Gibbes, W. R., c Ellis b Thompson	81	b Snedden	1
Baker, W., b Thompson	2	b Thompson	29
Mahoney, J. J., b Snedden	25	c Horpsool b Thompson	26
Midlane, F. c Henus b Snedden	31	c Mason b Snedden	7
Blacklock, J. P., b Thompson	1	c Ellis b Jones	51
Dickson, J., st Ellis b Snedden	8	b Jones	11
Robinson, C., b Thompson	14	not out	31
Grimmett, C. V., c and b Thompson	1	b Snedden	2
Berendsen, not out	8	b Snedden	3
Saunders, J. V., b Snedden	0	c Mason b Jones	12
Extras	15	Extras	11
Total	232	Total	192

Auckland Bowling.

	B.	M.	R.	W.	B.	M.	R.	W.
Thompson	210	12	72	5	186	7	85	3
Jones	84	5	31	—	66	4	30	3
Snedden	107	4	48	4	144	6	46	4
Mason	36	2	19	—				
Wallace	12	—	12	—				
Taylor	18	—	14	—				
Somervell	36	—	21	1	30	1	20	—

AUCKLAND.

First Innings.		Second Innings.	
Hemus, b Robinson	66	run out	38
Ellis, c Blacklock b Saunders	2	c Saunders b Grimmett	4
Horspool, b Saunders	5	c and b Grimmett	19
Snedden, b Saunders	32	c Gibbes b Grimmett	7
Thompson, c Robinson b Saunders	22	b Saunders	25
Taylor, b Saunders	6	lbw b Grimmett	0
Somervell, c Grimmett b Dickson	54	b Saunders	27
Wallace, b Saunders	1	not out	16
Mason, lbw b Gibbes	4	not out	28
Anthony, not out	32	c Blamires b Gibbes	3
Jones, c Saunders b Robinson	4	c Blamires b Saunders	3
Extras	25	Extras	4
Total	253	Total: 9 for	174

Wellington bowling.

	B.	M.	R.	W.	B.	M.	R.	W.
Saunders	174	6	86	6	115	1	84	3
Grimmett	132	7	68	—	102	—	48	4
Robinson	53	2	23	2	42	—	17	—
Gibbes	30	1	31	1	30	—	21	1
Dickson	12	—	20	1				

The first of 248 first-class games

lively pace. Saunders toured England with Joe Darling's 1902 Australian team: Victor Trumper's team! Grimmett liked the Australian-born Wellington coach very much. He loved to hear coach Saunders talk of the days he toured with the likes of Trumper, Warwick Armstrong, Joe Darling and Monty Noble. They were like gods to Clarrie. Saunders had a commonsense approach to the game. In that 1911-12 summer he was opening the bowling for Wellington and he was a man to keep in touch with, for not only did he coach Wellington's first-class team, but he was also the groundsman at Basin Reserve. Clarrie soon learnt that a spinner must have the ear of the groundsman on his home turf.

Clarrie's first-class debut proved to be quite a match. Wellington scored 232 and 192, while Auckland hit a first innings total of 253. The Auckland XI needed 171 runs to win the match outright. They scraped home, but only just; at one stage they had lost 9/137 and Wellington seemed sure to win. However, a gritty last-wicket stand between Mason and Wallace thwarted Clarrie, Saunders and company. Just prior to the game, Clarrie was the subject of a short newspaper report:

> A promising young player is Grimmett, who is getting his first chance in representative cricket. He played for East A for a long time, but as Hickey and Gibbs usually found little trouble in getting rid of the wickets, he did not get many chances to display his talent.
> He is considered to be the best googly bowler in Wellington, and in the East team has done well with the bat. He is well worth his chance.

Clarrie regarded Jack Saunders as the "finest left-hand bowler I ever saw and although he had then passed his zenith, he could spin the ball with amazing pace off the wicket. I have met other great left-handers such as Bert Ironmonger, but although he always bowled well and kept an excellent length, he was never as dangerous as Saunders."

Saunders got 6/86 in the Auckland first innings and Clarrie had to be content with 0/68. The breaks came for him in the Auckland second innings. Clarrie got 4/48 off 17 overs and Saunders 3/84 off 20.1. The pair bowled well enough in tandem to pull off an extraordinary win, but for that last wicket stand. The paceman Gibbs bowled only five overs for a modest return

1913-1914 — SIMS' AUSTRALIAN XI. v. WELLINGTON.

Played at Wellington, Feb. 13, 1914. Australian won by seven wickets.

WELLINGTON.

First Innings.		Second Innings.	
Howe, C., c Nobel b McKenzie	19	b Armstrong	4
Hay, D., b Armstrong	14	lbw b Noble	4
Midlane, F. A., b Collins	3	b Armstrong	2
Gibbes, W. R., c Collins b Armstrong	31	b Armstrong	0
Beechey, E. M., c Trumper b Armstrong	14	b Armstrong	8
McGirr, H., b Mailey	43	c Armstrong b Cody	16
Gimmett, C. B., c Noble b Mailey	3	st Waddy b Armstrong	18
Joplin, F., b McKenzie	7	not out	5
Robinson, C. W., not out	41	b Armstrong	0
Saunders, J. V., b Armstrong	1	c Collins b Armstrong	2
Southall, T. R., c and b Armstrong	4	c Trumper b Cody	1
Extras	_21_	Extras	_11_
Total	201	Total	71

Australian Bowling: — Ransford 54 — 4 — 11 — 0, 12 — 0 — 8 — 0; Armstrong 215 — 9 — 80 — 5, 102 — 10 — 17 — 7; Mailey 96 — 5 — 31 — 2, 12 — 1 — 5 — 0; McKenzie 96 — 4 — 37 — 2; Collins 54 — 0 — 21 — 1; Cody 98 — 2 — 22 — 2; Nobel 42 — 3 — 8 — 1.

AUSTRALIAN TEAM.

First Innings.		Second Innings.	
Dolling, b Robinson	2	b Robinson	74
Collins, c Howe b Saunders	11	b Robinson	11
Cody, b Southall	24	not out	35
Noble, c and b Saunders	35		
Trumper, c Hay b Southall	0	b Robinson	16
Armstrong, b Southall	0		
Ransford, run out	5	not out	6
Waddy, b Southall	14		
McKenzie, not out	8		
Sims, st Howe b Saunders	0		
Mailey, c Midlane b Southall	12		
Extras	_13_	Extra	_7_
Total	124	Total for 3 wickets	149

Wellington Bowling: — Saunders 96 — 6 — 40 — 3, 60 — 0 — 50 — 0; Robinson 48 — 3 — 18 — 1, 43 — 0 — 39 — 3; Southall 76 — 4 — 34 — 5; 36 — 2 — 29 — 0; Grimmett 24 — 0 — 19 — 0, 18 — 0 — 34 — 0.

Australia v. Wellington 1913-14

of 1/21. Clarrie's first big wicket was that of Auckland's Eric Horspool, who offered a return catch.

Saunders was the Wellington Cricket Association coach-cum-groundsman for five years. He had said a year prior to Clarrie's first-class debut that Grimmett had "perfected the Bosey ball" and success awaited him on the big stage of cricket. Saunders and Grimmett became firm friends. Years later when Clarrie left Sydney (after a three-year stay from 1914 to 1917) to live in Victoria, he stayed with Saunders at his South Melbourne home.

By then Saunders had been living back in Australia for a number of years. It was during the Auckland match that Clarrie's leg-breaks made a lasting impression on national selector L.G. "Chummy" Hemus. Hemus top-scored for Auckland with 38 in the second innings, but he was impressed with Grimmett's first innings bowling, though Clarrie failed to take a wicket. "The quality of Grimmett's work", said Hemus, "was in no way reflected in his figures." Hemus meant what he said, for when Hemus and M. Crombie, of Wellington, sat down to help choose the New Zealand XI for the 1913-14 tour of Australia, both urged the selection of C.V. Grimmett. However, the other three men on the five-member selection panel lived in the South Island and not one of that trio had seen Grimmett bowl. They overruled Hemus and Crombie, but Clarrie was made first reserve. He received a letter (dated 21 October, 1913) from the New Zealand Cricket Council secretary Frederick Raphael advising him of the decision: "you will therefore please note that it is necessary to be vaccinated at once, in order that you be fit and well before leaving New Zealand, should your services be required".

Grimmett later reflected rather cynically that "all bowlers selected remained healthy, so I stayed at home". Some fifteen years later Grimmett met up with Dan Reese, one of the trio of New Zealand selectors who had lived on the South Island, joining hands to outvote Hemus and Crombie over the selection of Grimmett for the Australian tour.

Reese told Clarrie how sorry he had been that he had not believed the glowing reports of his bowling they received from Hemus and Crombie.

Clarrie was crestfallen about missing that Australian tour. In Australia he would have had the chance to bowl to some of the great players, such as his hero Trumper, Armstrong, Noble, Darling, Ransford and Collins. Even before Arthur Sims' team arrived to play Wellington in a series of matches early in 1914, Clarrie had decided to leave New Zealand. Among the Australian stars was the Englishman, Jack Crawford. He was another of Clarrie's heroes. Crawford played a lot of cricket Down Under. He was a livewire in the field, whether batting, bowling or fielding. Grimmett regarded Crawford in the class of the great West Indian Learie Constantine as a fieldsman. Clarrie played for Wellington in both the matches against the Australians. He bowled in three innings and conceded 84 runs, but failed to grab one wicket. He also scored 21 runs in three innings.

Clarrie's greatest thrill was to bowl to his boyhood hero, Victor Trumper. "It was a great moment for me. Trumper took two runs off my over, but he showed lots of respect for my efforts. Sadly he got out the other end next over and that was the only time I bowled to him. I have always regretted that, but I was glad to have had the chance to bowl to that greatest of batsmen."

During the lunch interval on the first day of the first match, several of the Australian players indicated to the Wellington players that they would only be too happy to "give us any hints they could and they urged us not to be backward in asking".

In those days Clarrie could bowl both the Bosey and the leg-break with equal accuracy. His length or direction did not suffer, whichever ball he decided to bowl. However, Clarrie was interested in finding out how Arthur Mailey, the great Australian legend of leg-spin, bowled the Bosey.

"Mr Mailey, could you please show me how you bowl the Bosey?" Clarrie asked the leg-breaker. Without so much as a word to young Grimmett, Mailey picked up a ball, ran leisurely into the empty net and delivered a nicely spun Bosey, which, upon pitching, turned appreciably from the off. "This did not convey very much," Clarrie said, "so I asked Mailey if he didn't mind showing me again." Mailey didn't say a word. He sauntered in, bowled another Bosey, then walked away. Clarrie was livid. The Mailey snub belied his image as an entertainer and a man with a keen sense of humour. Significantly, some ten years later Grimmett took over from Mailey as Australia's best slow bowler. But as he watched Mailey walk away from Basin Reserve nets on that hot and clear summer's day in 1914, Clarrie stood dejected.

Depression fell heavily upon the young Grimmett. He decided to pack his swag of paint brushes and bowling tricks and set off for Australia, with those of his family who would come.

3 SYDNEY

The Grimmetts arrived at Circular Quay on a crisp, clear May day in 1914. There was a cloud over Europe, but the real storm would not hit the world until 28 June, in that year, the fateful day in Sarajevo when an assassin's bullet killed the Austrian Archduke Franz Ferdinand. War would soon strike, sending millions to their deaths.

For the little Kiwi signwriter, this was the start of a new adventure. He stood on the wharf, suitcase in hand, with his mother, Mary and sister, Eva. His father, Dick Grimmett, remained in Wellington; he would end his days as a recluse. Family troubles aside, Clarrie had his heart set on one day wearing the coveted green baggy cap of Australia. He heard over and over in his head the words of his coach and mentor, Jack Saunders: "Bowl imaginatively and with confidence, Clarrie. For your next ball will surely get a wicket."

In 1914, Clarrie's hair was thinning. Ever since leaving school he had bowled in a cap, but not, as some people thought, to hide his baldness. He was aged twenty-two, not twenty-one as he honestly believed. Clarrie thought he was born in 1892, but I have the official record of his birth; on Christmas Day, 1891. Grimmett dearly wanted to play Test cricket, and as New Zealand did not start playing Test matches until that first encounter against England at Lancaster Park, Christchurch, in January 1930, Clarrie had decided to try his luck in a land which not only played Test cricket but also produced the best cricket team in the world.

He was ambitious and he was developing a remarkable patience, for which he later became renowned. In Sydney Clarrie would have the chance to play with and against his cricketing heroes. He wanted to play for Paddington, where Trumper played before transferring to Gordon, in the summer of 1907-8. The dentist and talented Test all-rounder Monty Noble led Paddington. Communications must have been appalling in 1914, for the young Grimmett's idea that his hero, Victor Trumper, was still playing for Paddington was way off target. Clarrie persuaded his mother to rent a house in Darlinghurst, for that suburb, he thought, was well within the embrace of the Paddington Cricket Club. It was late in September, 1914, when Grimmett ventured out to the Paddington practice nets. He had settled down quickly, sauntering in to bowl his accurate brand of leg-breaks, when a man in a neat blue suit approached:

"Where do you live?" came the opening salvo.

Clarrie did not expect to be warmly welcomed, but he did expect common courtesy. The man asking the question held a position of power: he was none other than the Paddington Club secretary, Gordon Sale.

"Woolcott Street, Darlinghurst," Clarrie answered, half-expecting admonishment.

"You are not in the district and you can't play for us," Sale said bluntly.

Clarrie was shattered.

Sale's attitude turned him off Paddington. Clarrie went to Sydney at Rushcutter's Bay. There he found warmth and understanding. The Sydney Cricket Club (SCC) secretary George Stack made himself known the instant he set eyes on the migratory New Zealander. They shook hands.

"A Bosey man, eh? I've seen a few good 'uns from New Zealand. Brought your togs? Good. Put them on and come out to the nets. I'll introduce you to some of the boys."

Stack was batting when Clarrie reached the nets. He immediately walked out of the net and introduced Clarrie to a number of players. Among them was Herbie Collins, later to become Clarrie's first Test captain. Clarrie felt wanted and at ease. Kindness does wonders for the newcomer. Ironically Paddington, the club which did not want Grimmett, amalgamated with Sydney, the latter swallowing the former, a fact that did not go unnoticed in the Grimmett household.

In 1914 Herbie Collins was an ordinary member of the A

grade side. He opened the batting, but did not lead the team. That was left in the capable hands of wicketkeeper Carl Wright. However, Collins had ambitions to lead. He also admired the little Kiwi leg-spinner. His admiration for Grimmett grew stronger every year. Clarrie's modesty probably cost him dearly from the outset. He did not tell Stack that he had played first-class cricket in New Zealand.

"I thought such a statistic would have hardly impressed him very much," Clarrie said years later. Such thinking was consistent at that time, for New Zealand cricket was not particularly strong, certainly not strong in comparison with Australian cricket. Australians tended to look down on the Kiwis. Grimmett reckoned that the mere fact he had played first-class cricket for Wellington would not mean a bean in Australia. He was, of course, dead wrong. While Sydney grade cricket was hard-fought and a good standard, New Zealand often produced players of star quality. There was simply a greater depth of talent in Australia. Club cricket in Sydney was "something" in those days. There were few distractions for the young. Money was not as plentiful as it is today, and only the well-to-do could afford a motor vehicle. Cricket was a noble pursuit and a way for an ordinary bloke with cricketing talent to become famous, if not build a fortune along the way. Grimmett's Sydney club debut was a resounding success, but it was for the Third XI.

"The sides were chosen before you arrived tonight, Clarrie," George Stack explained, "so we couldn't pick you in any higher grade than the thirds. I'm sorry, but I expect your performance in that grade this weekend will give the selectors a better chance of judging your ability." What a comedown! Yet Clarrie wasn't upset. He was happy enough to be given the opportunity to prove his worth. All he ever wanted was the chance to show what he could do. The leg-break wizard spun Sydney to an easy win over University.

He bagged twelve student batsmen for 60 runs in the two innings and was the next week rushed into the Second XI. It was not until late in the summer that Grimmett got his chance in the First XI. All-rounder Dr Willcocks was too ill to take his place in the side and when Clarrie arrived at his home after work on the

Saturday morning of the match, George Stack was there waiting, his face beaming.

"Clarrie, you're in the side. You're in the As against Mailey's Redfern at the cricket ground." George and Clarrie shook hands. Grimmett was elated, but he masked his emotions. He would watch, listen and absorb. He would keep his own counsel, but he would scheme and plan and work hard. The Redfern batsmen were now his prey. This chance would not be wasted. His Second XI days were over.

Grimmett spun his way through the Redfern batting in a stunning debut on the Sydney Cricket Ground (SCG). He liked the atmosphere of this famous ground. In 14.2 overs Grimmett took 7/32. His success was praised, but not too loudly lest the Mailey spin crown be dented. Mailey bowled serviceably to take 3/45 from 12 overs, but Grimmett's performance was brilliant both in terms of the quality of his deliveries and in the result. Grimmett paved the way for an easy Sydney outright win with a follow-up 5/33 to complement his first innings haul of seven wickets. Grimmett had arrived. The elation Clarrie felt was shared by Jack Saunders. His first telegram of congratulations came from Jack, another from F.A. "Dimp" Hempelmann, his Mount Cook School sportsmaster.

Clarrie finished that first Sydney season in A grade with 28 wickets at 10.64 runs apiece. He bowled only 93 overs. Dr Willcocks, the man who withdrew from the team sick and created a chance for Clarrie to make his belated Sydney debut, captured 21 wickets at 15.27; Paddington's Monty Noble 33 at 12.39; Redfern's Arthur Mailey 51 at 14.41; Gordon's Charlie Macartney 34 at 15.91 and Glebe's Charles Kelleway, 26 at 15.92.

After his first success against Redfern, a newspaper report on Clarrie's debut appeared: "Grimmett — not to be mistaken for Grumitt of Redfern — was brought up from the Second Grade, in which he performed with credit as a bowler, and captured seven for 32. This is a record that even his efforts in Second Grade did not foreshadow."

The new year of 1915 began with the sad news that German submarines had torpedoed the HMS *Formidable*. In Australia, far from World War I, Clarrie was having his own battle as he clawed his way for recognition. Grimmett didn't have the charisma of Arthur Mailey. Mailey was Sydney's spin hero. He tossed the ball up and spun it hard, giving himself every chance of either being belted unmercifully or claiming a wicket. He experienced both, the former rather than the latter, but Mailey still managed to secure good "bags" of wickets every season. Grimmett's style was unique. He copied no-one. He was neither smooth nor awkward, yet he must have always possessed rhythm because he was accurate and was forever beating good batsmen with subtle changes of pace.

Clarrie was pleased with his season, although the war was a rude interruption to his cricket ambitions. From February 1915 until December 1919 no Sheffield Shield matches were played. During the winter, Clarrie played baseball to keep in trim. The first Anzac Day came and went, as news of the dead and dying filtered back to a concerned nation. Victor Trumper was dying. The great batsman succumbed to the ravages of Bright's Disease (a form of kidney ailment) on 28 June, 1915. Two days later Clarrie was among the twenty thousand mourners who lined the route from Circular Quay to Waverly. It was a cold and damp Wednesday. A long line of cricketers marched ahead of the cortege and young Grimmett joined them. News of Trumper's death shocked a nation that was already numb from the ghastly reports of the carnage at Gallipoli.

Grimmett played two more summers for the Sydney Cricket Club, taking 59 wickets at 20.7 in 1915-16 and 20 at 16.3 in 1916-17. Clarrie was frustrated in not being able to show his worth in interstate cricket. That frustration was soothed when he was selected at the end of the 1916-17 season to play in Syd Gregory's XI against Monty Noble's XI at the SCG. Alan Kippax, who was the "embodiment of Trumper in style", Tommy Andrews and Johnny Taylor were among his team-mates. Kippax was stumped off Mailey and Andrews thrashed the bowling for 102. Mailey took 3/102 off 15 overs and Grimmett took 3/79 off 15 overs: both were expensive, although the match was played as if they were troops on Gallipoli Beach and there was no tomorrow.

A week later Grimmett found himself in the same eleven as Mailey. They represented a New South Wales Cricket Association team against the St George Cricket Club. Clarrie picked up

5/18, bowling in tandem with the famous leg-spinner Mailey, who also excelled, taking 4/22.

Clarrie had spent a productive holiday in Melbourne, the previous winter. He arrived on 1 July, the very day the Somme offensive began. That day some 60,000 British soldiers were injured; 19,000 died. His old cricketing mate, Jack Saunders, had invited him to stay with him for a month. Saunders introduced Clarrie to Elizabeth Egan, the daughter of a friend of Saunders. That chance meeting was to change Clarrie's life.

4 A DOG NAMED JOE

Jack Saunders' advice to Clarrie found its mark: "Come to Victoria. In Sydney they can't see past Mailey. Once the war is over, you'll be left out in the cold there. Victoria needs a good Bosey man."

Clarrie thought long and hard about Saunders' words. Playing in the same team as Mailey, Clarrie felt a mixture of honour and envy. Some of the great men of Australian cricket almost worshipped Mailey. How could the little Kiwi leg-spinner hope to beat Mailey for a State berth? He had visited Melbourne in the early part of the 1916-17 summer and played a mid-week match for Saunders' old club, South Melbourne. Grimmett bowled steadily, wheeling away with that unerring accuracy, commanding total respect from the batsmen. But Clarrie might not have finally decided to leave Sydney to live in Victoria and play for Saunders' South Melbourne had it not been for the chance meeting with Elizabeth Egan. This time logic and his heart were pointing in the same direction, away from Mailey's Sydney.

That first season (1917-18) with South Melbourne saw Clarrie take 40 A grade wickets at just 14.4 runs apiece. World War I was winding down by the time the 1918-19 Victorian Cricket Association district season began. German U-boat warfare ended on 20 October, and the German Fleet surrendered on 14 November. State cricket was on everyone's lips. Clarrie had waited a long time to test his skill on the first-class stage in Australia. He practised even harder and was immediately among the wickets, taking 6/41 against University and 7/41 in combat with Prahran.

After the Armistice three matches were played: Victoria v.

New South Wales at Melbourne, Victoria v. South Australia at Melbourne and Victoria v. New South Wales in Sydney. These games were not deemed Sheffield Shield matches, but they were played in the same competitive way: hard but fair. Grimmett and young Bill Ponsford were selected in the last of these exhibition matches played in Sydney. Fast bowler Ted McDonald ran through the New South Wales batting with a brilliant 8/42, routing the Sydneysiders for 89. Left-arm spinner Bert Ironmonger mopped up alongside the leg-spinner, Philip Le Couteur, each taking a wicket. Edgar Mayne, the Victorian captain, did not have a great regard for slow bowlers (some Victorian skippers since have inherited that trait!) and McDonald's feat gave the slow men, Ironmonger, Le Couteur and Grimmett, few chances. Clarrie had a great regard for Le Couteur, who went to Oxford University as a Rhodes Scholar in 1909, 1910 and 1911. He played for the Gentlemen against the Players six times. He took 5/98 in such a game at the Oval in 1911, defeating all the professionals but Jack Hobbs. Le Couteur must have played under a more sympathetic captain in England, for Mayne virtually ignored his skill, even after McDonald and Ironmonger failed to make an impression in the New South Wales second innings.

"Le Couteur and I both wanted to bowl into the wind, but Mayne gave us two overs each with the wind behind us and then took us off," Clarrie wrote later. "In my second over Frank Highett missed an easy chance off James Bogle, who went on to score a century. But I did not get another chance until New South Wales had made 5/386 and wanted only 10 runs to complete the outright victory."

Bogle's 145 turned the match right around. He and Tommy Andrews stood up to McDonald; Andrews continually advised Bogle not to nibble at rearing McDonald deliveries outside his off-stump. Grimmett bowled a further three overs, but to no avail, and then the match was all over. He chuckled at the notation in the 1918-19 South Melbourne annual report, where his Victoria debut was briefly described: "C.V. Grimmett represented SMCC in the interstate match at Sydney and performed well". Clarrie's idea of "performing well" was very different. He continued to practise his tricks in club cricket, but the big matches eluded him. There was the odd game for the Victorian Second XI. In such matches against New South Wales, Grimmett took 11/263 at 23.90 runs apiece. He also played for the Second XI against various country teams, taking a further 19/215, his wickets coming at the average of 11.31.

During a seconds match against New South Wales, Clarrie took over the Victorian captaincy. The Victorian skipper, Andy Ratcliffe, who was keeping, and batsman Hughie Carroll collided in the first hour of play. Carroll was dashing to gain his ground and Ratcliffe was about to take a wayward return. Both suffered concussion and were taken to hospital, neither taking a further part in the match. Grimmett led the side well and was batting with young Bill Ponsford, the side nine down needing 30 runs to win, when "Ponny" fell.

The Versailles Treaty gave world peace and life was good for Clarrie Grimmett. On 1 November, 1919, Clarrie and Elizabeth Egan were married, at St Ignatius Catholic Church, Richmond. The Grimmetts moved into a new house in Prahran in 1920 and under the VCA district rules, Clarrie's change of address also required a change of clubs. In his last summer for South Melbourne, Grimmett took 40 wickets at 20.8. In three seasons with South Melbourne he had bagged 121 victims at 16.65 apiece. At Prahran Grimmett was immediately successful. His efforts with Prahran proved his most productive since he left Wellington in 1914, for Grimmett took 67 wickets at 14.95 in 1920-21. Highlights of his wicket-feast that summer were 7/54 against St Kilda; 7/59 versus Carlton; 8/61 against Richmond and 8/111 against Fitzroy.

Elizabeth Ann Grimmett was a dressmaker. Clarrie and Elizabeth were a good team. They were both fastidious, patient and believed in all things in moderation. They were teetotal. Elizabeth used to watch Clarrie bowl for South Melbourne. She would sit in the stand or, if it was very hot, under a shady tree. During knitting rest breaks Elizabeth would look up, and focus on her husband, who was either trundling down another leg-break or moving in briskly with the bowler at cover or mid-off.

*

Joe

The Grimmetts had a spacious backyard. There Clarrie built a full-sized turf cricket pitch, ensuring there was plenty of room to add a pace or two onto his run-up, if required. Elizabeth, (or Lizzy as Clarrie always called her) loved the indoors. She liked cooking and dressmaking. Gardening was never her favourite pastime.

Clarrie could have hardly expected his Lizzy to throw back the balls he would bowl for hour after hour in his backyard net. He needed someone else. Then he hit upon an idea. He would train a dog to fetch and carry for him. Clarrie selected a little black and white fox terrier and named him Joe. All Joe had to do was to lie quite still at the batsman's end, until the full complement of eight balls had been bowled. Joe sat still and watched his master spin the balls down, one by one. He didn't move a muscle until the eighth ball was delivered. Then he went into action, rushing to Clarrie with a ball in his mouth, depositing it at his master's feet, then dashing for number two. He did this, very rapidly, with all the balls until there were eight lined up for Clarrie to bowl another over.

In 1920 Clarrie was approaching thirty. The dreaded thought that age might rob him of his dream to play Test cricket was the spur that made him train summer and winter. If it was an obsession, Clarrie didn't show it. Only on the cricket field did he wear a sad face.

Summer Sunday mornings were happy occasions. The Sabbath was always set aside for a couple of hours of batting and bowling. He invited his cricketing mates to have a hit and a bowl. Willis, Lampard, Healy, Sutherland, Ellis and young Ponsford often turned up. Ellis sometimes kept, making Joe more than a little jealous. One Sunday, Jack Ellis threw a ball into the empty nets while the players were laughing and joking over a cool drink during a break. Jack whistled for Joe: "C'mon Joe, fetch the ball. C'mon get the ball…"

Joe was taking a nap under the big red gum at the end of the garden. It was a hot day and Joe showed not the slightest inclination to obey Jack's request. Jack called again and Joe condescended to open one eye. He focussed on Clarrie, who was as eager as everyone else to see what Joe might do. The dog had never before been tested in this way. Jack threw another ball into the empty net, then another. He repeated his call. Joe yawned, stretched and closed his eyes. Clarrie finished his drink, laughing: "Here's how to do it".

The master spinner picked up a ball and walked briskly to his mark. He skipped in to bowl and delivered. Joe opened one eye and then closed it, as if he was taking count. Seven to go. Clarrie then began to nominate the stump he intended hitting. "Bosey to pitch off and hit leg; leg-break to pitch leg and hit off…" Joe opened and closed his left eye with each ball delivered.

Clarrie's accuracy was sensational that morning. He hit his mark with each of those eight deliveries. Immediately the eighth ball had pitched leg and taken the top off the off-stump, Joe sprang into action. He leapt from his place of comfort under the gum tree and scampered to the empty net, grabbed a ball in his mouth and rushed back to place it at Clarrie's feet. Joe had an appreciative audience. When all eight were at Clarrie's feet, Joe was applauded and Clarrie clapped and laughed the loudest. Young Ponsford observed during a lull in proceedings, "That dog might be famous one day, yer know". Clarrie smiled.

Joe's enthusiasm to retrieve for his master equalled Grimmett's determination to become a great spin bowler. Clarrie's methods were different. Few other spinners practised for hours alone, having a dog as a constant companion. Those who didn't know Clarrie and had even less understanding of the exacting art of spin bowling were cruel. Elizabeth hated overhearing comments at the local shops about her husband, such as "that mad bloke with the dog". Clarrie had a tough hide; he was impervious to such comments. He continued to plug away, spinning and scheming; always scheming. In 1920-21 Clarrie again got the call to play for his state, this time against J.W.H.T. Douglas' MCC team at the Melbourne Cricket Ground (MCG).

"This match," he said later, "was my unluckiest time in cricket.

"It was Patsy Hendren's birthday and he had made 96 when I was given a bowl. In my first over he hit a ball to the outfield where George Davis dropped the easiest of catches. Patsy went on to score more than two hundred with beautiful strokes." Just after having Hendren missed, Frank Woolley swung hard at Grimmett and skied the ball over cover. Another near miss. It fell safely between two fieldsmen as they each hesitated, neither going for what should have been an easy catch and a Grimmett wicket.

"Bad luck, son," Woolley said. There were other near misses. Edgar Mayne was one of the culprits. Mayne dropped two chances off Grimmett's bowling. Clarrie was crestfallen.

"When I came in to bat, Parkin [Cecil Parkin the Lancashire slow bowler] sent down his mystery ball and it struck me on the left kneecap," Clarrie told me.

"He was somewhat of a comedian, this chap, and he roared laughing at my predicament. That painful blow hampered me for the rest of the match, but I still managed to get 35 runs." But Clarrie's tale of woe did not end with the hit on the knee. In the MCC second innings, the first ball he bowled to Jack Hobbs deceived the great man and he hit a firmly-struck return catch to Grimmett. In his excitement, Clarrie stumbled and misjudged the speed of the ball.

He grabbed too soon and suffered a badly split third finger, his main spinning finger! Grimmett's pride also took a hammering, for he had allowed the great Hobbs to escape. The injured hand forced him out of the action for the rest of the match. Clarrie took 3/160, which was a commendable performance given that he had an extraordinary run of bad luck. The Victorian selectors, however, didn't see it that way. They must have thought Clarrie short of big match temperament and prone to injury, for he was discarded from the State side for the rest of the summer and beyond. Grimmett put all his energies into performing well for Prahran. He was a key to the club's A grade premiership, taking a record 67 wickets at 14.9. Team-mate Carl Willis scored 520 runs at 74.5 and was one of the four Prahran players to play for Victoria in 1920–21. The others were Lampard, Ellis and Grimmett. Willis, Lampard and Ellis were also picked to represent Australia on a tour of New Zealand. Lampard snapped up the chance, but Ellis and Willis declined the invitation due to pressure of business. If only they had asked Clarrie.

Christmas Day 1921 and Clarrie turned thirty. His dream of playing a Test match was fading. Disappointment wasn't going to defeat him. He plugged on, bowling in the backyard with his faithful Joe fetching and carrying. His skill was impressive, his mind alert, honed to razor sharpness by his many setbacks.

In the season 1921–22 Clarrie starred for Prahran, as usual, taking 39 wickets at 14 runs apiece. He failed to gain a State spot and the Victorians won the Sheffield Shield. That made it all the tougher to force his way into the team. Clarrie began thinking about a move back to Sydney. Time was running out. Clarrie took two wickets to help Prahran dismiss Collingwood for 165 in the VCA grand final. Jack Ryder played a lone hand with a fine 92. Then Prahran thrashed the Collingwood attack, scoring 688 with Healy (230), Thompson (154) and Willis (110) taking full toll of the bowling.

While Clarrie retained extraordinary faith in his ability to bowl out the best batsmen in the world, he was frustrated in that he knew the Victorian selectors were making life impossible for him to make any headway in big cricket. He refused to lie down. In 1922–23 Clarrie took 60 wickets at 11.52, but his fabulous summer again failed to impress the State selectors. He was totally ignored and probably suspected there was a conspiracy mounted against him. The following year, 1923–24, Grimmett spun his way to a season's haul of 54 wickets (average 12.12).

On 17 December, 1923, Elizabeth gave birth to the Grimmetts' only child, a son, Victor Clarence. Lizzy and Clarrie were delighted. At that time rumours were rife about Grimmett's intention to quit Victoria and return to Sydney. Some suspected he might go in the other direction. They were on the right track.

The Adelaide Cricket Club secretary Eddie McCarron travelled to Melbourne mid-way through the season to offer Clarrie a place in the Adelaide district team. There was a signwriting job in the offered package, which amounted to a "guaranteed ten pounds per week for three years' working for Harry Lyons Pty Ltd". Under the terms of the offer Clarrie was told that he would be given time off (on full pay) should he play for South Australia or Australia. In addition, the club would pay forty pounds towards Grimmett's relocation costs. That was the carrot. Confirmation of the offer would not come until 10 May, 1924.

Meantime Clarrie pondered his future. He was now thirty-two. He had a devoted, loving wife and a baby boy. The prospects in Adelaide appeared too good to refuse. He was jolted back to earth when picked as thirteenth man for Victoria to play New South Wales in Sydney. Carl Willis (twelfth man) and Clarrie fielded for most of the time in place of Jack Ryder and Jack Ellis. Ryder was unavailable for the next match, the last of the season, ironically against South Australia in Adelaide. Clarrie was selected to play for Victoria against South Australia on the Adelaide Oval.

Edgar Mayne never thought much of Grimmett's bowling and Ernie Bean, VCA secretary from 1917–25, was one of the head-in-the-sand State selectors who had for so long ignored Grimmett's ability. Bean had a habit of rubbing people up the wrong way. He had a very public row with Warwick Armstrong, with whom he tangled for almost a decade after the 1912 debacle when Armstrong and five others, including Victor Trumper, refused to go on the tour of England unless Frank Laver was appointed manager of the side. Grimmett had nothing to do with that little aside, but his progress was apparently impeded because of men such as the power-hungry Bean. At Prahran, one of Clarrie's team-mates was a nuggety little fellow named Stan Stevens. He was a solid left-hand batsman and a wonderful fieldsman. Once when Grimmett was bowling to Bean, the State selector, Clarrie asked Stevens to move in very close at cover. Bean was outraged. He stood with hands on hips and bellowed: "Stand back or I'll knock your head off!"

Stevens laughed, Bean fumed and Grimmett watched. He sensed a kill. He forced Bean onto the back foot for three deliveries, then lured him forward and Bean drove low and hard straight to short cover where Stevens scooped it up on the half-volley and threw the stumps down in a twinkling. Bean was run out for a duck!

Clarrie turned up at the Adelaide Oval for what was destined to be a significant match in his career. Before the game got underway, a reporter found a number of prominent Victorians, including Bill Ponsford, and keeper Jack Ellis, praising the spin skill of Grimmett. They were soon joined by the likes of Arthur and Vic Richardson, all of whom claimed the Prahran spinner to be "the finest slow bowler in Australia, if not the world". Over the years the Victorian selectors had been criticised because Grimmett was continually being overlooked for State honours. What Clarrie needed was a star performance that would prove beyond doubt that he had what it took to become a great bowler. In the South Australian first innings Clarrie bowled sparingly, taking 1/12. Then in the second, Grimmett bowled magnificently, taking 8/86. Clem Hill was beside himself with joy, as was Vic Richardson, the South Australian skipper. These men were also South Australian selectors and they knew Eddie McCarron was chasing the services of Grimmett. Clarrie bowled 19.1 overs, getting Percy Rundell (34) and Eric Bowley (23) stumped by Ellis, although the Bowley stumping had the South Australians upset because they considered Ellis' histrionics were "over the top".

Clarrie regretted leaving Prahran, for he had forged many lasting friendships. In four years with the Prahran Cricket Club, Clarrie took a total of 258 wickets, his season's hauls in sequence 67, 39, 68 and 54, yet he played only a couple of big games for Victoria.

Prahran had had a spin genius pining in relative obscurity. Grimmett helped create history there; the club won a VCA incentive worth one hundred guineas. The club was the first in the VCA to win three premierships and a Victory Cup was the prize.

"We won three in a row, just to be sure," Clarrie said years later, "and we also succeeded in persuading the VCA into donating the funds to help us build a new press and scoring box at Prahran, instead of presenting a cup." The scorebox was designed by Clarrie Grimmett. Clarrie had won the hearts of the people of Melbourne. They loved a battler and knew their cricket and they were convinced Grimmett was a top-flight spinner. Back in 1919–20, in his last summer with South Melbourne, a Melbourne writer under the pseudonym of "lbw" declared: "Should any body of selectors rightly judge a man on 40 balls?" The author was referring to Grimmett's first match for Victoria, against New South Wales at the SCG, a game not deemed to be a Sheffield Shield encounter. Then the selection committee comprised Matt Ellis, Ernie Bean and Peter McAlister, who was made team manager for the 1909 Australian tour of England, much to the players' disgust. Among the disgusted team-mates were Victor Trumper, Warwick Armstrong and Edgar Mayne.

During a match for South Melbourne against Melbourne in 1919–20, Clarrie snared six wickets of the eight to fall with only the Big Ship, Warwick Armstrong, able to fathom the genius of Grimmett's spin.

Melbourne scored 8/227 and Armstrong was unconquered on 157 at the day's end. "lbw" said: "Grimmett deserves more encouragement than he is getting on this side" (meaning since he arrived from Sydney in 1917). Compliments began to drift across the seas. He had become the first New Zealand-born cricketer to make the big time in Australia. Readers were reminded that certain top Australian players made their mark in New Zealand with Jack Saunders at Wellington, Charlie Macartney (Otago) and Albert Trott (Hawke's Bay). When Grimmett reflected on all the hard work, he never regretted the toil. He loved every minute of it and he was convinced that someday he would be rewarded with a Test cap. Clarrie would say later that he thoroughly enjoyed his time in Melbourne; seven years of hard work, fun and camaraderie. Nor would he forget the part Joe played: Joe Grimmett, the alert little fox terrier, who became the most loyal cricketing companion for the master craftsman of spin bowling. Bill Ponsford was right. Joe Grimmett did become famous one day.

The Grimmetts moved to Adelaide in May 1924. They travelled in style, as stylish a passage as forty pounds would allow a man, his wife and baby child on the Melbourne-Adelaide train.

Joe was given a kennel with a new blanket. South Australians would soon appreciate the amazing skill, stamina and determination of the Wicket Fox.

5 THE HAVEN ADELAIDE

Clarrie Grimmett's face stared from a single column in an obscure left-hand page section of the Adelaide *Advertiser*. It was a serious study: tight-lipped, with the hint of a frown under the peak of his Victorian cap. It was the same cap which he wore during his epic bowling performance against South Australia, in the last game of the previous summer. His 8/86 in the South Australian second innings did not go unnoticed by a good many people who knew the game inside out. They included Vic Richardson, the South Australian captain, Clem Hill, the old left-hander who went in after either Victor Trumper or Reggie Duff started back to the pavilion. Hill was as capable a number three as Australia had possessed before Don Bradman happened along. Richardson was keen to have Grimmett in his State team attack. Bill Whitty, the left-hander, was nearing the end of the road, although he could still turn in the odd telling bowling spell. Tim Wall, destined to play for Australia, was just starting out and Richardson wanted a bowler who was both accurate and penetrative. In Grimmett he had those two qualities and more. It was May, 1924, just three months since Clarrie had routed the Croweaters in a perfect song of spin; the ball humming, batsmen falling like ninepins.

The newspaper article heralded the arrival of C.V. Grimmett for the Adelaide Club. Headlined "Melbourne Cricketer Arrived", the writer told how "South Australia should be able to give a better account of herself in interstate matches of the future", with Grimmett in the attack.

South Australia did not win a match in the 1923–24 season and Grimmett was seen as a saviour. Richardson was among the crowd of wellwishers at the Adelaide Railway Station. Others included J.A. Riley (secretary of the South Australian Cricket Association), J.F. Travers (a Colts selector), A.J. Lee, L.S. Kelly and Eddie McCarron (Adelaide Cricket Club), and H. Bridgman (West Torrens). Clarrie was accompanied by his wife, Elizabeth and son, Victor.

The day could not have started out better for Clarrie, because he was informed by Richardson that he had been selected in a Rest of Australia XI to play New South Wales at the Sydney Cricket Ground in celebration of Bill Howell's Benefit Year. "Farmer" Bill toiled long and hard for New South Wales and Australia, taking 177 Sheffield Shield wickets for New South Wales in 36 matches, plus 49 (at 28.71) in 18 Tests. He toured England in 1899, 1902 and 1905. In 1899 he took all ten Surrey wickets for 28 off 23.2 overs. Grimmett took 10/37 versus Yorkshire some 31 years later. Clarrie was elated. Perhaps this was the start of real recognition.

But the Howell Benefit was not for a few months. Clarrie needed to settle down quickly. He worked hard at his signwriting post with Harry Lyons and continued to train in the backyard with Joe, for whom Clarrie's affection continued to grow. Then one day, late in July, 1924, Joe was not to be found. Clarrie combed the Adelaide streets. It was dark and light rain was falling.

Clarrie was soaked to the skin when he slumped on the front doorstep; head in hands, he shed a silent tear for the dog who had meant so much to him. Clarrie loved that little black and white fox terrier. He knew Joe was not merely out of sight; he was dead, for Joe would not go willingly with another mortal soul. As he sat on the cold, wet slate floor at the top of the stone stairs leading to the Grimmett front door, Clarrie spun out the memories in his mind. How Joe would crouch ready to move into rapid action, returning the balls at his master's feet. How he disdainfully refused if anyone other than Clarrie issued a command. How he would yelp for joy when a Grimmett Bosey pitched perfectly and then spun to hit middle and leg stumps, or the inswinging leg-break pitched in line of leg then whipped across wickedly to hit the top of off-stump…. Clarrie reckoned Joe must have taken a bait. He never again saw his beloved dog.

The cricket season approached fast and Clarrie continued to

work hard on his bowling. Clarrie, Lizzy and their son, Victor, were then living in John Street, Adelaide. It was a small, comfortable city home, but not quite the ideal for Clarrie. He yearned for space where he could put down a pitch and a tennis court. At every spare moment Clarrie and Lizzy would scour the Adelaide area, searching for a home to suit their needs.

They soon found an established suburb called Firle, some eight kilometres east of Adelaide. Tall, healthy gum trees abounded, a good sign of ample water and rich soil. They wanted to find their dream home in this area. They would save. The first club match came round in no time and Clarrie was quickly involved. He scored a first-up duck (run out) for his new club, Adelaide, against Vic Richardson's Sturt, but he made amends with the ball, taking 5/104, ending the Sturt innings with a hat-trick. Clarrie's team-mates dropped many chances off his bowling, and according to the newspapers he should have returned figures of "8/50 but for the fielding of his fellow clubmates".

"Farmer" Bill Howell's Benefit Match came to the fore and Clarrie found himself in the same side as Vic and Arthur Richardson, Percy Hornibrook and Clem Hill, the latter looking fit and sprightly at the age of forty-seven. Their opponents were led by Herbie Collins, Clarrie's old Sydney skipper, and now Test captain, plus a formidable array of talent, especially batting talent. Clarrie was delighted. He would be confronting some of the cream of Australia's batting, including such notables as Tommy Andrews, Alan Kippax, Charlie Macartney, the man good judges reckoned the best since Trumper, Warren Bardsley, Johnny Taylor, Charles Kelleway and Jack Gregory. It was a great challenge and one Clarrie looked forward to with utter relish. He was itching for a good battle.

On the eve of the match, Hill said of Grimmett: "I think he will turn out to be a very good bowler this season." Prophetic words.

Clarrie enjoyed the match although he suffered at the hands of the strong New South Wales batting line-up. Kellaway, Collins, Taylor and Kippax all scored centuries. A.G. (Johnny) Moyes, the former New South Wales and South Australia right-hander, who was selected in the 1914–15 Australian team to tour

South Africa (the tour was cancelled due to World War I), wrote warmly of Grimmett's bowling:

> I thought Grimmett bowled the best, and he had one purple patch when he got Bardsley and Andrews in one over. Right through the day his length was good and he swung in with the wind in disconcerting fashion. Kippax and Taylor used their feet cleverly and scored freely off him, but at no time did he lose his length. On a faster wicket he would have done even better. At mid-off he did many fine things and was one of the stars in the field.

Clarrie noted the styles of all the batsmen and he learned that Kippax, in particular, did not "read" his top-spinner. He would store that information away for some future battle. While he was not right on top of his form, the match did much for his confidence and it was good to have a tough encounter before the Sheffield Shield season got underway. Often during the match old hands Clem Hill and Vic Richardson were seen deep in conversation. They were, no doubt, discussing the merits of the South Australian newchum Grimmett.

He had made a favourable first impression on both men the previous February when his leg-spinners for Victoria brought South Australia to its knees. Now the wily spinner had shown remarkable stamina and temperament in wheeling them down in the oppressive heat, on a hard strip with the batsmen in total control. Clarrie did not waver once. His control was immaculate and he never complained about the odd shoddy piece of fielding. Three easy catches were turfed, but the Fox kept his own counsel: inwardly his screams would have deafened the soul. Clarrie worked hard on his fielding and found no humour in shoddy work in the field.

The big match against Victoria finally arrived and Clarrie was asked to bat higher in the order than expected. He went in as a night-watchman first day and wound up hitting a superb 49 at number 5 in a batting line-up which amassed 518. The Victorians faltered first time up, mainly to Grimmett's untiring leg-spin. He took a debut 5/97 off 42 overs, 10 of which were maidens. His victims included Edgar Mayne (12), the Victorian captain who had little truck for slow men, Frank Tarrant (86), lured down the track and stumped, Jack Ellis (69), Bill Ponsford (10), clean bowled and Hunter "Stork" Hendry (18).

South Australia batted again and were bundled out for 223, Arthur Richardson getting 46 and Clarrie himself getting 22.

This gave Victoria the winning target of 409. South Australia was favoured to win the match, but they had not allowed for the steel of the Victorian batting. Ponsford opened and hit freely to register 77 before Clarrie bowled him a beauty. Bill Woodfull made amends for a first innings score of 6 to hit 67 invaluable runs before Clarrie claimed him, but it was "Stork" Hendry who won it for Victoria. He hit a magnificent, unconquered 109. Grimmett had bowled a total of 96 overs for the match, returning 9/267. It was a performance to put him right before the Test selectors.

On the Sunday players from both teams visited a near-Adelaide winery in the foothills, where a sheep was turned over the hot coals. The players and officials tucked into their meal with relish, but Clarrie reserved the skeletal head of the poor beast for the Victorian captain. Edgar Mayne was a prized scalp for Clarrie. The Fox never forgot the "enemy" and he regarded Mayne thus, for Mayne's non-recognition of his bowling skill in Victoria. It was Mayne who gave Clarrie only five overs for Victoria in the match against New South Wales at the SCG back in 1919; as Victorian captain he had showed scant respect for Clarrie's ability. Clarrie slammed the sheep's head in Mayne's empty soup dish and laughed: "There you are, Mr Mayne. Your head on a platter...caught and bowled!" There was the odd snigger among the Victorians, but nothing to the roar of delight from the South Australian corner. If Clarrie hadn't won his team-mates with his marvellous bowling, this timely act against Mayne was something they'd never forget.

Victoria had the last laugh (in the collective sense), winning the match; however, Clarrie helped to turn attitudes in his adopted state. He showed that they could stand up for themselves against any opponents. Tony Lock helped turn Western Australia into a formidable cricketing state in the 1960s with a similar attitude.

South Australia's first innings total of 518 brought some caustic comments from the Melbourne cricket commentator "Old Boy", who wrote of the Victorian selectors' incompetence in not selecting the two St Kilda spinners, Don Blackie and Bert

"Dainty" Ironmonger, the former an off-spinner and the latter a left-handed finger spinner. Neither made the Victorian team and "Old Boy", lamenting the dreadful Victorian bowling in Adelaide, wrote of the St Kilda spin pair's bowling efforts since October 1922:

> Blackie has taken 98 wickets at 14.95 runs apiece and Ironmonger, 93 wickets at 13.16.
>
> No less a judge than H.S. Love said recently that the Blackie-Ironmonger partnership was the best in the land. The remarkable thing has been that Blackie has been consistently overlooked. He can bowl all day, never tires, is a good field and a better batsman than most bowlers. So far this season he has an average of 74 runs per innings and twice in succession has batted well in a pinch.
>
> When, on Saturday, he made 39 like a tradesman and saved his side, a St Kilda supporter questioned whether the State selectors should not look at Blackie as a batsman, considering they do not class him good enough to play State cricket as a bowler.
>
> I have no hesitation in saying that Blackie has been the best bowler in Victoria and has more than earned his inclusion. One has waited so long for the Colts to get a chance that one is constrained to urge that the best veterans should be picked when their merit is outstanding.
>
> Ironmonger has had interstate opportunities, Blackie has not. A trial against the Englishmen might give the selectors some valuable information. They got it from Grimmett last season.

After the remarkable match against Victoria in Adelaide, the teams were destined to meet again in Melbourne just three weeks later. Again Victoria won, with Ponsford hitting a classic 166 and Clarrie getting 5/97. Under fire Grimmett was proving cool and calm. New South Wales hit 510 against the South Australian attack in Sydney, with Kippax scoring 127 and Grimmett snaring yet another bag of five wickets, this time 5/137. He still reckoned Kippax was not "reading" him — perhaps next time. Vic Richardson got a century in each innings, but Jack Gregory (7/88) and Arthur Mailey (6/99) in the respective South Australian innings proved too much and New South Wales won by 9 wickets.

However, South Australia convincingly won the return encounter in Adelaide, recording its first Sheffield Shield win since 1914. South Australia hit a first-up 389 and New South Wales replied with 408. Clarrie took 3 wickets. Then New South Wales collapsed for 226 in the wake of South Australia's second innings of 406. Grimmett took 6/103 and even the Victorians were calling for him to be rushed into the Test team. While Grimmett starred with the ball and in the field, and Arthur and Vic Richardson continued to do well with the bat, South Australia's lone win of the summer did little for the majority of enthusiasts in Adelaide.

Australia was dominating the Test rubber against Arthur Gilligan's England team, winning the first Test in Sydney by 193 runs, the second Test in Melbourne by 81 runs and the third Test in Adelaide by 11 runs. Yet the cry for Grimmett was getting louder. That first Test in Sydney was also Vic Richardson's Test debut and Bill Ponsford's first big match. Vic scored 42 and 18 and Ponny hit a debut 110 and 27. The push for Grimmett grew stronger and stronger as the days passed, especially after England beat Australia in the fourth Test in Melbourne. Arthur Mailey's 4/186 off 43.6 overs was not sufficient to stop England's run glut. The English total of 548 was more than enough. Australia hit 269 and 250, Maurice Tate being the chief destroyer for the visitors. Australia needed bowling support for Mailey. Grimmett was the man.

6 TEST DEBUT

Clarrie Grimmett was coaching youngsters on the picturesque St Peter's College Oval (where Clem Hill once hit 360 in an intercollegiate match) when a breathless, ruddy-faced young man rushed up to him. In his quivering hand he held a copy of *The News*, the afternoon daily newspaper which Sir Keith Murdoch began in 1924 and later handed to his son, Rupert (the very platform young Rupert used to launch his now rocketing media empire).

"Mr Grimmett…Mr Grimmett!" the ruddy-faced man yelled, "You're in…you're in the Test team!"

The Test team was in the "Stop Press" section at the back of the newspaper: no sweet tasted better to Grimmett. News didn't travel quite as swiftly in 1925 as it does today.

For most of the summer the critics had urged Grimmett's selection, so his belated inclusion did not come as a surprise, but for all his outward nonchalance, the Fox was delighted.

Apart from his sensational bowling for South Australia, Clarrie was also in fine fettle for the Adelaide club. He took 5/104 against Sturt, plus 5/49 and 6/51 against the North Adelaide team. Clarrie was rarely not at the top of his form.

Clarrie's dedication and extraordinary grit had paid off. He was well-satisfied. He received dozens of telegrams from friends, team-mates and opponents, even some from strangers. Clarrie sought the quiet life; he soon learned there was a price to pay for fame. An adoring public could also be a constant and maddening menace.

Two men were to make their Test debuts: Clarrie Grimmett and the New South Wales batsman Alan Kippax. The team was: Herbie Collins, Bill Ponsford, Jack Gregory, Charles Kelleway,

Tommy Andrews, Johnny Taylor, Jack Ryder, Alan Kippax, Bert Oldfield, Arthur Mailey, Clarrie Grimmett and Vic Richardson. Clarrie spoke of his reaction:

> I was getting a fair swag of wickets for South Australia while Gilligan's team was out here in 1924–25, but I never imagined I would play in a Test that season. Had anyone suggested to me that I would do so, I would have laughed at them because, in Mailey, Australia already had a spin bowler of considerable experience.
>
> From the time that fellow rushed up to me at St Peter's College and told me I was in the Test team I was very surprised and excited. By the time I got home telegrams from friends were starting to pour in. Some of the wires were from Sydney friends asking me to keep certain nights free so they could entertain me during the match.

Clarrie's dream of wearing the coveted green baggy cap would soon be realised. The little Kiwi had made it. He was measured for his blazer, sweater and that all-important cap. The measurements were then telegraphed to Sydney and the clothes were awaiting collection when Clarrie arrived at the Grosvenor Hotel. The hotel has since been demolished. It was pulled down to make way for the approaches to the Sydney Harbour Bridge in 1932.

The crowd flocked to the ground, although Australia already held a 3-1 lead in the series. England had won the previous Test match and there was much ado about the new men, the little spin wizard Grimmett and Kippax, a serene stroking batsman many argued was as stylish as Victor Trumper himself.

"We stepped from our cars and the autograph hunters were upon us," Clarrie told me. "But once through the turnstiles it is impossible to remain calm. Although the Ashes had been won by Australia, there was a big crowd by the time I arrived. The atmosphere was electric."

He was a bit tense, but nerves never entered the picture. Clarrie was as quietly confident as always. He had worked hard for this day. He would continue to strive for spinning excellence. Grimmett's South Australian captain, Vic Richardson, was made twelfth man. Clarrie was not worried about performing to a good standard, given the chance; he was more tense about the naming of the eleven. When Richardson was named to carry the drinks, Clarrie's heart pounded. He was playing!

He might not have realised it then, but Grimmett was only the second New Zealand-born cricketer to play a Test match for Australia. The first was Thomas Underwood Groube, a medium-pacer and batsman, who was born at Taranaki and became a last-minute replacement for Charles Bannerman in the Australian touring team to England in 1880.

Bannerman became ill on the preliminary tour of Australia before the team sailed for the Old Country. Groube, who had played only two eleven-a-side matches for Victoria in the 1879–80 season prior to the 1880 tour, batted at the coveted number three spot for Australia in that first Test match on English soil. Groube scored 11, before Steel uprooted his off-stump and Morley got him for a duck in the second innings. Groube never again played Test cricket. England won that first encounter by five wickets, W.G. Grace getting 152 in the first innings, but Australia missed Frederick Spofforth, the demon, who two years later brought English cricket to its knees with a match-winning performance at Kennington Oval, taking 14/90, prompting the *Sporting Times* to carry a mock obituary, stating that the body would be cremated and the Ashes taken to Australia. But on this day, 27 February, 1925, the day of Grimmett's Test debut, Spofforth sat in the members' stand, as a director of the England-based Star Tea Company, a guest of the New South Wales Cricket Association.

Collins won the toss and Australia batted first on a good track. Yet Maurice Tate (4/92) and Roy Kilner (4/97) bowled well to restrict Australia to 295. Kippax hit a promising debut 42, with Ponsford top scoring with a solidly-compiled 80. Clarrie was pleased with his 12 not out, despite the indignity of batting below Mailey in the order.

Clarrie watched every ball until his turn came to bat. He hoped to discover the way in which a bowler was likely to trap a batsman, so he might be on guard against the wiles of each bowler. He was ever the cricket student.

Grimmett believed there was much to learn by watching play when his side was batting. He could never understand any player in the pavilion being preoccupied and missing seeing the action.

"When the ninth wicket fell, my turn came to bat. The uppermost worry in my mind as I walked onto the arena was a fear that I might not break the duck. Had I made a duck in front of all those 39,000 people the walk back would have been torture," Clarrie said. Batting at number eleven wouldn't normally have displeased Clarrie, but it did this time, for Arthur Mailey was batting above him. Mailey got 14 and Grimmett 12 not out in a modest Australian total of 295.

Finally the Australians walked onto the field and Clarrie wondered where he would be placed in the field as the captain, Collins, went quietly to work arranging his field placements. He eyed Clarrie and said: "Will you take the drive?" That gave Clarrie as much confidence as Collins' New South Wales team had given him a few days earlier. Clarrie had just arrived in Sydney for the Test match. He ventured down to the SCG where New South Wales were playing the Englishmen. The players were having afternoon tea on the last afternoon of that game and Collins was sitting on the far side of the changeroom when he noticed Clarrie. Immediately he spotted the new Test spinner, Collins rushed to his side, extending a congratulatory hand-shake. This gesture was important to Clarrie. He lived and breathed cricket; harmony among players was essential and obviously mutually beneficial. His State captain, Vic Richard-son, was strong on team harmony and Clarrie was grateful that Collins shared this attitude towards good team spirit.

The famous Jack Hobbs, Herbert Sutcliffe partnership was at the wicket, but it wasn't long before Hobbs fell to a marvellous leg-side catch by Bert Oldfield. Jack Gregory sent the first ball of the innings to Hobbs who leg glanced it wide of Oldfield. It seemed a certain four, but Oldfield leapt across to take the catch. England one for none! Oldfield's swift footwork had him in the perfect position; he did not have to throw himself frantically to his left in the manner of a soccer goalkeeper.

Andy Sandham was in next. On sixty-three occasions Sand-ham assisted the man he passed at the gate (J.B. Hobbs) in century opening stands for Surrey. As with his Surrey colleague, Sandham didn't last long. He was brilliantly run out when he hammered a ball from Gregory between Andrews at cover and Grimmett at mid-off. Clarrie swooped on the ball and returned it smartly to Gregory near the stumps.

It was the sort of throw one would expect from a baseball infielder. Grimmett's baseball paid off. He was quick to the ball, whether at mid-off or cover and had the ball back in a flash. It could have been the perfect throw from short stop to first base. Clarrie thought his throw might have hit the stumps had not Jack Gregory's huge right arm shot out to grab the ball and swing the hand which held the ball against the stumps, with Sandham stranded well out of his ground. Frank Woolley, that tall, graceful man of Kent, strode to the wicket. With Woolley, a left-hander, and Sutcliffe, a right-hander, at the crease frequent field changes were needed. Clarrie kept his wits about him, lest he miss a veiled signal from the skipper. Collins never telegraphed field changes. His team had to keep an eye on him, for Collins, the Sydney bookie, made field changes with a subtle nod or wave of the hand. It could have been brushing a fly when he really meant his mid-off to "give himself a few yards" or move deeper for Woolley.

Clarrie feared missing a Collins signal. It would have been an annoyance to the captain and that fear remained as one of his clearest recollections of that biggest day of his career. Sutcliffe (22) fell to Kelleway and Patsy Hendren (10) to Gregory before Collins threw Clarrie the ball. England was 4/89, with Woolley having blazed his way to 43 and Jack Hearne on 8. Back in 1915 Collins had suggested Clarrie toss up a higher, slower delivery to a Redfern batsman when Grimmett was making his Sydney club debut.

The slower one was to follow a series of deliveries which forced the batsman to retreat on to the back foot. Collins said then, "Do that and I'll catch him at cover for you." The plan worked. Collins took time out to discuss field placings and to help settle him down. Collins suggested a series of leg-breaks to Woolley, then a well-pitched Bosey, hoping for a catch to Jack Gregory at slip. Clarrie listened, but he already had his strategy worked out. He knew Woolley would be on the lookout for the Bosey, so Clarrie was going to disappoint him. Collins sensed Grimmett was in total control, so he wisely decided to leave the little man to his own devices. Clarrie described it later:

> I was thrilled at being given the ball but I was not really nervous because I have always had supreme confidence in my bowling and

in my ability to maintain a length.

The more important the match, the better I can concentrate. Even though I have been knocked about, I have never lost my head. I have never felt beaten by any of the marvellous batsmen to whom I have bowled. Everyone else might have thought I would never get them out but I have always felt there was a chance of a mistake. No matter how well a batsman had been shaping, I never gave up hope of dismissing him.

That first ball in Test cricket was a tester for Clarrie. He said he had felt a little anxious as he approached the crease.

"I felt I was going to put the ball where I wanted it to go but I did not know what the batsman would do with it." Clarrie's figures stood at 0/4 when he again prepared to bowl to Woolley. "Woolley was on 47. A boundary would give him his half-century and he was a man whose bat would flash and send the ball racing to the pickets, but it has been my good fortune to get him on most of the occasions we have met."

In the 1920–21 summer when Clarrie played for Victoria against MCC, he should have had Woolley caught at cover, but the two fieldsmen couldn't make up their minds which of them would make the catch. It was the Grimmett Bosey. Woolley might have picked it, but Clarrie knew the elegant left-hander could be beaten with a subtle change of pace, and he knew the Kent man would be on the search for the ball turning away. Clarrie decided to bowl only leg-breaks to Woolley. If he was, as Clarrie suspected, on the lookout for the Bosey, he might just leave a gap between bat and pad. Grimmett aimed to clean bowl Woolley in just that fashion. A couple of well-pitched leg-breaks had Woolley stretching and driving firmly to Collins at cover. Grimmett then purposely got one to swerve away late: "I sent down an ordinary leg-break and he seemed to lose sight of it. Then came the death rattle of the stumps falling — the sweetest sound a bowler knows."

The ball curved slightly away from the left-hander, effectively opening up a gap between bat and pad.

As with all the successful Grimmett plans, Clarrie had "seen" the dismissal in his mind's eye. The actual dismissal was almost an action replay. Woolley tried to drive through cover, but the ball found its way through the "gate" to clean bowl him and present Grimmett with his first Test wicket.

A photograph of Clarrie's first Test wicket was presented to him by Herbert Fishwick of the Sydney *Mail*. Team-mates gathered round the newchum Test spinner offering congratulatory pats on the back and handshakes. It was a precious moment in his life.

Hearne and Whysall fell lbw to Grimmett's dipping top-spinner, Roy Kilner was stumped by Oldfield after leaving his crease in an unsuccessful attempt to drive a Grimmett Bosey and Gilligan made an uncouth airswing to become Clarrie's fifth victim, also courtesy of an Oldfield stumping.

Grimmett had stunned England and delighted the nation. In just 11.7 overs, he had claimed 5/45 in a display of spinning wizardry seldom seen on the SCG.

Clarrie loved to talk of his Test debut; his pride shone, yet he did not boast. He simply told it as it happened. "It must have been my lucky day because as we left the field some friends called me over to the grandstand dividing fence to congratulate me," Clarrie recalled. "As we chatted, there was a heavy thud. I looked down and saw a heavy battery box at my feet. It had been accidentally dropped by the broadcasting technicians from the balcony above."

Clarrie's first Test outing with the ball almost proved his last, but he reckoned that near miss was a good omen, for his bowling proved even more devastating for Gilligan's men a second time.

As he left the SCG, well satisfied with his bag of five English scalps, a large, black limousine pulled up. A man sitting inside waved his hand at Clarrie and called, "Congratulations, Grimmett". The car was some distance away before Clarrie realised that the occupant was Lord Forster, the Australian governor-general. A night out with his old Sydney baseball mates, which included dinner at Circular Quay and the theatre, rounded off a great day in the life of Clarrie Grimmett. Australia rattled up 325 in the second innings with a late-order rally by Kelleway (73) and Bert Oldfield (65 not out) ensuring Collins' men were very much in the box seat. Clarrie was brought back to earth with a thud, getting a duck, bowled by Tate.

Set 454 runs to win, England was immediately in trouble.

With the score at 3, big Jack Gregory blasted through Herbert Sutcliffe's defence to clean bowl him for a duck. Hobbs was settling in well against Gregory and Kelleway, but with the introduction of Grimmett the tide turned again in Australia's favour. Clarrie had Hobbs stretching. He persistently lured him forward to drive, Collins cutting off a couple of powerful strokes. Then Clarrie got a ball to curve in and spin past the Hobbs forward defensive prod. Hobbs was at full stretch. He overbalanced and his back foot slipped forward and over the popping crease. Oldfield had the bails off in a flash. Umpire Bob Crockett, the same man who nearly caused a riot by ruling Clem Hill run out on that very ground when he and Victor Trumper were in full flight more than twenty years before, had no hesitation in giving Hobbs out. However, controversy raged. A photograph showed Hobbs' foot just behind the line, yet Clarrie always maintained that the photograph was captured after Hobbs had regained his ground. The scorebook had the final say. It read thus: "Hobbs st Oldfield bowled Grimmett 13".

Grimmett cut through the rest of the England batting like a scythe, having Sandham lbw to his top-spinner, and getting Hendren, Hearne, Whysall and Strudwick to finish with 6/37 off 19.4 overs. It was the perfect answer to all his critics. Curiously Arthur Mailey bowled only five overs (0/13) for the entire match, while Clarrie's match figures stood at 11/82.

Fittingly, it was Mailey who took the catch, off Grimmett, to dismiss Strudwick and provide Australia with victory by 307 runs.

Clarrie was grateful for Bert Oldfield's keeping in that game. Oldfield stumped four batsmen (Kilner, Gilligan, Hobbs and Whysall) and caught one, Hendren, of Clarrie's eleven wickets. The New South Wales Cricket Association presented Clarrie with the ball he used in the England first innings. A small silver shield, with his figures engraved on it, was attached to the ball. However, Bert Oldfield, who took the wonderful catch down the leg side to dismiss Hobbs in the England first innings, dearly wanted that ball. Clarrie gave Olfield the ball used in the first innings. He then pleaded with Bob Crockett for the ball used in the England second innings and attached the shield to it.

In Adelaide the people hailed Clarrie's Test feats with such enthusiasm that *The News* opened a subscription list to make him a presentation during the approaching England v. South Australia match. The premier, the Hon. J. Gunn said: "His performance was phenomenal. The Adelaide bowler is entitled to be proud of it. It will rank high in the record feats of the cricket world." Adelaide lord mayor, C.R.J. Glover, was emphatic that Grimmett be recognised in a tangible way. "I recommend the idea of a presentation and I commend it to the whole of the sporting community."

Mr Glover's words meant that all South Australians, not just the local association, could take part in donating towards the fund. SACA president Harold Fisher spoke in glowing terms of Grimmett, the bowler and the man. "Grimmett is a young fellow who has put in and made the mark in a remarkable manner. I think we should take notice of his performance and do something to mark the occasion. In my opinion the cricket association will be glad to assist in making him a presentation."

It was probably the Australian Board of Control chairman (also the then SACA treasurer), B.V. Scrymgour, who made the most significant remarks, reported in *The News*, 5 March 1925, relating to Grimmett's bowling strategy. "The great feature of Grimmett's bowling is that he does not wait for the batsmen to make mistakes. He beats them with the ball. The fact that a South Australian bowler has done so well, allied to the success of the two Richardsons [Vic and Arthur], will make a lot of old cricketers reminiscent of the days when at one time we supplied George Giffen, Ernest Jones, Joe Darling, and Clem Hill to the Australian Eleven." He later added, "Grimmett is such an unassuming quiet type of man that his success will not spoil him, but rather will induce him to still greater effort."

The man mostly responsible for Clarrie moving from Victoria to South Australia, Adelaide Cricket Club president Eddie McCarron, was quoted in *The News* as saying: "Grimmett's success must be applauded throughout the land. Players of the Grimmett type do much for the game. He is always ready and willing to assist young crickets, many of whom have already derived benefit from his sage advice. I will do all in my power in the matter." Joe Lyons, the former international and one-time SACA secretary, said, "I know what pride he [Grimmett] must

On the encouragement of bowlers — by Wells. A cartoonist slams the
Victorian selectors after Clarrie's brilliant Test debut in 1925

have felt in the achievement because I remember how elated I
was when I took 5/31 in a Test match at Lord's in 1893. I received
a presentation from my fellows as a result of that feat."

In Melbourne a cricket writer put the question; "What about
Mayne, Bean and the rest of the officials who refused to listen to
the clamouring for the inclusion of Clarrie Grimmett in the
interstate cricket team? When the question was put by the
people of Melbourne there was no answer." Perhaps Clarrie
rubbed salt into the wounds in Melbourne. He told a representative of *The News* in Melbourne, "I'm told the crowd in
Sydney was excited by my performance, but I did not notice
much of it myself." Clarrie spent a few days in Melbourne on
his return from the Sydney Test match, attending a ceremony at
Prahran Cricket Club where the scoreboard he designed was
officially put on show.

The Wolfe Schnapps Company prize scheme for the 1924–25

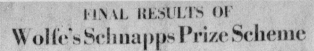

Clarrie's special prize of £10 for his 11/82 bag in his first Test. He also
collected a further two shillings for hitting a boundary

season was announced, with Johnny Taylor picking up fifteen pounds eighteen shillings; Bert Oldfield, twelve pounds fourteen shillings; Bill Ponsford, seven pounds eighteen shillings and Arthur Mailey, four pounds sixteen shillings.

Charlie Kelleway won twenty-five pounds for his best bowling average. The rules were that the player must have competed in at least three Tests and have taken no fewer than ten wickets.

Kelleway took 14 wickets for 413 runs; an average of 29.5. Company executives must have pondered over this win, for Grimmett took 11/82 in just one match, his average being a shade over seven, and Wolfe Schnapps awarded Clarrie a special prize of ten pounds. In addition, he got the mandatory two shillings for hitting a four.

Clarrie returned home to a fabulous welcome at the Adelaide Railway Station. The South Australian team were about to play England, the last match of the tour for Gilligan and his men. The euphoria of being back in his adopted state had hardly subsided when there he was out with the South Australian team, wheeling away against Gilligan's Englishmen. England were trundled out for 179 first up, with Clarrie hardly making an inroad. He took just 1/40 off 17 overs. Arthur Richardson's slow-medium off-breaks did the damage. Richardson took 5/52 off 13 overs. South Australia rattled up 443, Rymill getting 146, Percy Rundell 90, Dave Pritchard 87 and Vic Richardson 43. Clarrie stroked his way to 39 before Tate had him caught at slip. Batting again, England made a better fist of things with Sutcliffe (75), Hearne (78), Woolley (90) and Hobbs (59) all getting into run-making mode. Grimmett got himself a "bag", accounting for Sutcliffe and Hearne, before clean bowling Woolley, a repeat of his first Test effort.

At the tea adjournment, SACA president Harold Fisher presented Clarrie with a cheque for two hundred and twenty pounds. The sum total of the Testimonial Fund was two hundred and twelve pounds seventeen shillings and sixpence, as reported in *The Advertiser*. However, Clarrie was adamant that he received a cheque for two hundred and twenty pounds, a princely sum in 1925. Nine pounds were raised at the Abattoirs when a two hundred and eighty pound sheep was auctioned on the bugler system. E.W. Pearce, of the Model Meat Store, King

William Street, purchased the animal outright for the sum of three pounds ten shillings. A further five pounds ten shillings was raised by sundry contributions. At Adelaide's Floating Palais the previous night, Grimmett was presented with a cheque for ten pounds, when dancing was suspended to perform formalities. England cricketers Tate, Sutcliffe and Freeman received presentation sleevelinks for their Test heroics. After the presentation ceremony, Clarrie walked on to the Adelaide Oval and almost immediately clean bowled Percy Chapman with his top-spinner which hurried through to claim the off-stump. Life was good.

7 ENGLAND

It is every Australian boy's dream to play Test cricket in England. Although not Australian-born, it was also Clarrie's dream, almost an obsession. Johnny Moyes described Adelaide as "so often a haven for unwanted bowlers and a staging-post on the way to England". Grimmett felt unwanted in Sydney because the prevailing attitude towards Mailey before, during and just after World War I and Victoria's selectors had made it impossible for Clarrie to build a first-class career. At the age of thirty-two Clarrie sensed his days as a cricketing nomad were numbered. Adelaide was his last chance. Clarrie and Lizzy settled down to the quiet Adelaide lifestyle.

Lizzy had a trick or two up her sleeve, but she confined most of them to playing bridge. In her leisure hours she knitted, cooked or played cards. She cooked good, wholesome and balanced meals. Every morning Clarrie consumed a huge serving of porridge. He was an avid tea drinker. Long after Grimmett's time as a player, little Alan Knott, arguably the greatest wicketkeeper of them all, developed a similar passion for tea.

Clarrie's eye for detail, so often displayed in cricket, was part of his job as a signwriter. His ability to draw beyond the sort of skill required for his signwriting job was largely unknown. Grimmett sketched profiles of little-known characters. He drew a caricature of himself when he was at the height of his fame in 1934, but there is no evidence that he sketched his team-mates at any time in his career. Clarrie did not want to be linked with his old adversary Arthur Mailey, for he feared the press might take him to task for copying Mailey, the leg-spinner-cum-artist. Mailey was much loved, a spinner with flair; he managed to put on a public face of one who could laugh at himself. Grimmett did not approve of Mailey's attitude to the spinning craft, having a scant respect for a bowler who allowed batsmen to belt him unmercifully, even applauding a batsman for hitting a boundary.

Often after the evening meal, Clarrie would sit in the kitchen with Lizzy, as she knitted contentedly , and sketch someone's profile on the back of an invoice or an envelope. Grimmett wasted nothing, not one delivery, not one precious piece of paper, not one stroke of the brush.

The winter wore on. The 1925–26 season was fast approaching, at the end of which was the 1926 England tour. Clarrie's new-found fame as a Test hero brought many requests to coach, even in the middle of winter. He coached for the South Australian Cricket Association and privately. He needed to keep trim, so he used to walk the Adelaide streets, rugged up against the cold and the rain, running through his mind yet another bowling plan.

He joined the East Torrens Baseball Club, playing on Saturday afternoons immediately after a round of golf. During the week, he bowled in the small backyard at John Street, although mid-way through the winter Clarrie and Lizzy moved to a more spacious home in Halifax Street, still in the heart of the city. Halifax Street had a bigger backyard. He always found time for at least two hours' bowling every day, either before or after work. Clarrie always trained, even when it rained. He was never worried when having to bowl in a match with a wet ball. Clarrie Grimmett was a fielding captain's dream.

Clarrie bowled only 91.2 overs for Adelaide in the 1925–26 summer, but he managed to take 27 wickets at an average of 12.88. For South Australia Clarrie took 49 wickets at an average of 31.63. It proved to be the Fox's second highest average, his highest being recorded the following summer (30 at 34.33). Critics said he bowled better than his figures; however, Clarrie was not interested in merely bowling well; he wanted results. If he was picked for the England tour, he and Lizzy planned to buy a house on his return to Australia. Lizzy was contented, and their little son, Victor, was a joy to them both.

Clarrie felt secure. All he had to do was to bowl well and that dream of an England trip would be his, at long last. The first big

match of the season was in November, 1925 with South Australian turning the tables on the old foe, Victoria. Despite Don
Blackie's 7/71 and South Australia being bundled out for 170,
the Croweaters fought back with a second dig of 410 and bowled
the Victorians out for 275 (Grimmett 5/59) and 182 (Jack Scott
6/58). In December South Australia came up against powerful
New South Wales, again on the Adelaide Oval. In the New South
Wales first and only innings of 554, Grimmett failed to take a
wicket and conceded no fewer than 174 runs! Charlie Macartney
hit 112 and all of the New South Wales players got starts. Their
line-up included Bert Collins, Warren Bardsley, Johnny Taylor,
Charles Kelleway, Alan Kippax, Charlie Macartney, Jack Gregory and Bert Oldfield. "I had several chances missed off me,
but I kept plugging away in spite of the horrible figures against
my name on the scoreboard," Clarrie said later.

"I kept my length and when stumps were drawn Collins and
Macartney came to our dressingroom and congratulated me.
They were impressed with the way I stood my ground in the
face of heavy punishment."

In the last match of the season for New South Wales, Kippax
belted 271, but he missed the boat for England. Competition for
places was extraordinarily tough. Clarrie always maintained
that he was responsible for Kippax being left out of the touring
side. There was a Test trial in Sydney. Clarrie had just removed
Tommy Andrews with a big-turning leg-break. The Fox watched
Andrews trudge off towards the Pavilion. He couldn't miss
Andrews indicating to the incoming batsman, Kippax, with
arms outstretched just how far the ball was turning. So the Fox
decided to do the unexpected. He would toss down a top-spinner and hope for the best. Kippax played back and across for the
expected amount of exaggerated turn, but the ball went straight
on and cannoned from his pad onto the stumps — out for a duck
first ball. It proved a crushing blow for Kippax. Clarrie considered Kippax, the man some thought the very embodiment of
Trumper because of his grace and style, to be one of the hardest
batsmen to bowl against. Clarrie was considered among the
certainties for the 1926 Australian Touring Team and was duly
picked, along with some great names in Australian cricket,
including Charlie Macartney, Warren Bardsley, Bill Ponsford,

Tommy Andrews, Bill Woodfull, Johnny Taylor, Bert Oldfield, his old Prahran team-mate Jack Ellis, and Arthur Mailey.

"When we were on the ship [the *Otranto*] en route to England, Collins told me my bowling against New South Wales in Adelaide, when I was clobbered to the tune of none for 174, went a long way to my selection to tour England," Clarrie said. During the voyage Clarrie spent most of his time on the sports deck or swimming, and he danced in the evening. He found the time passed quickly and the Test team seemed to enjoy special treatment by the shipping people with regard to on-board entertainment.

"We arrived at Colombo, first contact with Asia and its teeming millions," Clarrie noted in his diary. "The natives are keen on their cricket. We played a match at Colombo. So efficient were the waiters at our hotel I found it did not pay to put my knife and fork down for more than a couple of seconds because these diligent chaps were ready to pounce on a plate and whisk it away. We were each given a pith helmet to wear on the field, for the regulation Test caps are not proof against the fierce rays of the tropical sun."

Soon they were underway again, getting ever closer to the Mother Country. Clarrie was on the deck when the *Otranto* approached Naples, and later described the scene:

> I got a thrill when we arrived in Naples, the fog restricting our view of that beautiful harbour. Then the fog lifted, revealing high cliffs and castles, relics of old feudal days.
>
> Mount Vesuvius was smoking, the oarsmen faced the way they were travelling, dozens of different uniforms could be seen on shore and there was every indication I was in a strange land. We went overland from Naples, through Pompeii, to Florence, with its marble, to Milan with its glorious cathedral and La Scala opera house, and then through a tunnel into Switzerland. When we went into the tunnel we left behind a country of green fields and sunshine. We emerged into a land of snow.

Although Vic Richardson, Alan Kippax and Charlie Kelleway had been unable to win a tour place, the team, under Collins' captaincy, played pretty well, although it lost the only completed Test match, with England regaining the Ashes after fourteen years. Clarrie did well, taking 116 tour wickets at an average of 17.20 while his old spinning mate, Arthur Mailey, took 141 wickets at 18.70. The spinners were the bowling mainstays, with Macartney's left-hand slows getting 56 wickets at 16.14 and off-spinner Arthur Richardson taking 63 wickets at 17.66. The first Test match was a disaster. England batted first and was none for 32 when the heavens over Trent Bridge opened up. Rain did not let up for the entire scheduled three days. Clarrie did not come into the side until the third Test at Leeds. Harold Larwood made his debut for England in the second match at Lord's. Arthur Mailey took 0/96 off 30 overs in an England total of 3 declared for 475, Jack Hobbs (119) and Patsy Hendren (127 not out), Frank Woolley (87) and Herbert Sutcliffe (82) caning the Australian attack.

Almost forty-three years old, Bardsley carried his bat in the Australian first innings of 383, with a fine knock of 193. Jack Gregory's knee was troubling him, but he struggled on. Australia batted first at Leeds, with Bill Woodfull getting a solid 141, but it was Macartney's century before lunch on the first day which stole the glory. Dropped at slip before he had scored, Macartney flayed the Englishmen, to emulate Trumper's century before lunch at Manchester in 1902. Grimmett was destined to see another such event, at Leeds in 1930, when young Don Bradman notched the coveted century before lunch. The third Test was drawn, but Clarrie bowled superbly, taking 5/88 off 39 overs in the first innings, claiming Herbert Sutcliffe, Roy Kilner, Maurice Tate, Macaulay and Herbert Strudwick, while Mailey accounted for Jack Hobbs and Patsy Hendren. In the second innings Grimmett took 2/59 off 29 overs, clean bowling Hobbs for 88 and getting Frank Woolley for 20. Woodfull and Macartney again hit centuries in the Manchester fourth Test, but the match ended in a tame draw. Clarrie got one wicket (Hobbs for 74), conceding 85 runs off 38 overs, and Mailey took 3/87 off 27 overs.

Four tests had been played for four draws. England took a gamble, bringing in a new captain, Percy Chapman, and recalling Wilfred Rhodes, then aged forty-eight. Rhodes had made his Test debut at Nottingham in 1899, W.G. Grace's farewell Test appearance. That match was also Victor Trumper's first Test match. Rhodes bowled superbly in the match, taking 2/35 off

25 overs and 4/44 off 20 overs to win the game and the rubber for England.

A fabulous 172-run partnership between Hobbs and Sutcliffe on a rain-affected track set up the game, after England's first offering of 280, only slightly worse than Australia's 302. Grimmett took five wickets for the game, but Mailey excelled, taking 6/138 off 33.5 overs and 3/128 off 42.5 overs. However, the Englishmen revelled in the damp conditions. Rhodes proved the ogre, getting Bardsley, Ponsford, Collins and Richardson cheaply. Larwood, also recalled for this last match, took 3/34, the perfect foil for Rhodes. The Kennington Oval crowd acclaimed their heroes, as they were destined to do in 1953 when Jim Laker and Tony Lock "rolled" Australia for England to win the only completed Test match and regain the Ashes after a nineteen-year wait. The 1926 tour established a record for they lost only one match, but the one they lost happened to be the Test match which cost Australia not only the rubber but the coveted Ashes.

"In this match I saw one of the best exhibitions of slow bowling in my experience," Clarrie said on his return. "Rhodes had acquired all there was to know about the bowler's art. He took only two steps, right foot, left foot and then appeared to send the ball gently on its way. What a marvellous, curving sinuous flight he had. Every ball pitched where it should be and each fieldsman was in exactly the right place. I was not interested in his average, that day, but I shall always remember seeing bowling at its best."

Between them Grimmett and Mailey took 27 of the 41 English wickets to fall in the rain-marred series. Before the tour, critics had begun to compare the relative merits of each bowler, but Mailey decided to retire from Tests after this tour, although he played on for New South Wales. One of his last wickets was Jack Hobbs, bowled Mailey for 100. It was a high full toss. Hobbs must have misjudged it in the shadow of the Oval gasometer for he swiped and missed, the ball landing on top of the off-stump. How Mailey loved it. Clarrie was delighted to see Hobbs on his way but rather annoyed to see the great man fall to such a terrible delivery.

It took Clarrie time to adjust to the hard, bouncy wickets of

Australia. As it turned out Clarrie's 30 wickets for South Australia in 1926–27 came at the high average of 34.33. It was in December, 1926 that Bill Ponsford, the boy who attended Grimmett's Sunday morning practices at Prahran in the early 1920s and now Clarrie's high-ranking Test team-mate, hit 352 in Victoria's world record score of 1107 against New South Wales in Melbourne. It was Mailey, with the figures of 4/364, who jested that his figures would have been much better had the fellow in the felt hat not dropped a dozen catches in the outer! Clarrie spent his thirty-fifth birthday watching Arthur Richardson slay the Queenslanders at Adelaide Oval, hitting a faultless 232. Grimmett got a belated birthday present, 5/107 to steer South Australia to a 10-wicket victory.

Ponsford scored 104 for Victoria in the game against South Australia at Melbourne and Clarrie notched 5/180, but he was not bowling quite like his old self. In the South Australia–New South Wales match in Sydney, South Australia's Karl Schneider hit 146 and Archie Jackson an unconquered 104 for New South Wales. Both were destined for early stardom and an early death. This was the year Queensland came into the Sheffield Shield competition. Because of the extra side in the Shield, matches were restricted to four full days and a portion of a fifth day. Matches not completed within that timeframe were drawn. If Clarrie wasn't quite the same on the field, perhaps there was an off-field reason.

There was. The Grimmetts were about to move into their new five-roomed house at 155 Glynde (now Glynburn) Road, Firle. They had been searching for months. They liked Firle, a leafy Adelaide suburb. The home account was with Goldsbrough Mort and Coy Limited (which had merged with Bagot, Shakes and Lewis Limited). The asking price was one thousand seven hundred and seventy-five pounds. Clarrie and Lizzy had one thousand pounds on a first mortgage and two hundred and seventy-five pounds on a second mortgage. They paid four hundred and seventy-three pounds, nine shillings and ninepence cash which covered the balance owing. Cricket came first, but there was much to do at Firle. Physically the move mid-summer took its toll on Clarrie. He felt jaded.

After a long spell in the field in Adelaide, Clarrie trudged off the ground and slumped into a chair. Bill Whitty, the left-hand bowler who had acounted for Trumper some seven times in his career, was not playing but he was in the dressingroom, there specifically to have a chat to Grimmett. He advised Clarrie to shower.

Then he gave the little spin wizard a brisk rub down with a towel, followed by a massage. Before Whitty's intervention, Clarrie had never dreamed of getting onto the massage table. He considered it tantamount to a declaration of weakness, the last frantic diversion before hauling up the white flag. But the massage felt good. Clarrie continued the practice for the entire season.

At the end of the summer, Clarrie got stuck into the garden at Firle. He worked slavishly to prepare the bed for a cricket pitch and by the end of September, 1927, the couch grass was ready to cut. Clarrie wanted to erase the memory of his performance the previous season. Only twice did he take a five wicket haul and thirty wickets was not good enough.

The 1927–28 season would prove another successful campaign for Grimmett. He was back to his best, taking 42 wickets at 27.40 runs apiece, a mighty performance on the uncovered wickets, which were flint hard in a summer almost bereft of rain. Ponsford had an extraordinary summer hitting a sequence of 133, 437, 202 and 336, extending the broadest of blades to all bowlers, even the cunning Grimmett.

The ravages of the Great Depression had yet to hit the world, but Clarrie had worries of his own. The year was a mixture of success and looming failure. Success came with the move into the house at Firle and his bowling on the first-class stage, but Clarrie would experience failure in a new business venture, the Clarrie Grimmett Bag Store, right in the heart of Adelaide, in Gawler Place. Clarrie still dabbled in signwriting, coaching and writing for the newspapers, mainly the morning paper, the *Adelaide Advertiser*, yet his move into the fashion world was probably made to cash in further on his fame as a world-class bowler. Clarrie and Lizzy worked the partnership. When Clarrie was there he would sit and sketch the profiles of women. His attention to detail was no more remarkable than the meticulous care he took over his spinning art. Some of the sketches he later transformed to oil on canvas. They are quite outstanding works of art. However, the bag store began to decline in early 1927. Grimmett was the subject of a number of official and unofficial meetings of the South Australian Cricket Association Ground and Finance Committee during 1927–28.

Joe Travers, the old South Australian bowler, told of Grimmett's financial difficulty with his shop in Gawler Place; he was selling off his stock at a discount because of continuing losses. He also told of Grimmett having been offered the job as a travelling salesman in the country, even about a good job offer coming to Grimmett from Victoria. The "find me a job or I'll move elsewhere" ploy had worked before and has worked since, but the SACA was not interested in taking chances. They simply had to retain Grimmett's bowling services. Grimmett wound up the bag business in early December, the SACA having secured for him a job with Stevens and Rowe, a sports equipment wholesaler.

The season saw the coming of Don Bradman, the greatest batsman the world has ever seen. Young New South Wales star bat Archie Jackson pulled out of the Adelaide match because of a painful boil on his right knee. This gave Don Bradman his chance.

Clarrie felt secure again. The closure of his shop, the move to Firle and having to cope with world-class batsmen on good tracks would have been more than enough for the average cricketer. But this was Grimmett. Now he had to contend with a youngster named Bradman. Clarrie had noted the name, and although Macartney had spoken of a budding genius, Clarrie was relieved that Jackson was sidelined and Bradman would be playing. Bradman slammed 118, playing Grimmett with great skill, sometimes with scant respect, before he felt to Jack Scott's bowling.

Clarrie watched Bradman closely; his eyes never left the young master. The Fox knew this lad was something very special, but he did notice an almost boyish urgency to get after the bowling. Clarrie struggled to make an impression on the Don in the first round. He liked the boy's batting and he warmed to Don's pleasant nature and ready smile. Clarrie invited Don and a few of the New South Wales team to his home at Firle.

There he delighted the audience by spinning a table-tennis ball on a table. Clarrie could get the ball to turn all manner of ways; the angle of his wrist was critical and the Don picked up on that essential straight away.

Yet young Bradman was fascinated; perhaps mesmerised because if Clarrie failed in the New South Wales first dig of 519, he demolished them in the second dig with 8/57, bowling Bradman with his famous top-spinner, the ball cannoning off the Don's pads and onto his stumps, for 33.

South Australia won the match, but Bradman won the hearts of cricket lovers, not only because of his brilliant debut century, but also with his natural charm and attitude to the game. Clarrie celebrated his thirty-sixth birthday on 25 December, 1927. His Christmas stocking included a little bag, entitled; "Queensland 315, Grimmett 5/101" to complement his 5/85 a day earlier.

In Melbourne Victoria thrashed South Australia to the tune of 637, with Woodfull (106) and Ponsford (336), yet Clarrie plugged away to snare 5/170.

Archie Jackson got a century in each innings in the Sydney match. Clarrie bowled well and was keen to get another overseas tour, this time closer to home than any cricket tour in his international experience.

8 HOME AGAIN

Grimmett was picked in a near full-strength Australian XI for the 1928 New Zealand tour. South Australian captain Vic Richardson led the team, which included some Test-hardened stalwarts in Bill Woodfull, Bert Oldfield and Bill Ponsford, as well as talented youngsters Karl Schneider and Archie Jackson. Alan Kippax, who missed the 1926 England trip chiefly because Clarrie bowled him first ball in the Test trial at the SCG, also gained selection. Five household names — Mailey, Collins, Andrews, Bardsley and Macartney — were absent. For Clarrie, the trip meant a return to his birthplace after an absence of fourteen years. He was elated and proud.

The Australians played two unofficial Tests and Clarrie took a total of 74 wickets on the tour at an average of 13.86. Second best wicket-taker was Don Blackie (the St Kilda off-spinner who spun virtually unnoticed until Grimmett left Victoria to play for South Australia) with 38 wickets at 16 runs apiece. Tall, wiry and bow-legged, Blackie was born in Bendigo in 1882. Blackie joined Prahran Cricket Club a year before Grimmett began his sign-writing apprenticeship in Wellington in 1907. The man they called "Rock" had to wait until the 1924–25 season (when he was forty-two) to win a State cap. But Blackie could bowl. He curved the ball away from the right-hander and he put plenty of work into spinning the ball hard. After years of non-recognition, Blackie quit cricket in the 1920s and took to mowing his lawn on Saturday afternoons. He was lured back after a few years, joining St Kilda and teaming with Bert Ironmonger, the left-hand orthodox spinner.

Stevens and Rowe were delighted to have Grimmett as an employee; however, they were not so happy to fork out full pay

R.G. 100

NEW ZEALAND

CERTIFIED COPY OF ENTRY OF BIRTH   № 147218

IN THE REGISTRAR-GENERAL'S OFFICE

Place of Registration: DUNEDIN

1. Surname ... ... (Where shown on entry.)	−
2. Christian or first names (If twin, state whether elder or younger.) (If stillborn, state so.)	Clarence Victor
3. Sex	M
4. When born	25 December 1891
5. Where born ... ... (Town or locality only.)	Caversham
Father	
6. Name and surname ...	Richard James Grimmett
7. Profession or occupation	Bricklayer
8. Age	44
9. Birthplace	Farringdon Berkshire England
Mother	
10. Name and Surname ...	Mary Grimmett
11. Maiden Surname	McDermott
12. Age	28
13. Birthplace	County Roscommon Ireland
14. Name and Surname of child if there has been any addition or alteration after registration of birth.	−

Certified to be a true copy of the above particulars included in an entry of birth in the records of the Registrar-General's Office.

Given under the seal of the Registrar-General at Lower Hutt, the

.......27............ day of ......May.................................. 19 .91...

Certified copy of entry of birth (Courtesy Registrar-General, New Zealand)

Basin Reserve, Wellington, New Zealand. The ground Clarrie lived near, and bowled his leg breaks with the Harris boys on, before the turn of the century. (Courtesy Vic Grimmett)

C.R. Grimmett, Clarrie's stern grandmother (Courtesy Vic Grimmett)

Victor Trumper, Clarrie's
hero, at Lord's, 1909
(Courtesy
S.S. Ramamurtny)

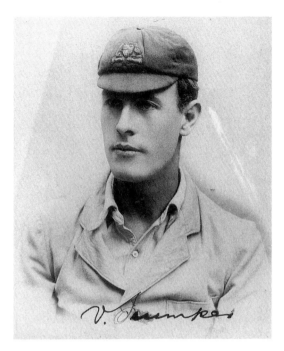

Grimmett as a member of
the Wellington
YMCA boys team,
New Zealand, 1907
(Courtesy Mr G. Adair)

Clarrie Grimmett, 1909
(Courtesy Vic Grimmett)

Picnic Match, New
Zealand. Clarrie, aged
seventeen, is seated
second from the left.
(Courtesy Vic Grimmett)

Clarrie Grimmett, 1909
(Courtesy Vic Grimmett)

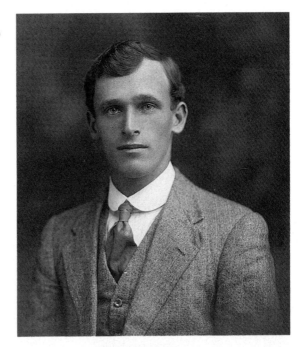

Below: Clarrie and
Elizabeth Grimmett,
1921
(Courtesy
Vic Grimmett)

Below right: Clarrie and
Elizabeth Grimmett
with young Victor after
arriving in Adelaide
(Courtesy
Vic Grimmett)

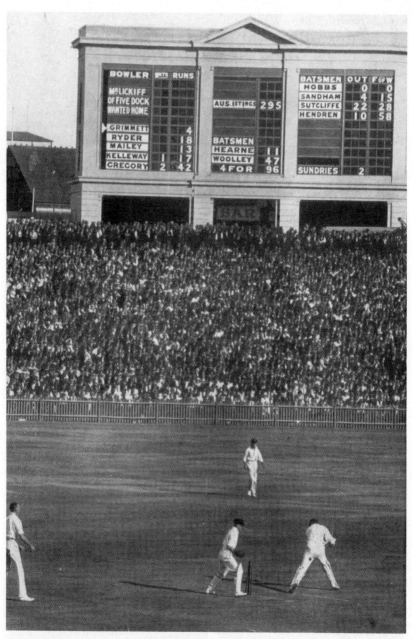

Clarrie Grimmett's first Test wicket, SCG, 1925 (Courtesy News Ltd)

Clarrie's faithful fox terrier, Joe
(Courtesy Vic Grimmett)

Clarrie receives a cheque after his Test
debut at the SCG (Courtesy News Ltd)

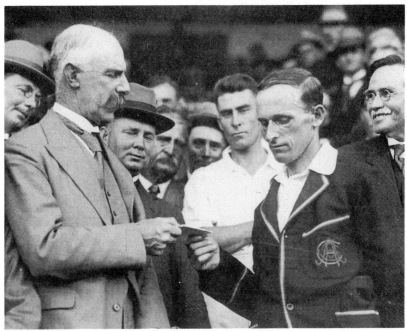

Poster — Australian cricket team for England 1926 (Courtesy *The Referee* 3.3.26)

Clarrie in 1926, bowling, with Herbert Sutcliffe at the non-striker's end watching intently (Courtesy News Ltd)

Richard (Dick) Grimmett with son Clarrie, Wellington, 1927 (Courtesy Vic Grimmett)

Grimmet in England, 1930. Seated is Arthur Richardson. To his right Bill Ponsford, to his right behind, Jack Ryder, and to Ryder's left, captain Bill Woodful. (Courtesy News Ltd)

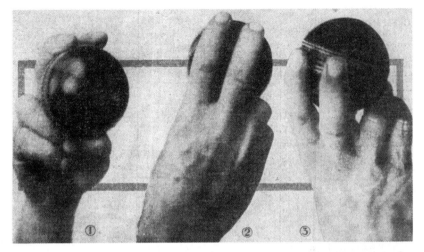

C.V. Grimmett's grips (Courtesy *Sporting Globe* 3.9.30)

Bradman and Grimmett, 1934
(Courtesy *Auckland Star* 26.5.34)

Bill O'Reilly, 1934 (Courtesy News Ltd)

O'Reilly and Grimmett,
1946–47 Test (Courtesy
News Ltd)

Grimmett claims another
victim in Hammond
(Courtesy Vic Grimmett)

Grimmett bowling (Courtesy Vic Grimmett)

V. Hazare, 1939
Grimmett Collection

Grimmett bowling (Courtesy Vic Grimmett)

Clarrie Grimmett
(Courtesy Vic Grimmett)

Clarrie with some old Test
and State teammates and
opponents at Adelaide Oval
early in 1971. From left,
'Nip' Pellew, Andy Smith,
Bill Whitty, Frank Woolley
(Clarrie's first test wicket),
Clarrie, and Tim Wall.
(Courtesy Vic Grimmett)

to him while he was away playing cricket in New Zealand. They offered to pay him a small retainer while he was away, but it was not enough to satisfy Clarrie. The SACA, fearful that Grimmett would pack his swag of bowling tricks and go elsewhere, came to the rescue with an offer to pay him ten pounds a week while he was away. Already SACA had offered to pay him for his captain-coach role with the Colts' team. After three seasons with Adelaide (110 wickets at 15.86 runs apiece), Clarrie took on the Colts job. He took 19 wickets for Colts at 13.57. He stayed only one summer, joining Kensington in 1928–29. This change probably came about in the winter of 1928 when the SACA by-laws were revised and boundaries amended.

When all the benefits were totalled, SACA was paying Clarrie more than sixty pounds per month. The money came at a time when the Grimmetts really needed it to establish the home at Firle after their not-so-successful foray into the business world. The SACA package helped Clarrie to relax. Peace of mind is essential for a bowler toiling on the Test stage.

Everywhere Clarrie went he was feted. He revisited his old school, Mount Cook Boys', and met many old and valued friends, including the man who insisted he become a leg-breaker, Dimp Hempelmann. The Australians arrived in New Zealand in March, 1928. Clarrie found that it was not customary to have massage at the cricket grounds in New Zealand. He described his reaction.

> I soon found my muscles going as tight as a drum, because I had come to rely on massage to keep them in trim. When we were in Dunedin, Eastman, an old Essex player, who had done massage work in England, jokingly felt my shoulder muscles when I was changing after practice. He was amazed at their tightness and told me I stood a great risk of straining them. I accepted his offer to try and get them back into working condition and, although he succeeded, I resolved to do without massage the following season.

Clarrie would start with fifteen minutes' bowling and gradually increase his time at the practice crease. He found this gradual build-up best for him and he never again had a rubdown before, during or after a match. Despite his arduous summers Down Under and his later tours of England (1930 and 1934) and South Africa (1935–36) Clarrie remained in perfect muscular condition. He never smoked and, until 1935, he did not touch a drop of alcohol.

The Australians had great fun on the New Zealand tour. There was an unwritten law among Clarrie's colleagues that anyone who hit a century against one of the weaker teams should retire, providing there was a reasonable score on the board; Clarrie described it thus:

> We were playing North Otago. Ron Oxenham got his hundred then went on batting as though the Ashes were at stake. In the pavilion, as we saw him reach 110, then 120, we were all asking, "Why doesn't Ron get out?" Finally we decided that someone should go in and run Ron out. I was next in and Ron hit a ball to square leg. I yelled, "Yes," and rushed towards his end. Ron began to run and then I turned to race him back to my end but, in turning sharply, I twisted my ankle and he reached my crease first, so I was the player to be run out. My fellows who followed did their darndest to run Ron out, but he refused to be drawn again and went on to hit 169.

Two of Clarrie's team-mates, Karl Schneider and Archie Jackson, were almost killed in New Zealand. "Jackson was hurled into the freezing and murky waters in a cave near Mt Cook and Schneider collapsed in the snow attempting to walk to Ball Hutt, some twelve miles from The Hermitage, our lodgings." Both men were destined to die tragically when in their early twenties. Schneider was born in Victoria, but he was lured to South Australia for the start of the 1926–27 season by the South Australian coach, England Test batsman Patsy Hendren. Patsy called Schneider the "coming Warren Bardsley". A short and compact left-hander, Schneider died of tuberculosis on 5 September, 1928, three months before his twenty-third birthday and only six months after the Mt Cook mishap.

Jackson was also to die of the same ailment, but five years later (in 1933). Jackson's family always suspected Archie had contracted the disease from Schneider at Mt Cook in 1928.

That New Zealand tour meant a great deal to Clarrie. New Zealanders were justly proud of this little man of spin who would never give up. Two unofficial Test matches were played, a rain-marred match at Auckland where Australia had the better of a draw and a second match at Dunedin, where Grimmett and Blackie spun Richardson's men to an easy victory. Clarrie took

3/85 (off 35 overs) and 0/15 off 8 overs in Auckland and 6/47 off 28.2 overs and 3/52 off 28 overs in Dunedin. Carisbrook Park, Dunedin is only a short distance from Caversham, where Clarrie was born. He enjoyed that match. So too did Blackie, whose second innings bag of 5/27 off 16.1 overs completed the rout by the spinners. There were few times in his international career that Grimmett could lay claim to having bowled in tandem with a man nine years his senior.

Clarrie's mother was living in Adelaide, his sister Eva in Sydney; his father, Dick Grimmett, contacted Clarrie during the Australian tour of New Zealand. They met, they talked and Clarrie kept it all to himself. That brief meeting in Wellington in April, 1928 was the last time Clarrie saw his father.

Woodfull hit 284, the highest score of the tour, in the first unofficial Test match at Auckland, Australia declaring at 5/573.

Jackson and Schneider averaged in the mid-forties, both hitting at least one century. Oxenham's 169 was his highest score in scoring 346 runs at 45.5 and Ponsford took honours on aggregate with 915 runs at an average of 61. The tour failed to give much direction in terms of new blood for the coming Ashes series in Australia, for Kippax and Richardson disappointed with the bat; the big guns such as Woodfull, Ponsford and Grimmett were certain selections. An exception was Don Blackie.

Percy Chapman's Englishmen were due and Clarrie wanted to renew his battles with Jack Hobbs and Herbert Sutcliffe. He would also come up against a man who would provide the sternest opposition of all the Test players he confronted, Walter Hammond. Hammond made his debut for England against South Africa. He did little of note against the Springboks, then played in three Tests against the West Indies at home. Hammond was a solid type of batsman, who drove with great power. He was merciless on anything short or wide of the stumps. Don Bradman had missed the tour of New Zealand, just as Grimmett had done in New Zealand in the summer of 1913–14. He was then the Kiwi first "reserve" for the tour of Australia.

The Don was made first reserve for the tour, his only chance of touring if a player fell ill. Bradman stayed at home in 1928, just as Grimmett stayed at home in 1913–14.

Chapman's Englishmen were a tough bunch. England won the series 4–1. Grimmett took 23 Test wickets, but his was a lone effort. Jack Gregory (cartilage problems) and Charles Kelleway dropped out of cricket. Australia lacked a pace spearhead. Hammond's 251 at Sydney was the blazing start of a long and successful career. Bradman was twelfth man for this match, but he played in the Melbourne third Test and hit his first Test century, the first of 29 centuries in just 52 matches. Grimmett lacked bowling support, so in came Don Blackie, the off-spinner, aged forty-six who bowled so well in New Zealand. Blackie took 4/148 off 59 overs to outbowl both Grimmett and Ironmonger in the first innings. He got 6/94 off 44 overs in the next Test in Melbourne, then took only three wickets in the Adelaide fourth Test and was promptly axed, never to return. Grimmett thought Blackie might have been a sensation in England, but others thought the Victorian had left his run too late. He had fallen foul of Victoria's selectors, Bean, McAlister and Ellis, plus the biased captaincy of Edgar Mayne. Archie Jackson hit a magnificent debut 164 in Adelaide and stirred the national soul, but even that knock failed to prevent a win by England.

Clarrie picked up 5/102 off 52.1 overs in the first innings against England, but he did not claim Percy Chapman as one of his victims. Chapman, in fact, hit a big six off Grimmett which struck a young woman, walking on the eastern boundary, quite unaware of events on the field. Margery Nicholls was taken to hospital, having sustained mild concussion. Miss Nicholls happily made a full recovery. However, upon her recovery she presented the SACA with a bill for her medical expenses. At that time the SACA was not insured for such claims. Legal advice was sought. Eventually Miss Nicholls received a cheque to recompense her fully for the medical expenses incurred as a direct result of being struck by a cricket ball bowled by Clarence Grimmett and despatched by Percy Chapman. The covering letter read: "This payment is purely a voluntary one and is not in any way to be taken as admitting the association's liability".

Wally Hammond's brilliant double of 119 (not out) and 177 gave England the narrowest of victories. The English left-arm spinner Jack White took 5/130 and 8/126 to give his team the winning edge. Bradman was run out for 58 when Australia appeared certain to win. The Don said later he believed the wicketkeeper, George Duckworth, "took the bails off without the ball. But he had his back to the umpire and the umpire could not see what I had seen".

Tim Wall, the tall South Australian, came into the side for the fifth Test in Melbourne and his 3/123 and 5/66 helped win the game for Jack Ryder's team.

Grimmett reckoned he had a long run of bad luck, especially when bowling to Hammond in the series. "In the first Test in Brisbane, the usually reliable [Bert] Oldfield missed a stumping chance offered by Hammond. Altogether Bert missed five chances of stumping Hammond off my bowling during the season and I never got Wally's wicket in any of the five Test matches," bemoaned Clarrie.

In the Sydney second Test, Alan Kippax was given out bowled when a ball from George Geary appeared to Clarrie and his team-mates in the dressingroom to have richocheted onto the stumps off the wicketkeeper's pads, as Clarrie later retold:

> Kippax was standing with his right foot behind the batting crease and he cocked his left leg with the intention of leg glancing. He missed the ball and it hit his stumps, but, in my opinion, it bounced off Strudwick's pads before hitting the stumps. It was the last ball of Geary's over and George Hele, the umpire at the bowler's end, said "not out!" Then Jack Hobbs appealed. While the players were moving into position for the next over, Hobbs appealed again, this time to the square leg umpire, Dave Elder, and without consulting Hele, Elder ruled Kippax out, bowled Geary.

Grimmett pleaded with the skipper, Jack Ryder, to go out onto the field and make inquiries, but "he refused to do so".

During the fourth Test in Adelaide, Hammond cocked a ball up on the on-side of the wicket and Clarrie moved to his left in an attempt to catch the ball, but Douglas Jardine, the non-striker, blocked Grimmett's progress. "Jardine blocked me, perhaps not intentionally, but quite effectively when I tried to get around him to make the catch," Clarrie said.

"At the time it did not strike me that I should have appealed for obstruction, but in discussing the incident afterwards with the umpire he said he would have had to give Hammond out for obstruction by Jardine."

If only they had known what Jardine was *really* like. But this was 1928–29, not yet the bodyline series of 1932–33. Clarrie's consistency with South Australia continued; he took 37 wickets at 31.25. The following year he bowled superbly, spinning to 58 wickets at 26.27 for South Australia, plus 31 wickets for Kensington A grade at an average of 16.12.

For South Australia Grimmett took 7/136 against New South Wales at Adelaide); 6/146 (against Queensland at Adelaide, yet another top-notch birthday present, his thirty-eighth) and 5/55 and 5/155 (against Victoria at Adelaide). There was great interest in the summer, for Australia was about to tour England. A largely young and untried XI was favoured to be sent "home". In January 1930, Don Bradman hit an unbeaten 452 against Queensland on the SCG. It beat Ponsford's 437, but no-one, other than Ponsford, has hit two scores of more than 400. Ponny hit 437 against Queensland in December, 1927 and in only his third first-class innings, in February, 1923, Ponsford hit 429 in just 477 minutes against Tasmania. In Sheffield Shield cricket Ponsford hit 5413 runs in 43 matches, with 21 centuries and an average of 80.27. Clarrie always regarded Ponny as having the "widest" bat of them all, certainly the "hardest to spin past".

Another hectic season was underway. Clarrie's Rover motor-car (registration SA 76772) was always parked on match days under the huge pepper tree at the northern end of Adelaide Oval. He found he could drive Lizzy into town from Firle in a quarter of an hour. Young Victor was just starting school, too young yet to introduce to the serious business of spin bowling. Clarrie continued his trade of signwriting, but he found his cricket fame brought more and more coaching requests. He coached at St Peter's and Prince Alfred College, Rostrevor School, where Victor spent his schooldays, Adelaide High School, and Scotch College. Clarrie was geniune in his desire to teach spin to the young and eager. He went on coaching trips in the country areas of the state with Vic Richardson. Always welcome, Clarrie delighted young and old who crowded round to watch him run through a few spinning tricks with a tennis or a cricket ball.

In 1929 a Sydney newspaper caused a mild sensation by alleging that Grimmett was forty-four, not thirty-seven as he claimed. Grimmett was very upset. He offered five hundred pounds if anyone could prove he was over the age of forty. Johnny Moyes wrote in the *Sporting Globe*: "I may say that more than once when I have been in Sydney I have heard the view expressed in certain circles that the popular little South Australian is more than the age he claims to be, but I am convinced that such views are wrong. Grimmett has always said he was born on 25 December, 1892 and that makes him 37." Moyes' argument was reinforced by a photograph reproduced on the page alongside his article.

It depicted a shot of the Wellington YMCA Boys' Team in 1907. "Now if Grimmett's present age were 44," Moyes continued, "it would mean that at the time he was in this boys' team he would have been at least 21 years of age. That settles the argument, for no 'boy' of 21 would be in the YMCA Boys' Team." The picture was reproduced from the Auckland *Weekly Times* and showed Clarrie sitting padded up, ready to go to bat. It also showed the face and physique of a teenager. In fact, no-one was correct. The Sydney paper was years out and Moyes was one year astray because Clarrie honestly thought he was born in 1892, not 1891 (his real birthdate).

Clarrie was always interested in photography. In the winter of 1929 he set up a darkroom in the kitchen at Firle. There was a little niche in the corner and he managed to improvise amazingly well. There he would develop prints from the camera he took on tours with him. He began with a Kodak folding Autograph camera. It was easy to operate but not small enough to slip into his pocket. While he dabbled with a quarter plate camera, Clarrie hit upon his most prized little whiz of a camera, the Kodak Ensign Midget. It never failed him. The Midget was destined to find itself in the presence of royalty on the noble green sward of England, and in the hands of a pilot of a bomber flying over German-occupied Europe in World War II.

In 1929 Patsy Hendren's contract as full-time state coach ended. The SACA advertised in Australia and overseas for a replacement. The offer was five hundred pounds, and the brief was: "To act as coach under the instructions of the association in respect to the coaching of university, college and high school players; the SACA Colts team, interstate and district players;

selected juniors and in such other directions, if any, as may be instructed from time to time. The coach also to play for, and captain, the SACA colts team in district matches".

Some twenty-four applications came from England, of which fourteen were Test cricketers. Four were received from Australia; Clarence "Nip" Pellew, Joseph Taylor of Sydney, Hubert Myers from Hobart and Clarrie Grimmett from Firle. Clarrie missed out, the job going to the equally popular Nip Pellew. Pellew had been a member of Warwick Armstrong's legendary 1921 side and before that he played with the first AIF team under Herbie Collins in England. Many of the appointment committee were possibly swayed Pellew's way because the 1921 Australian team had an air of immortality attached to it, rather like Joe Darling's 1902 team and, much later, Don Bradman's 1948 side. Nip had been born in Port Pirie and he attended one of the very best schools, St Peter's. Undeterred, Clarrie continued to sell sports goods, dabble in signwriting, coach budding spin bowlers, write articles and practise on his backyard pitch at Firle.

9 BRADMAN V. GRIMMETT

Don Bradman and Clarrie Grimmett were both masters of their art. Bradman, of course, is universally acknowledged as the greatest cricketer of them all. The pair dominated the first-class scene in the run-up to the 1930 Australian tour of England. Grimmett starred with the ball for South Australia, taking 7/136 against New South Wales at Adelaide; 6/146 against Queensland at Adelaide; and 5/55 and 5/155 against Victoria in Adelaide. In the South Australian game against New South Wales, in Adelaide, Clarrie gave Bradman a thorough going-over. It was a searching test, a lesson from the master to a batsman so gifted he hit a world record score of 452 not out just two weeks later. Bradman acknowledged Grimmett's bowling of 24 December, 1929: "In our second innings Grimmett bowled with tremendous effect. Some of the balls he sent down to me were the most difficult I had ever been called upon to play; I was absolutely tied up and made to look like a schoolboy." Bradman finished with 894 Shield runs and Grimmett 43 wickets.

The Australian Tour of England in 1930 became known as Bradman's Tour. Bradman hit no fewer than 974 Test runs, including 254 at Lord's which he would later described as "the best innings of my career" and 334 at Leeds, having hit an unconquered 309 the first day, joining Victor Trumper (1902) and Charlie Macartney (1926) as one of three Australians to have scored a century before lunch on the first day of a Test against England. Bradman's batting mastery was complemented by Grimmett's spin.

Clarrie took a record 29 Test wickets in the series and 142 wickets at 17.09 for the tour, including 10/37 against the might of Yorkshire. The 1930 team had only four veterans of previous

tours; Grimmett, Bill Woodfull, Bill Ponsford and the keeper
Bert Oldfield. There was depth in batting, with the young lion
Don Bradman, Bill Woodfull and Bill Ponsford, Alan Kippax,
Stan McCabe, Archie Jackson and Vic Richardson. However,
Grimmett would carry the attack. Fellow South Australian Tim
Wall toured and he bagged 58 tour wickets at 29.25. Percy
Hornibrook took 93 wickets at 19.37, but without Grimmett, the
bowling looked, and was, decidedly thin. Even at the age of
forty-eight Blackie would have been invaluable in the Austra-
lian attack. The average age of the team was twenty-seven.
Clarrie was then in his thirty-ninth year, at the very zenith of his
spinning powers.

In 1928–29 Wally Hammond came of age in the cricketing
sense. He proved himself a world-class bat, hitting double centuries in successive Test matches. If he worried about Grimmett's spin, it was not reflected on the scoreboard. Clarrie did
bemoan stumping chances, but he also thought that he had
allowed Hammond too much room to hit on the off-side. The
Fox never forgot. England won the first Test in 1930 at Trent
Bridge. Bradman got 8 and 131 and twice in the match Clarrie
trapped Hammond with his wickedly-dipping top-spinner,
trapping him lbw for 8 in the first innings, and in the same
manner for 4 in the second. Australia bounced back at Lord's to
win by seven wickets. Clarrie got 2/105 off 33 overs and 4/167
off 53.

Again he claimed Hammond, bowled for 38 and caught at
cover for 32. This was the match where Bradman played an
innings which will live in the memory of those who saw it as the
most masterful batting in the history of Test matches. He scored
254 and he would say later that there was not one occasion that
the ball did not go precisely where he had intended. It was an
innings of genius. Clarrie told me in 1967 that he had taught the
Don how to late cut on the ship going to England in 1930 and
he added, "Bradman learned fast!" With scores of 6 declared 729,
566 and 695, the Australian batting was considered too strong
for any county team. Even Hammond conceded that his
Gloucestershire XI might be struggling. Yet the county's Goddard and Parker had already taken 293 wickets that summer
between them by the time Woodfull's men arrived in Bristol.

Hammond considered Bradman and company might set a winning total in quick time, with the Fox (Grimmett) to devour the Gloucester batting. Wally Hammond wrote about Grimmett's play:

> Grimmett had trundled England out in the Tests and proved himself the most formidable bowler of his class that the world had ever seen.
>
> We batted and Clarrie began to swing down those slow leg-breaks, almost round arm, with the ball curling in towards the batsman as if answering some enormous magnet, and then whipping off the pitch like lightning. He evolved the ball by bowling round a soapbox; if he could pitch the ball beside the box, and the break sent it darting behind out of sight, that one was satisfactory.
>
> At Bristol that day there was a very damp, heavy air, and he used this to make the ball swing more than ever I saw it do anywhere else. Until our second innings began, though the struggle was fierce, it was fairly even. They [Australia] led by 85 runs on the first knock, but we felt we could make a game of it. But when our second innings opened the pitch was falling to bits. And there was Grimmett, bowling the most deceptive stuff I have ever seen, varying it now and again with an unexpectedly wicked top-spinner or a googly. It is not vanity, I hope, for me to say now that I realised that the game might depend on my innings. From the first ball I knew Grimmett was in such form as I had never seen him, and that this would try me more than any Test innings I have ever played. Yet it was my duty to keep Clarrie to myself and protect my partners by keeping the strike.
>
> He knew it as well as I, and brought every trick out of the bag, especially at the end of each over. Presently I found I had scored 20, and stopped to wipe the perspiration from my eyes. That innings became almost like a nightmare. I find it difficult to recall, except as an endless period of gripping my bat, wiping my hands, and trying to score off balls, every one of which struck off the pitch like a viper. Then my castle went down and I recall creeping into the pavilion as exhausted as if I had been batting all day. I had got 89, and was too done-up even to regret missing the century. Our total was 202, leaving Australia 118 runs to win.

Goddard and Parker did the job and the match ended in the first tie Australia had played against an English county team. Hammond vividly remembered the glory of his county doing what All England struggled to come close to doing; beat the

Aussies; but it was Grimmett's exacting skill he remembered most.

In nine innings that 1930 Test series, Grimmett snared Hammond on five occasions. As Hammond said, "When making a selection of great bowlers, I always think first of sad-faced Clarrie Grimmett. Of all the bowlers I have met he [Grimmett] was the one I could take least liberties with."

The Wall Street crash of 1929 plunged the western world into a financial abyss, the Great Depression. On 18 February, 1930 the world celebrated a new and wonderful discovery, a planet beyond Neptune, named Pluto. The cricket world's new "discovery" was Don Bradman, about to shine like no other cricket star in Test history.

On 24 April Amy Johnson became the first woman to fly from England to Australia. While Amy winged her way into aviation history, Bill Woodfull's men were sailing to England. The Great Depression was hurting everyone. In faraway Australia the people yearned for a hero to help ease their pain, to help them forget the increasing burden for families of coping with day-to-day living. Bradman was the man of the moment with his incredible batting feats, and Grimmett wheeled away in his silent, deadly way.

Bowlers are limited to the number of wickets they can get in any one innings. A batsman has no such limit. On 10 May, 1930 Grimmett wrote his name into cricket history with a ten-wicket rout of Yorkshire. By bowling out all ten Yorkshire batsmen for a paltry 37 runs, he had emulated Arthur Mailey's like performance against Gloucestershire in 1921. Grimmett's ten came at a lower cost than Mailey's 10/66. An opportunist, Mailey entitled his autobiography, *Ten for Sixty-Six and All That*, a play on words referring to William the Conqueror's invasion of Britain in 1066.

It's an extraordinary feat for any bowler to get all ten wickets. Usually the wickets are shared, the lion's share going to the one who performs the best. This is not always the case; often a bowler can beat the bat, while the man up the other end takes the edge and claims the wicket his bowling partner might have deserved. Yet over a period of time a fellow who bowls consistently well for long enough periods will earn his rewards. Think then of Tony Lock, some twenty-six years on at Manchester in

1956, when he took one Australian wicket while his Surrey spin twin, Jim Laker, took the other nineteen to not only rewrite the record books but to claim a record which may never be beaten. Grimmett came on second change. Wall and A'Beckett opened the bowling against the formidable Percy Holmes and Herbert Sutcliffe. Together the pair recorded a century opening partnership sixty-nine times.

THERE WON'T BE ANY NEED TO SEND A TEAM TO ENGLAND IN THE FUTURE—
JUST BRADMAN AND GRIMMETT
WILL DO.

Two years after the Grimmett attack, Holmes and Sutcliffe hit a record stand of 555 for Yorkshire versus Essex at Leyton. Bramall Lane was packed with eager Yorkshire supporters. They were a vocal lot, but knowledgeable, in the manner of the Victorian crowds, usually the most knowledgeable in Australia. Percy Hornibrook came on first change, but there was no breaking the stand.

Eventually skipper Bill Woodfull called on his ace card, the Fox. Yorkshire's score stood at 59 when Grimmett bowled the perfect leg-break. It curved in late and alarmingly and Holmes stabbed in hope. The ball pitched on the line of the leg-stump, turned easily past Holmes' hopeful forward stab and found the top of the off-stump. Keeper Charlie Walker beamed and clapped as the bail flew over the skipper's head at slip. That began the procession of Yorkshire batsmen. Some of the best players to set foot on Yorkshire soil, Holmes, Sutcliffe, Leyland, Macaulay and Bowes, all fell to Grimmett's wiles. The old hand, Wilfred Rhodes, back down the list at number ten, survived on six, but he ran out of partners, young Bill Bowes suffering the same fate as Holmes, albeit making 31 runs less. Bowes was bowled for a duck. The card read thus:

YORKSHIRE

first innings

Holmes		b Grimmett	31
Sutcliffe	c Walker	b Grimmett	69
Oldroyd		b Grimmett	2
Leyland	St Walker	b Grimmett	9
Barber	St Walker	b Grimmett	1
Mitchell		b Grimmett	3
Robinson	c Bradman	b Grimmett	2
Wood	c Richardson	b Grimmett	17
Macaulay	St Walker	b Grimmett	1
Rhodes		not out	6
Bowes		b Grimmett	0
Sundries			14
			159

Fall: 59, 84, 120, 125, 126, 130, 130, 132, 155, 155.

Australian bowling:

	O	M	R	W
Wall	16	3	42	0
A'Beckett	12	6	11	0
Hornibrook	12	4	49	0
Grimmett	22.3	8	37	10
McCabe	3	2	2	0

Australia v. Yorkshire May 1930

Clarrie's performance was, of course, much publicised, but some critics blamed the combination of smoke from the industrial furnaces and low cloud which had defeated the pride of Yorkshire batsmanship that day. Yet at the day's end Australia was a comfortable 1/69 with Ponsford having been trapped lbw for six and Woodfull being unbeaten on 37; Bradman, who had been there for just 38 minutes, was 24 not out. Grimmett was proving as much an asset for Australia as was Bradman.

This was more noticeable to the Australian team than it was to the legion of Bradman fans in England and at home. The team knew full well that it mattered not how many runs a side compiled; if they couldn't get twenty opposition wickets the game could not be won. Bradman's golden worth was not only in getting runs in big lots; it was the speed with which he scored his runs. Usually they came at the rate of a run a minute, or better. The Bradman run rate enabled a captain to give his bowlers ample time in which to bowl sides out twice.

Against Lancashire it was Grimmett again with his guile and flight, who helped to dismiss the opposition for 176. Bradman had his leg stump knocked out of the ground by Ted McDonald, the Tasmanian-born fast bowler who had served Victoria and Australia so well in past days. McDonald was considered to be one of the best fast bowlers Australia ever produced. The McDonald-Gregory pace partnership of 1921 ranks alongside Lindwall and Miller (1948) and Lillee-Thomson (1974). The side tripped down to Lord's and Clarrie was a real hit when he walked to the crease. "This was the time I established a record by receiving continuous applause during an innings. My 10/37 against Yorkshire led to me being cheered all the way to the wicket; it continued when I square cut the first ball from Maurice Allom to the fence and there was another cheer when the next ball destroyed my castle. They were still applauding when I reached the boundary."

The 1930 Australians revelled in the rich history and character of London. London was vibrant and alive, almost a decade before Hitler unleashed his madness upon the world. Woodfull's men spent a fabulous night at the Royal Albert Hall, where they marvelled at the singing of Australian Harold Williams, who played the title role of "Hiawatha". Bradman and Grimmett, the 1930 Test superstars, were photographed sitting on either side of Williams. The cricketers were splendid in their dinner suits, Williams in full chief's headdress and matching accessories. It was the night of 19 June, 1930, two days after England had taken the first Test at Nottingham and just eight days before the start of the second big game at Lord's, where Grimmett spun Australia to victory after Bradman's magnificent 254 in Woodfull's team's score of 729. The Lord's win equalled the series. Lord's is a special place, although Clarrie was less than impressed the first time he saw the old ground back in 1926. He wrote about it:

> I was very disappointed with the headquarters of English cricket. The ground has no shape and the surroundings are poor. There is no fence around the arena at Lord's except in front of the members' stand. Depressing as the surroundings are, there is nothing depressing about the turf. It has a fine playing surface, like that of practically every county ground. What did impress me about Lord's was that I was continually being brought into contact with relics of bygone days or meeting cricketers who had thrilled the crowd when I was running about in knickerbockers. Even at Test matches many spectators at Lord's leave their coat or stick or lunch basket on the seat they have occupied and stroll out during the luncheon interval to inspect the wicket. They parade all over the ground, except on the wicket itself, the pitch being fenced off with a light line.

During the tour the Australians created another record by talking directly to Australia from England via the wonders of modern science, the radiotelephone link. This fascinated all of the Australians, none more so than Clarrie, who loved to dabble in photography and the wireless. He learnt morse code as a young man in New Zealand and was always interested in a new idea. During one such radio link, Bill Woodfull, Bill Ponsford and Clarrie Grimmett spoke directly to their respective wives. Clarrie and Lizzy might not have realised the full impact of their affectionate chat. Half of Australia did, as they warmed to the radio reunion.

Clarrie's form with the ball was outstanding, but he had done little with the bat by the time the third Test came around. A pair at Nottingham and not getting the chance to bat at Lord's was none too great a lead-up for Leeds, yet he got 24. There he took 5/135 (his fourth bag of five or more wickets) and 1/33 but the match was drawn. Manchester proved a draw also, but it was a Test where Grimmett outscored Bradman. The Don was fiddled out by the leg-spinner Peebles for 14; so too was Grimmett but only in the wake of hitting a Test fifty.

"Grimmett, c Sutcliffe by Peebles 50". Rain prevented all but 45 minutes' play on the scheduled third day and there was no play on 29 July. However, Clarrie won more than one fan with his maiden half-century in Test cricket. He received a letter penned by a resident of Leeds, Irish-born lass, Ida Burke.

Dear Mr Grimmett,

Why I am writing you I do not know, except that it is just a whim on my part. Being Irish, I am told, I do a lot of mad things, and evidently this is one. I expect I am writing you because I'm especially prone to bowlers and you do seem to be a bit of a trickster. I've watched cricket for ages and usually I'm more thrilled with the ball than the bat and with good fielding most of all.

You remind me of Puck or Punch for you are rather tiny, aren't you? Or of some sort of Irish Leprecauns, that live at the bottom of Lakes Killarney — dear little folk they are, but all alive, and up to mischief.

You know you would make a cute little Irishman. This letter is to wish you luck with the ball. I would like to read of you doing something really startling. Can't I then read of Grimmett breaking all records — Bradman becomes boring — even all the school girls know of Don Bradman, who does seem to be a bit of a darlin' but — I began this because I had nothing to do. I will finish for I now have nothing to say.

Yours, with best wishes,

Ida Burke.

An Australian cricketer in England is looked after extremely well. He is invited to all manner of social functions, Ascot, the Derby, meeting Royalty at Lord's (in 1930 it was King George V), attending the Wimbledon singles final, the FA Cup final, the House of Commons, Westminster Abbey, perhaps even a trip to Buckingham Palace.

Those who perform to a reasonable level without setting the world on fire can cruise through such a tour, enjoying everything to the full. The demands made on the likes of Bradman and Grimmett in 1930 were very different.

They were the real playmakers: Bradman tearing the English bowling to bits and Grimmett, planning and executing the destruction of the English batting. Each player received a tour payment of six hundred pounds, fifty of which was to be paid to help equip them for the tour ahead, four hundred while on tour, and, "upon a satisfactory report on their conduct at the end of the tour by the manager", the balance of one hundred and fifty pounds upon their return to Australia.

Six hundred pounds in 1930 was the equivalent of about $30,000 today; a veritable fortune to many people in 1930, for during the Great Depression a family man on five pounds a week could live comfortably. In home Test matches, the players were paid thirty pounds a Test, plus expenses. The England tour allowance was also supplemented by an amount of thirty shillings per week for "incidental expenses". It was a far better deal than that enjoyed by, say, the 1972 Australians who received $2400 for a five-month tour of England.

Bradman's incredible 334 at Leeds led to great fame, and some fortune. An Australian, Arthur Whitelaw, wealthy soap manufacturer, sent a telegram to skipper Bill Woodfull and asked that Bradman accept one thousand pounds "as a token of my admiration".

The Don thought it was a practical joke, at first, but Woodfull and manager Kelly assured him it was genuine. Imagine how young Bradman felt! One thousand pounds in 1930 was equivalent to $50,000 now, or at a comfortable wage of five pounds weekly, some four years' work in the Great Depression.

Right at the end of the tour, when their fame was at fever pitch, Clarrie Grimmett and Don Bradman were offered five hundred pounds to give bowling and batting demonstrations at the London Palladium. Their contract stipulated that each of fourteen performances by each man must run for at least ten minutes. B.J. Kortland was the lecturer and the General Theatre Corporation Ltd managed the deal and provided all the necessary equipment.

It was during his second tour of England in 1930, his most triumphant, that Clarrie began a new adventure, taking movie film. Much of that film exists today, showing his colleagues of the 1930s during matches or at the nets.

During the tour he sold his reels of film to news houses. They paid well. The old Fox reckoned if the newspaper photographers and cinematographers did not obtain sufficient quality material he was happy to fill the void. So long as he kept the best interests of the game in mind, the authorities did not seem to mind Grimmett's media pursuits.

At Sandringham Palace, Bill Woodfull's 1930 team turned up to be greeted by King George V and Queen Mary. It was the

Sunday rest day of the match against Cambridge University. First Viscount Downe and Lady Downe arranged for the team to meet His Majesty's representatives outside Sandringham. They attended the church the Royals attended and then motored on into the palace grounds. The sun shone gently; the warming hand of God.

"Two men walked towards our party," Clarrie told me. "At first they were too far away to recognise. Soon we could identify one of the men. It was the King. As soon as he saw us, he changed direction and walked briskly to our group. Our escort introduced Bill Woodfull and we stood to attention, like Palace guards, as the two chatted casually. Then we were each introduced to King George V. We shook his hand."

Clarrie was chatting to the King when he noticed two women in the distance.

"Ah, excuse me, Clarrie," the King said. "Here's the Queen. I must go and meet her and introduced her to the boys."

Queen Mary and her lady-in-waiting joined the group and the King suddenly announced: "It is hot, so please put on your hats, boys. I suppose, as you will have cameras, you would like to take some photos."

King George scanned the sky and took his Queen by the arm, creating the "right" position in relation to the sun for the small army of Australians, taking their photographs with the enthusiasm of a band of eager schoolboys. Clarrie's faithful Ensign Midget was in action first.

The King was fascinated by spin bowling and he asked Clarrie to explain the Bosey. Grimmett demonstrated with an orange. Nobody could find a cricket ball when it was most needed, but the well-spun orange gripped and turned on the sun-drenched Sandringham turf. Woodfull's men pooled their photographs and had them inserted in an album for His Majesty, accompanied by team photographs and a letter from the team management.

Clarrie arrived home in plenty of time for the 1930–31 series against the West Indies. He starred with successive figures of 7/87 and 4/96 (first Test at Adelaide); 4/54 and 1/9 (second Test at Sydney); 4/95 and 5/49 (third Test at Brisbane); 2/46 and 2/10 (fourth Test at Melbourne) and 3/100 and 1/47 (fifth Test at

Sydney). He also took 36 wickets for South Australia at 19.52. Clarrie's Adelaide performance came hot on the heels of his twenty-nine wicket Test haul in England in 1930, a record. Clarrie weaved a cunning web around the West Indians, who couldn't fathom the spinning depth of this little leg-break genius. Traditionally West Indians like the ball coming on. They are impatient to hit out and Clarrie picked that immediately. He teased and then he pounced.

Grimmett took 33 wickets in the West Indian series, while the Don had a run of scores; 4; 25; 223; 152 and 43 and 0, a total of 447 runs at an average of 74.5. Bradman was human after all!

The next series against South Africa was to be at home and this time both Grimmett and Bradman championed the Australian cause. Grimmett again came up with a series haul of 33 wickets and Bradman hammered the Springboks to the tune of 806 runs at an average 201.5; he didn't bat at all in the rain-marred fifth Test in Melbourne. Bradman hit 299 not out in the fourth Test in Adelaide, while Grimmett took 7/116 and 7/83 in the same game. Ironically Clarrie did not bowl a ball in Melbourne, where the South Africans were bundled out for 36 and 45, Ironmonger taking 5/6 and 6/18 and O'Reilly, the only other spinner used, taking 3/19 off nine overs in the second dig.

Bill O'Reilly developed into a great bowler, one whom Bradman affords the "greatest bowler of them all" tag. The Grimmett-O'Reilly spin partnership is described in the chapter "The Tiger and the Fox". When Grimmett, O'Reilly and Bradman were on the same side, heaven help the opposition: they were a champion team in themselves. O'Reilly was in the mould of the great Sydney Barnes, who opened the bowling (on and off) for England just after the turn of the century. Barnes operated at a brisk medium pace. He could swing the ball and turn it from the leg at an uncomfortable pace.

Experts still argue as to the relative merits of Barnes and O'Reilly, great bowlers both, but they regard the best slow leg-spinner of them all as being Clarence Victor Grimmett. In 1930 there was no television, so a player could not be always immediately identified as he walked the London streets in his "civvies". Bradman just might be spotted, for his photograph was paraded on almost every newsstand in the country, every day. Grimmett's fame was widespread too, but he tended to melt into a crowd; the Don stood out.

Late in that fabulous English summer of 1930 a man was holding forth in a crowded tramcar on the glory of English cricket and how lucky the Australians had been in winning the Ashes. He was particularly aggressive when talking about Grimmett, and spotting an inoffensive-looking little man in a grey suit sitting opposite him, he said: "Grimmett only gets wickets by taking a mean advantage of batsmen. Why, he'd even take advantage of a little bloke like you!" Clarrie Grimmett was the inoffensive little man in the grey suit. He held his peace.

Twenty-five times Grimmett bowled to Bradman and on ten occasions he got his man. Hedley Verity, the English spinner, also got Bradman ten times. They share that record.

Bradman took England by storm, thrashing the England bowling unmercifully. It was as if the shy, blond twenty-one-year-old Australian had achieved what the nation had been trying to do since 1788: throw off the cloak of colonialism and belt the British.

That the pride of England was savaged by one so young inspired the fledgling nation crippled by the Great Depression. The English Press compounded Bradmania with posters such as "BRADMAN versus ENGLAND" and the most famous after his great 334 at Leeds, "HE'S OUT". Grimmett was doing the equivalent with the ball that Bradman was doing with the bat, dominating the English. However, little Clarrie's trickery in a deft change of pace might have confounded batsmen, but nothing stirred the blood so much as a ferocious Bradman hook or cover drive.

Few people would realise that the Grimmett bowling record is (dare I say it) better than the Bradman batting record. The answer is found in the records.

Bradman's career statistics have been recorded, researched, dissected and digested by numerous people, young and old, over a long period. Yet Grimmett's amazing record appears lost to the age. He played big cricket from 1911–12 until 1940–41; from Scott's historic Antarctic expedition to the miracle of Dunkirk and beyond. In that time, Grimmett took 1424 wickets. However, the full realisation of the Grimmett bowling achievement does not really hit home until it is compared with the figures of Don Bradman, whose batting feats are quite astounding. Before I set down the comparable bowling and batting statistics, I would point out that these figures are merely the bald facts. They do not represent any attempt by this writer to place Grimmett above Bradman as a cricketer.

However, the comparison is essential for the modern reader, especially the young who yearn for greater knowledge about the history and tradition of the game of cricket.

In first-class cricket

Clarrie Grimmett's first-class bowling record

Matches	Runs	Wickets	Average	Best	5 wkts/inns
248	31,740	1424	22.28	10/37	127

Don Bradman's first-class batting record

Matches	Runs	Average	Best	Centuries
234	28,067	95.14	452*	117

*not out

If you equate a five-wicket haul in an innings with that of a century, the records of Grimmett and Bradman, as you can see, are almost identical. Grimmett's 127 "bags" of five wickets in 248 matches is slightly better than Bradman's 117 centuries in 234 matches.

In Test cricket

Clarrie Grimmett's Test bowling record

Matches	Runs	Wickets	Average	Best	5 wkts/inns
37	5231	216	24.21	7/40	21

Don Bradman's Test batting record

Matches	Runs	Average	Best	Centuries
52	6996	99.94	334	29

Again the statistics come out slightly in Grimmett's favour. Divide the number of five wicket hauls by Grimmett into the number of Test matches he played (21 into 37); readers will find that he took a five-wicket bag every 1.76 Tests.

The same process can be applied to Bradman. Divide the number of centuries the Don scored into the number of Test matches he played (29 into 52); the result is that he scored a century every 1.79 Test matches.

It is fairer to deal with the Tests as a whole and not to look at the individual innings. My point is to show, by such comparison, that Grimmett was not merely a fine leg-spinner, he was the best. By both his superb skill in the art and by his amazing consistency, Grimmett was the veritable Bradman of Spin.

Bradman dominated the game to such an extent that, while Grimmett's incredible record was appreciated by some both within and out of the "inner circle" of cricket, the cricket public did not understand fully the impact Grimmett had on the game some four years before and for the better part of what was to become known as the Bradman Era.

The Great Depression hurt all Australians and the public yearned for a hero to call their own. Don Bradman was a natural. He was young, adventurous, and he wielded the cricket bat with magical flair. But the Depression did not make Bradman; the Don's extraordinary batting feats made the Depression more bearable for cricket lovers.

Bradman was a youngster who made good against all odds; he was an inspiration, and he helped lift the national spirit. During the height of the Depression (1930–34), South Australia recorded the highest rate of unemployment in Australia. For the 1931–32 season, the SACA's expenditure outweighed its income by a long chalk, yet the association, in addition to dealing with such necessary help to country associations, was prepared to look after its best men. Two cricketers' names appear on the expenditure list for that summer: Vic Richardson, the South Australian captain, and Clarrie Grimmett, the South Australian and Test leg-breaker. Richardson and Grimmett were paid (in honoraria) amounts of £187.10.0 and £152.12.4 respectively.

Bodyline 1932–33

When Douglas Jardine unleashed his Bodyline tactics in 1932–33 (a cold and calculated strategy to reduce the Bradman run-getting to managable proportions), the public saw Jardine as the enemy, a dark and evil figure trying to plunge a dagger into their hero's heart.

Those who forgot that it is "bowlers who win matches", were brought instantly back to reality when Harold Larwood started to deliver his bouncers. In tandem with the burly left-hander Bill Voce, Larwood had a devastating effect on the Australians.

There were some who played Larwood well at times and Stan McCabe's 187 not out in the first Test in Sydney was the greatest example of raw courage and skill against the rearing deliveries arriving at hurricane force. McCabe showed that Larwood could be hit, but despite his epic innings, Australia lost by ten wickets.

While the people heckled and batsmen ducked and weaved throughout the early onslaught of the Douglas Jardine-inspired Bodyline, a master craftsman struggled. Grimmett was wheeling away with his usual nagging accuracy, but the results were not coming his way. Bradman missed the first Test in Sydney, through illness, but was fit to play in the second Test.

Grimmett and O'Reilly did the bulk of the work, with Clarrie taking 1/118 off 64 overs and O'Reilly 3/117 off 67. Australia hit back in the Melbourne Test with a great win. Bradman was bowled for a duck first ball in the first innings, dragging a Bill Bowes short delivery onto his leg stump. He made amends with an unbeaten 103 in the second innings. O'Reilly carved his name on the Test with a match haul of ten wickets; 5/63 off 34.3 overs and 5/66 off 24 overs. The Bradman-O'Reilly performance clinched it for Bill Woodfull's team, with the sluggish MCG track helping to nullify Larwood's hurricane pace. It suited O'Reilly and Grimmett; Clarrie only bowled 16 overs in the first innings (1/21) and four in the second 0/19).

Then came the Adelaide Bodyline Test where emotions ran to fever pitch.

Larwood struck Woodfull a fearful blow over the heart and Bert Oldfield was hit in the head. The press had written a great deal about Jardine's "unsportsman-like" handling of his England attack. The crowd was, in a psychological sense, a human powder keg: one spark was all that was needed for the situation to become explosive. The Larwood thunderbolts which downed Woodfull and Oldfield turned the normally placid Adelaide crowd into an angry mob. Only swift and expert horsemanship by dozens of mounted policemen prevented the mob jumping the fence to attack the villain of the piece: Jardine. Despite the fury of the crowd, only one man actually got onto the field, and that was a fellow hell-bent upon shooting Jardine, not with a gun, but with a camera. The police brought the man down and he was hauled off to court and fined two pounds, with fifteen shillings costs, but he refused to pay the fine and went to jail for a few days.

Immediately after play, the joint MCC managers Pelham "Plum" Warner and Richard Palairet went to the Australian dressingroom where they offered Woodfull an apology for what had happened and their sympathies. Woodfull was curt to the Englishmen and he stated that he did not wish to see them. "There are two men out there. One is trying to play cricket and the other is not. The game is too good to be spoilt. It is time some people got out of it. Good afternoon!"

Someone was suspected of leaking this story to the newspapers. Jack Fingleton, the Test opener, was a professional journalist and the prime suspect. Fingleton in later years placed the blame on Bradman, alleging that Bradman had a clandestine night-time meeting with sports writer Claude Corbett and leaked the story of the exchange between Woodfull and the English team managers.

The story rocked the cricket world. Fair play was, after all, the very rock upon which the grand old game of cricket stood. Woodfull's words attacked the foundations of cricket, established by the forefathers of a hurt Pelham Warner and a smarting MCC. Lord's was further infuriated when the Australian Board of Control for International Cricket sent the MCC a cable:

BODYLINE BOWLING HAS ASSUMED SUCH PROPORTIONS AS TO MENACE THE BEST INTERESTS OF THE GAME, MAKING PROTECTION OF THE BODY BY THE BATSMAN THE MAIN CONSIDERATION. THIS IS CAUSING INTENSELY BITTER FEEL-

INGS BETWEEN THE PLAYERS AS WELL AS INJURY. IN OUR
OPINION IT IS UNSPORTSMANLIKE. UNLESS STOPPED AT
ONCE IT IS LIKELY TO UPSET FRIENDLY RELATIONS EXISTING
BETWEEN BRITAIN AND AUSTRALIA.

There seems to have been a lot of ill-feeling over who really
did leak the Woodfull-Warner exchange. Who dunnit? Journalist Fingleton had the motive and the contacts, although according to all the available evidence he was not in the room at the
time of the exchange. There were two others present in the
Australian changeroom, twelfth man Leo O'Brien and a room
attendant, whom everyone thought to be stone deaf.

The joint MCC managers Warner and Palairet must be ruled
out. They would hardly have leaked a story which attached an
"unsportsmanlike" tag to them and their team. O'Brien denies
leaking the story.

One of the players, an old hand, had been making a few bob
on the side by selling photographs and movie film to the highest
bidder for years. Clarrie Grimmett has never been accused of
leaking the Bodyline story, but I wonder if the controlling body
(the Australian Board of Control for International Cricket) suspected it could have been the old Fox who spilt the beans. Next
day, Grimmett found himself dumped from the Test side. That
Bodyline Test match was the last Test match Grimmett played
on Australian soil. Since his brilliant eleven-wicket debut
against Arthur Gilligan's English team in March 1925, Grimmett
had bowled magnificently for Australia. He had failed to pick
up bags of wickets in the first three Tests of the rubber, but in
the MCG second Test he hardly bowled at all. If star bat Bradman
failed three times in successive Tests, would the Don get the axe?
Not likely. In Adelaide Clarrie bowled with guile, but the wickets didn't come. He took 2/94 off 28 overs and 1/74 off 35,
modest in the extreme for a bowler of Grimmett's ability, but he
was not thrashed by the Englishmen. The wickets, he knew,
would return. They might as well have cut off his spinning
finger. Australia decided to go into the fourth Test at Brisbane
with a team laced with seven batsmen. Richardson and Woodfull opened, with Bradman number three.

Then came McCabe, Ponsford and newchums Ernie Bromley
and Len Darling. O'Reilly opened the bowling with Tim Wall

and Bert Ironmonger bowled first change. The team was too thin in the bowling ranks, and it showed. England won by six wickets.

Clarrie's depression deepened when, on 16 February, 1933, the last day of the fourth Test of the Bodyline series, the sad news of Archie Jackson's death was announced. He was only twenty-three years old. A nation crushed by the Depression mourned.

Larwood was made the scapegoat for Jardine's Bodyline. The ex-coal miner was given the dirtiest job and when he had completed that task to the tune of 33 wickets at 19.51 runs apiece to head the aggregate and averages for a bowler on either side, Larwood was axed from Test cricket forever. In his last Test at Sydney in February, 1933, Larwood took 4/98 and 1/44 and scored 98. Jardine retired from first-class cricket after leading the 1933–34 MCC team to India. As England captain he won nine matches, drew five and lost only one, the MCG Bodyline Test when Bradman and O'Reilly combined to beat England virtually by themselves.

Grimmett suffered silently over his Test axing. He kept his own counsel, although he did let go occasionally, saying in private what his legion of fans were unafraid to say openly in public. He was far from spent as a top-line bowler. Clarrie bounced back with a rich haul of wickets in 1933–34, taking 55 wickets at 20.01, including six bags of 5 wickets or more in an innings.

It was Clarrie's best first-class summer since 1929–30, the one prior to his triumphant 1930 tour of England.

He toured England in 1934 and again, this time with O'Reilly, bowled superbly. That tour is described fully in the chapter "The Tiger and the Fox". At the age of forty-three, Grimmett again proved his greatness. O'Reilly and Grimmett each collected 109 wickets on the England tour, with the left-armer Leslie "Chuck" Fleetwood-Smith also bowling beautifully with 106 tour victims. However, it was Grimmett and O'Reilly in the Test matches, with Fleetwood-Smith not getting one Test match. In the Tests Bradman hit a run of 29 and 25; 36 and 13; 30; 304 and 244 and 77. Australia clinched the Ashes it had lost in the Bodyline series.

Bradman was beset with illness during the tour. He became

gravely ill after what was first thought to be a routine appendix operation. However, the Don had to fight the battle of his life after the surgeon found infection had already set in before he began to remove the appendix. The world's greatest batsman had "hovered on the brink of eternity", but the immediate danger passed. The Don was still recuperating at the Sir Douglas Shields Private Hospital in Park Lane, London, having been joined by his wife, Jessie, when Woodfull's Australians sailed home, the Ashes safe. Clarrie wrote a cheery note to the Don and Bradman answered the letter promptly and courteously, as he always responded to fans and friends alike.

C/- Sir Douglas Shields Private Hospital
17, Park Lane,
LONDON, W. 1.

24th October 1934

C.V. Grimmett, Esq.,
C/- S.A. Cricket Association,
ADELAIDE, AUSTRALIA.

Dear Clarrie,

It was very kind of you to remember me after you had got away from England, and to send me along a few lines. At the time of my writing this you will be very near Fremantle, and although I have my compensations over here, I do envy you very much being back home once more.

From all accounts your sea journey home was a fairly comfortable one, and I trust you did not spend much time in your cabin, for the same reason as I undoubtedly would have done, and will probably do when my turn comes.

It seems ages since you left England, and yet we find Scott in Australia long before you. It only goes to show how small this world of ours is really becoming.

I have had a particularly bad time with this old appendix of mine, and although the worst is now past I am still in hospital, and do not know for certain when I will be leaving even though it is over a month since the operation. Naturally it will take some time to regain my strength, and I have no idea just how long it will be before the doctor will permit me to return to Australia.

Everybody in England has been extremely kind to me, but still I have missed the familiar faces of the members of the Team. I am sorry I spoiled the little party for the return journey. However, I hope to be back in due course, and will be looking forward to seeing you once more. Meanwhile, as ever you have my very best wishes.

With kindest regards.

Yours sincerely,

Don Bradman

Bradman missed the entire 1934–35 Australian season and was lured to Adelaide from his native New South Wales. The Bradmans arrived in Adelaide in the winter of 1935. He agreed to work for Harry Hodgetts, a leading Adelaide sharebroker and a SACA member. He signed for seven hundred pounds a year, although that amount was reduced to five hundred pounds during the time he was overseas playing cricket. According to the history of the SACA (published by Sports Marketing, 1990), the association's contributions to Bradman's annual salary was five hundred pounds. In 1935 the Don had still not completely recovered from his near-fatal illness on the 1934 England tour. Under the terms of his contract with the SACA, Bradman had to live in a certain area and his district club would be Kensington: Clarrie Grimmett's club. He reluctantly made himself unavailable for the South African tour of 1935–36, taking heed of medical advice. However, missing the Test tour of South Africa did not prevent the Don from turning out for South Australia, leading the State side and helping them to win the Sheffield Shield. Vic Richardson, the incumbent South Australian captain, was Test captain in South Africa at the time. Grimmett, the side's best bowler, was also in South Africa. Bradman had brought with him his St George leg-spinning team-mate, Frank Ward. Bradman must have had a high opinion of Ward. Grimmett was still bowling well for South Australia, although Bradman would have known Grimmett would go to South Africa and the South Australian team would need a good replacement spinner. The Don might also have been looking ahead to the day when he was leading Australia, when perhaps Clarrie was too old?

While Grimmett and O'Reilly spun havoc in South Africa, Bradman took Adelaide by storm. Bradman hit 117 in the first Shield match under his leadership against New South Wales. Ward took 6/127 and South Australia won by an innings and five runs. He scored 233 against Queensland 369 against Tasmania, a season's tally of 1173 runs at an average of 130.33. Bradman was back! Meanwhile, Clarrie wheeled away in South Africa, taking 44 Test wickets at 14 runs apiece. It was an outstanding effort for any bowler, let alone a man aged forty-four.

The 1936–37 Test season

Grimmett's bowling record in South Africa was simply cast aside when the selectors sat down to pick the first Test team against "Gubby" Allen's England side. Frank Ward replaced Grimmett. England won the match by 322 runs but Ward got 2/138 and 6/102 to keep most of his detractors quiet. There must have been a certain amount of resentment amongst the "old guard" in South Australia. While Richardson and Grimmett were away in South Africa, Bradman had led South Australia to its first Sheffield Shield in nearly a decade. Ward had also bowled well for South Australia; the pair had dominated. That Bradman was to continue leading South Australia might have upset the Richardson-Grimmett alliance. They had worked well as a team and the old never like giving way to the new, in any walk of life.

Clarrie couldn't believe his treatment. Richardson too was disturbed over his old friend's harsh handling by the Test selectors. Grimmett had played such a lone hand in Australia's attack in England in 1930 that it was written, with justification, that his bowling was more vital to his team than even Don Bradman's batting.

As Don scored 974 runs in that series, the full measure of this tribute can be imagined. In the 1936–37 season, England won the first two Tests, but Fleetwood-Smith came into the third Test

at Melbourne and with 5/124 in the second innings, helped to
turn a win Bradman's way. Australia won the following two
Tests in Adelaide and Melbourne to take the series, 3/2. Fleetwood-Smith took 4/129 off 41.4 overs in the first innings of the
Adelaide match and 6/110 off 30 in the second to crush effectively the opposition batting.

Clarrie took a season's tally of 36 wickets at 25.55. No gold at
the end of his rainbow: no gold in the form of a 1936–37 Test cap.
Ward played in two more Tests that summer, taking 2/132 in the
SCG second Test and 1/60 in the MCG third Test. He was then
discarded. Although Ward was dropped, there was no recall for
Clarrie. Australia turned the tables on Gubby Allen's men; after
being two-nil down, Bradman's men won the last three Tests to
win the rubber. O'Reilly was doing it alone.

Grimmett claimed that Bradman, South Australia and Test
captain, had told him that he had "lost" his leg-break. To a man
of Grimmett's professionalism the alleged criticism from Bradman would have cut him to the quick. But he would not have
lashed out; Clarrie always kept his own counsel. On 1 October,
1937 an appeal was launched to raise money by way of testimonial for Richardson and Grimmett. Their contribution to South
Australia and Australian cricket was to be formally recognised.

And in November 1937, Bradman's XI met Richardson's XI
on the Adelaide Oval. That Bradman had told Grimmett to bowl
more leg-breaks and even suggested to the old Fox that he had
lost the power to spin from the leg ensured that this testimonial
would be a grudge match between Grimmett and Bradman,
even if Clarrie was the only person aware of it. At that time
Clarrie had finally, after twelve years, brought his new toy, his
flipper, into play. He always reckoned his top-spinner to be his
most lethal delivery, as the batsman fumbled and stumbled,
searching desperately for the leg-break's breadth of turn, only
to see the ball skid on straight and trap him lbw or be clean
bowled.

Bradman arrived at the crease soon before lunch. It was a
Saturday and the people would swarm the ground after the
interval to watch Bradman in full flight. The Don got to 17 when
he faced Grimmett. Clarrie had intentionally bowled Bradman
a series of top-spinners and leg-breaks, which hardly turned at

all. His plan was taking shape. Then he changed tack. He sauntered up to the crease and swung his arm over, giving the ball a big tweak and following through vigorously, his right arm whipping across his body and right down past his left side.

The ball fizzed. It curved slightly towards leg stump, pitched on a perfect length and completely beat the Bradman forward defensive stroke. Grimmett's big-spinning leg-break, however, did not miss the top of Bradman's off-stump. Clarrie danced a little jig, his excitement, however, a mere trifle in the bigger scheme of things.

Bradman bowled Grimmett 17. Poor Vic Richardson. He sidled up to Clarrie, glad that his comrade had proved a point, but also rather bemused: "Well bowled, Grum, you old fox. But hardly well done! You've just cost us a thousand quid!"

But to Clarrie Grimmett, Bradman's wicket was priceless. Bradman's XI scored 184; Brown 42, Sievers 4/27, Grimmett 3/39. Richardson's XI replied with 9/380; Badcock 102, McCabe 72, Richardson 42, Chipperfield 41; Ward 4/71. Clarrie took 33 wickets at 21.42 runs apiece that summer.

The 1938 bombshell

The cricket world was stunned when Clarrie Grimmett was not selected for the 1938 Australian tour of England. Don Bradman, Test captain and selector, has never conceded that the selectors made a mistake in not taking Grimmett to England in 1938.

Sir Donald said recently: "I thought we might have made a mistake in not taking Don Tallon on this tour, as he probably became the best wicketkeeper Australia has ever had. And I have always regretted that Christ [the Queensland left-arm spinner C.P. Christ] did not tour. I think he would have done very well on the English wickets."

The Don might well have regretted the absence of keeper Tallon and spinner Christ, but Bradman's explanation of Grimmett's non-selection does not match the commonsense approach and logic he has always displayed in the public arena. The following quotation is taken from ABC interviews of Don Bradman by Norman May:

Bill O'Reilly was our spearhead, while Fleetwood-Smith was our up-and-coming spinner, then you had Grimmett and Frank Ward; Grimmett was, at that stage, I think, 46 years of age.

Now that is getting pretty old for a tour of England and he had already been dropped from the Australian team as far back as 1932.

So whatever happened, O'Reilly was going to be number one; Fleetwood-Smith was going to be number two and whoever the next spinner was would have to be number three, and you didn't have room for four.

I don't think people realised just how well Frank Ward did on that tour. I think he took 92 wickets and he was high up in the bowling averages. But the important thing that has been overlooked is the strike rate. And it is very important on a tour of England that you get the opposition out quickly. It gives you less time in the field and more opportunity to rest. Now Ward bowled 526 overs on tour, taking 92 wickets and his strike rate was that he got a wicket every 5.7 overs.

That was better than Grimmett achieved on any of his three England tours, it was a better strike rate than O'Reilly achieved, great as he was, and I think Frank was one of the great successes on the tour because he filled this gap very well indeed. I believe now, after all these years, that we still did not make a mistake in taking Frank [Ward] instead of Grimmett in 1938.

Grimmett toured England three times — 1926, 1930 and 1934 taking hauls of 116, 142 and 109 wickets respectively. As the Don says, Ward took 92 first-class wickets on the 1938 tour.

The Test records of C.V. Grimmett and F.A. Ward in England

	Year	Tests	Wickets
C.V. Grimmett	1926	3	14
	1930	5	29
	1934	5	25
	Total	13	68
F.A. Ward	1938	1	–
	Total	1	Nil

N.B.   Ward played in the Nottingham first Test in June, 1938. He failed to capture a wicket in 30 overs and conceded 142 runs.

Would Clarrie Grimmett have done better than Frank Ward in 1938? An overwhelming majority of his peers say an emphatic "yes".

O'Reilly has never forgotten the 1938 Test selection committee for its apparent shortsightedness over Grimmett's non-selection. Tongues no doubt wagged behind Bradman's back. He would have been used to that, for the Don's brilliance brought out the odd bit of envy in a number of his peers. Human nature does that. Yet if Bradman was the driving force behind Grimmett getting the boot from Test cricket, why, in Heaven's name, would he do it for a tour which was so vital to him because it was his first tour of England as the Australian captain? Bradman was one of a trio of selectors. His co-selectors were "Chappie" Dwyer and Bill Johnson. Bradman was not a member of the selection committee which dropped Grimmett in 1932–33, but neither was he on the committee which reinstated Grimmett for the 1934 tour of England and the tour of South Africa, in 1935–36. In his last ten Tests Grimmett took no fewer than 69 wickets (25 in England and 44 in South Africa). During his last three Test match innings in South Africa Grimmett reaped wicket hauls of 7/40 off 19.5 overs at the Old Wanderers, Johannesburg (his best Test bowling in an innings), 7/100 off 45 overs and 6/73 off 48 overs at Kingsmead, Durban. To axe him from the 1936–37 rubber did not make sense, nor did his 1938 tour non-selection.

It defied the Bradman logic for the Don to want a man he genuinely thought would be a great asset out of his team. Bradman obviously thought that Grimmett, at the age of 46, was either too old or past it, or both. They appeared on good terms when this article by Don Bradman appeared in the *Sunday Sun* on 4 April, 1932:

> Watch him walking down the street. One might imagine this slimly-built and short fellow to be anything but what he actually is. Confer on him the title of "world's greatest slow bowler" and nobody would disagree with you (except perhaps Clarrie himself). It is only natural he would disagree, for a more modest, unassuming cricketer never breathed.
>
> Scarlet, or Grum (to use some of his nicknames) is, as they call him, grim and wily. Have we not seen him over after over, day after day, match after match, toil in the hot sun, bearing the brunt of the

bowling for Australia, yet never wilting or complaining?

I love to sit in the pavilion and watch him bowling to a man who is well set and playing good cricket. Every time Clarrie walks back, getting ready to deliver the next ball, one can almost see him thinking out something new or planning out just how he intends to try to get this man's wicket. I don't think any bowler has made such a study of bowling as Grimmett. A few moments' conversation will soon convince you of this. He will explain scientifically why a ball [to] which overspin has been imparted will drop quickly in the air. He will tell you that a ball will swerve in the air because of the spin imparted to the ball, which way it will swerve and why.

Clarrie only needs a table and a ping-pong ball or tennis ball and he is a real entertainment. It is remarkable the spin he can impart to a ball, making it turn at various angles.

There is no player to whom I would rather go when seeking genuine, sincere advice than Clarrie. Go to him yourself in all good faith and he in turn will honestly and conscientiously give you what he considers the best advice and help you all he possibly can.

One of the main reasons for Grimmett's continued and outstanding success is his consistency. Bowling for the first time in a match, cold and stiff, against two batsmen well set, I have seen Clarrie come on and bowl four consecutive maiden overs.

That immaculate length, ball after ball, is tantalising to the batsman who is anxious to make shots, but can't. In desperation he often hits out wildly, but always with fatal results.

There was an incident after the Grimmett-Richardson Testimonial match which might have had a bearing on Grimmett's eventual non-selection for the 1938 tour of England. Vic Richardson attended a SACA cricket committee meeting on 15 December, 1937. He told the group that he had heard that two fast bowlers in the Grimmett-Richardson Testimonial match had been approached by the umpires and instructed not to bowl fast short balls; if they did, it would mitigate against their chance of selection for the 1938 English tour.

"On whose authority were such instructions given?" Richardson demanded.

The umpires for the match were the ex-New South Wales and South Australian fast bowler Jack Scott and A.G. Jenkins. Jenkins said he did not raise the matter. Scott explained in January, 1938 that he had indeed approached two bowlers, Ernie McCormick and Ginty Lush. "I had received instructions from the SACA office that Law 48b was to be enforced. In such a match as this I decided it was better just to have a quiet word to the players. I told them that if there is any bowling deliberately at the man, I am going to stop it straight away. I told them G.O. 'Gubby' Allen had said to me at the end of the last English tour that this type of bowling was still bowled in Australia." (Allen played under Jardine in the Bodyline series and was one of the England players to stand up his captain against the tactic. He refused point-blank to bowl at the body. He captained England in the next tour Down Under in 1936–37.) Scott added that both McCormick and Lush assured him that they would not indulge in such bowling. He said that was the end of the matter.

For Clarrie the 1930s were wonderful years, despite his setbacks. There was the 1930 tour, a triumph, 1934 in England, South Africa, plus the two successful home series against the West Indies and South Africa, although the Bodyline series hit hard. On the home front, Clarrie continued to lead a quiet life, enjoying Lizzy's home cooking, developing his photographs in the darkroom, or showing movies of his tours. During the height of his career, Clarrie hated being photographed; he shunned the camera (unless he was the one taking the picture). Clarrie's son Vic could never understand why his father would make a hasty retreat when the photographers were about when he and his mother would greet the returning hero from another campaign on the platform at the Adelaide Railway Station. He describes his feelings for his father:

> I was often upset when dad would make good his escape from the glare of publicity. I was over the moon whenever I had my picture taken with my father. I was so proud of him.
>
> He was a gentle man; I can recall only once when my dad hit me and even that was a cuff behind the ear. For him to do that I must have done something awful. Gentle, but very firm in his way. He wouldn't hit me, but he did have a very effective method of making me toe the line. My greatest fear was to be locked in the broom cupboard.

Young Vic's childhood fear manifested itself into the most horrific dreams. Even during the darkest days of World War II, when Vic Grimmett flew bombing missions over German-occupied Europe, he never experienced fear or terror quite so shocking as that he felt when locked in the Grimmett broom cupboard in Firle.

In many ways Clarrie Grimmett and Don Bradman were alike. They both had a burning passion for the game and a hunger for success that was seemingly insatiable. Both were canny and confident, the supreme artists. Bradman was the greatest batsmen of them all. In the cricketing world, if Victor Trumper was the sun in all its glory, Wally Hammond the earth and Graeme Pollock a shooting star, Bradman was the universe itself.

Bradman defeated all opposition and Grimmett was never beaten. He remembered old Jack Saunders' words: "Your next ball will surely get a wicket".

While Grimmett and Bradman had genuine and lasting respect for each other's ability, Grimmett never forgave Bradman for his omission from the 1938 tour. He blamed the Don, and O'Reilly, among Clarrie's peers, heartily agreed. Whether in anger, or bitter resentment, Clarrie always maintained batsmen such as Trumper, Ponsford, McCabe, Hobbs, Kippax, Hammond, Chapman and Macartney were tougher to combat than Don Bradman.

> When the old Fox was discarded from Test cricket in 1938 he
> was cut to the quick. He carried the scars forever.

10 *THE TIGER AND THE FOX*

Ask Bill O'Reilly who was the greatest bowler of them all and he has no hesitation. He gives the palm to his old mate, the little spin wizard he always has called Grum.

> Grum was my treasured bowling partner. He was, perhaps, as responsible for my success as I was, for we bowled as a team. In Grum's early life in the Shaky Isles he harboured ideas of succeeding in cricket, the game he loved, as a fast bowler. (I am at a loss over why every ambitious youngster in cricket starts off with his mind set on bowling fast. Must be the primitive appeal of violence, a hangover from the Stone Age.) Thank goodness his schoolmaster, Frank Hempelmann, saw the potential of the young Grimmett's leg-breaks and insisted upon Clarrie bowling slow. He began to concentrate on leg-spin and to think it all out with the supreme self-confidence that never forsook him throughout his life.

O'Reilly first saw C.V. Grimmett a day after the first interstate encounter between Victoria and New South Wales at the SCG after the end of World War I. It was the summer of 1919. On their way home the Victorians agreed to a match at Goulburn. Young O'Reilly was attending Goulburn High School and he ventured along to the local sports ground to watch the action. He was surprised to find the leg-spinner, Grimmett, opening the innings for Victoria with the manager Matt Ellis. "This fellow Grimmett must be good going in before the likes of Vernon Ransford, Jack Ryder, Les Keating, Basil Onyons and Phil Le Couteur," Bill thought. "When his name went up on the miniature makeshift scoreboard (I'd never seen one before) the local lads misspelt it 'Grummett'."

O'Reilly continued: "From that time on he was Grummett to me, a term which was abbreviated to 'Grum', and which all his

friends eventually used as a term of endearment and un-
bounded respect. Grum got 38 in painfully slow time, before he
was caught and bowled by the local champion, George Tickner.
He did, however, impress me with his dexterity in getting the
ball away through the slips, with a shot which at that time I had
only associated with the name of Alan Kippax."

Grum was one of Clarrie's many nicknames. In Sydney in
1919 Matt Ellis called him "Scarlet" because when all attempts
to have the Victorians join him in song failed, he turned to
Clarrie to help him out. "You remind me of the Scarlet Pimpernel," Ellis said. Clarrie might have reminded the Victorian selector of just that fact a few years later when his constant haul
of wickets in grade cricket failed to win him more than a few
State appearances. He was also known as the "Gnome", but
universally he was called the Fox.

O'Reilly and Grimmett met up, as already recorded, in the
Adelaide Test of 1931-32, when Bradman hit 299 not out and
Clarrie took 14/199. "I learned a great deal watching Grum
wheel away," said O'Reilly. "I watched him like a hawk. He was
completely in control. His subtle change of pace impressed me
greatly."

The West Indies tourists the following year proved to be easy
meat. O'Reilly had done most of the work in the Bodyline series,
with Grimmett being axed after the Adelaide match, so the pair
did not really show the world their mastery in tandem until
1934.

Let O'Reilly describe it:

It was on that tour that we [Grimmett and O'Reilly] had all the
verbal bouquets in the cricket world thrown at us as one of the
greatest spin combinations Test cricket had seen. Bowling tightly
and keeping the batsmen unremittingly on the defensive, we collected 53 (Grimmett 25, O'Reilly 28) of the 73 English wickets that
fell that summer. Each of us collected more than 100 wickets on tour
and it would have needed a brave, or demented, Australian at that
time to suggest that Grimmett's career was almost ended.

O'Reilly believed that he and Grimmett bowled in perfect harmony, each with a careful eye for the other:

With Grum at the other end I knew full well that no batsman would
be allowed the slightest respite. We were fortunate in that our styles

supplemented each other. Grum loved to bowl into the wind, which gave him an opportunity to use wind resistance as an important adjunct to his schemes regarding direction. He had no illusions about the ball "dropping" as we hear so often these days, before its arrival at the batsman's proposed point of contact. To him that was balderdash. In fact, he always loved to hear people making up verbal explanations for the suspected trickery that had brought a batsman's downfall. If a batsman had thought the ball had dropped, all well and good. Grimmett himself knew that it was simply change of pace that had made the batsman think that such an impossibility had happened.

Clarrie Grimmett and Bill O'Reilly had already formed a great spin liaison by the time the good ship *Orford* docked in Southampton one cold grey day in April, 1934.

The eighteenth Australian team had arrived; that is if you don't count the 1868 side, comprising an all-Aborigine outfit, led by the Englishman Charles Lawrence. While the 1868 side does not get official status in the records, English fans have since been disappointed with the Australian cricketers' inability to hurl a boomerang. Boomerang displays were popular when the Aborigines toured in 1868. They played 47 matches, winning 14, losing 14 and drawing 19. However, they won everyone with their displays of athleticism in throwing spear and boomerang.

Bill Woodfull's 1934 team comprised an ordinary pace attack, led by South Australia's Tim Wall and Victorian Hans Ebeling, the man who conceived the idea of the 1977 Centenary Test match at the MCG. However, in spin, Woodfull was able to call upon three able men, Grimmett, O'Reilly and the up-and-comer Leslie "Chuck" Fleetwood-Smith. A left-hand unorthodox spinner, Fleetwood-Smith gave the ball a big flick. At times he spun prodigiously, but he often suffered because of lack of control. Yet he took 106 tour wickets, but was not called upon to play a Test. That's how tough it was to displace a Grimmett or an O'Reilly. The Tiger and the Fox each claimed 109 tour wickets.

In the first Test at Trent Bridge, Arthur Chipperfield scored a debut 99 and Australia was never headed throughout, hitting a first innings 374, then 273, with England going for 268, then a lowly 141. Woodfull's men won by 238 runs, but events may have been different had not Woodfull switched his champion spinners on the last day.

As the players left the field for lunch, Woodfull said to O'Reilly, "I'm going to put Old Grum on at the River End next over, Tiger, and switch you up here to the Pavilion end".

The Tiger awoke to the ploy. Giving Grimmett the end most likely to respond to his leg-breaks was fair enough. Grum was the tried and true match-winner; he deserved the spoils. Bill was a newcomer to England; the apprentice. However, the big man knew it hurt his skipper to have to tell him of his plan to switch ends, for Woodfull never once looked Bill in the eye and that, Bill and everyone else knew, was not Woodfull's usual way.

In O'Reilly's first over from the Pavilion End he got the ball to bite and bounce disconcertingly. Grimmett's eyes narrowed at cover, for the very end which Woodfull thought would not suit Old Grum was destined to be just right for the Tiger. O'Reilly spun at remarkable pace and had the old hands in the Members' Stand talking excitedly about the days of Sydney Barnes, the English swerver and spinner who is generally acknowledged as the greatest bowler of them all.

The Tiger savaged the lion. He took 7/54 off 41.4 overs while Grimmett, at the other end, snared 3/39 off 47 overs. For the match O'Reilly bagged 11/129 and Grimmett 8/120.

"Never did I let Grum forget that day we switched ends, but you can take it from me that there was never any need for him to do that type of finessing. He was the most competent bowler I have ever set eyes upon," O'Reilly said.

The second test at Lord's brought the Australians back to earth. England hit 440, with centuries to the left-hander Maurice Leyland and wicketkeeper Leslie Ames. Grimmett toiled for 53.3 overs to take one wicket (Hedley Verity) at a cost of 102 runs and O'Reilly fared little better, taking 1/70 off 38 overs. It was Verity's match. The left-hand orthodox spinner took 7/61 off 36 overs and 8/43 off 22.3, claiming Bradman's wicket cheaply both times, to destroy the Australians on the rain-affected wicket, known as a "sticky dog". England won by an innings and 38 runs.

Light relief was required during this match, so O'Reilly, along with Stan McCabe, Alan Kippax and Arthur Mailey, on tour as writer and cartoonist, visited the apartments of Sir James Barrie, famous author. Barrie was barely 150 centimetres tall. He had a boyish look, fresh-faced with a bushy moustache which seemed stuck on and at odds with his look of youth. He was constantly surrounded by a pall of tobacco smoke, emitted by an old bent-stemmed Captain Petersen pipe, fashionable in those days. O'Reilly and company dined with Barrie at his Pall Mall apartments, near Trafalgar Square in London. His home away from the bustle of London was in Kent and it was there that Barrie's love of cricket evolved. He told O'Reilly that he had formed his own team — called something like the Wanderers as far as I can remember. "He [Barrie] said he was an active and very proud member of the eleven. Then talking to Mailey and me about his bowling prowess, he was inclined, it seemed to me, to let his imagination run loose.

" 'I was the slowest bowler, in fact I still am, that ever rolled the right arm over,' Barrie said. 'So slow indeed that if after delivery I realised that something was wrong with the trajectory, I could retrieve it and set it properly on its course. One day, bowling at the opposite's top batsman, I sent down a curly one and on letting it go, I cried out, "My God, he's out!" so I sat down and watched it take its course. And sure as I stand here now, it went up, evaded the bat and leaned up against the off-stump!' No wonder he wrote about Peter Pan."

O'Reilly's love of literature was fired in 1914, just before World War I, when he met Henry Lawson — introduced by his father outside a pub near where the Milson's Point Railway Station now stands. Meeting Sir James Barrie was a great highlight for him, but his spin twin Grimmett would not have had the same sense of fun over the "toss the ball up in hope and fantasy" that so entranced Barrie and the likes of Arthur Mailey.

Australia's first great leg-spinner was Herbert Hordern, who, like Monty Noble, was a dentist. Hordern was faster than Grimmett, but he turned about as much. Critics of the time argued that Hordern was the best of them all.

He played only eighteen first-class matches but managed 14/295 in two Tests against South Africa in 1910–11, and against England in 1911–12 he took 32 wickets in the series, including 5/85 and 7/90 at the SCG. But his dental career won out; Dr Hordern's clever fingers were saved for his patients. Batsmen the world over sighed relief. Hordern played too little to assess his place in the list of spinners.

Arthur Mailey tossed the ball up to invite the batsman to attack. His attitude to bowling did not impress Clarrie or Tiger O'Reilly. Once Mailey advised O'Reilly to change his grip for the leg-break, "if he ever wanted to get anywhere in the game". O'Reilly thanked Mailey for his interest and said resolutely: "I think I shall continue with this grip, Mr Mailey". In the shadows of the net stood a little, rugged-faced man with gnarled hands. "Good on yer sonny. They tried to change me, yer know. Follow yer own instincts." The voice belonged to Charles Thomas Biass Turner. It was the same C.T.B. Turner who was a legend in Australian cricket in the 1880s, the man who took 993 first-class wickets at just 14.34 runs apiece.

Mailey was probably at his best before World War I. It was a time of cricket chivalry, when batsmen such as Trumper would hit a fabulous century and then, with the bowlers at their mercy, pick out the most deserving bowler and simply get out to him. A few years later batsmen got meaner.

Bill Ponsford began an era of big scoring. The Maileys of this world became a back number. A bowler couldn't be confident about tossing runs away in the sure knowledge that once he got to his hundred the batsman would obligingly hole out. Ponsford batted on and on. So too did Bradman. Mailey's strategy of buying wickets worked on the tailenders. He swept through the tail effectively and swiftly.

In 1920–21 Mailey took 36 wickets in the England-Australia series, including a haul of 9/121 in one Test innings, still a record for an Australian. But by the mid-1920s Mailey's expensive style became unfashionable. Grimmett's mean offerings kept things tight, yet he also attacked. O'Reilly too was all-out attack, yet his control was such that he kept it tight as a drum. As a pair Grimmett and O'Reilly were unbeatable, yet their styles differed greatly.

O'Reilly was big and lumbering, over 180 centimetres in height. He charged up to the stumps with an awkward gait, bellowing aggression. His was a "boots'n'all" commitment. A driven four and the Tiger snarled in rage. In his early days, O'Reilly lacked finesse. He learned the art of change of pace from his old spin comrade, Clarrie Grimmett. The Fox was entirely O'Reilly's opposite in style. O'Reilly stormed straight for the heart of the enemy; Grimmett schemed and toiled, luring the enemy into a false sense of security, then he struck with deadly accuracy. Bill preferred to operate with the wind, Clarrie against the wind.

There was Clarrie spinning with unerring accuracy into the wind, luring the lead-footed ever forward and driving the fleet-footed back, all the while plotting his trap. At the other end, O'Reilly bowled at a lively pace, getting his leg-break to turn and lift, then bowling the Bosey, which bounced disconcertingly and often forced a batsman into giving an absurd popped catch to Jack Fingleton or Len Darling who lurked in close on the leg-side.

After the Verity debacle at Lord's, Woodfull's men drew the Tests at Manchester and Leeds, with Grimmett and O'Reilly carrying the attack and Bradman hitting a great 304 at Leeds, in the lead-up to the fifth Test at Kennington Oval.

There Australia crushed England by 562 runs. Ponsford (266) and Bradman (244) set up a record second wicket partnership of 451 in 316 minutes and Australia raced to 701. England struggled to 321 in reply, with Grimmett taking 3/103 off 49.3 overs and O'Reilly 2/93 off 37 overs. Australia hit 327 a second time, with Ponsford, in his last Test knock, getting 22. England, needing a virtually impossible 708 runs for outright victory, were bundled out for 145. Clarrie took 5/64 off 26.3 overs and O'Reilly again snared two wickets, conceding 58 runs off his 22 overs.

Sadly that Test was Grimmett's last in England. It was also Frank Woolley's last Test. Woolley, Grimmett's first Test wicket, had been recalled, at the age of forty-seven, to again don the England cap.

Woolley made his debut for England on 9 August, 1909 against Noble's Australians on this very ground. It was a sad farewell for Woolley, caught off O'Reilly for 4 and a last innings duck, caught Ponsford bowled McCabe. Clarrie was saddened by Ponsford's decision to retire. He was a grand bat, hitting 2122 runs in 29 Tests at an average of 48.22. In first-class matches Ponsford hit 13,819 runs at an average of 65.18 and for Victoria in Shield matches he averaged 80! He remains the only man to have hit two scores in excess of 400 — 429 against Tasmania in 1923 and 437 against Queensland in 1927–28 — in first-class cricket. Just before the Kennington Oval Test, Neville Cardus wrote this tribute to Clarrie Grimmett. It appeared in the *Manchester Guardian* on 12 August, 1934:

He is an unobtrusive little man, with a face that says nothing to you at all; seldom is he heard by the crowd when he appeals for leg-before-wicket. He walks about the field on dainty feet which step as though with the soft fastidiousness of a cat treading a wet pavement.

He is a master of surreptitious arts; when he hides his skill, and sometimes when he is on guard at cover, he seems to hide himself. He knows every trick of getting himself unobserved, and he darts forward to run a man out like somebody emerging from an ambush.

"Gamp is my name and gamp is my natur'." That is a dark metaphysical saying; the meaning cannot be put into words, but none the less we can grasp it by the instinct for eternal substances.

It is like that with Grimmett; the name penetrates to the quiddity, like "cural", "twist", "slithery"; his name is onomatopoeic.

I love to see him bowl a man out behind his back, so to say — round his legs; the ball gently touches the stumps and removes perhaps only one bail. The humorous cunning of it reminds me that the Artful Dodger used to walk stealthily behind the master and extract the handkerchief from the coat tails without making a tinkle on the little bell!

Compare Grimmett with the wonderful leg-spin bowler he succeeded in the Australian eleven, Arthur Mailey. An Australian wit once said to me: "Mailey bowled the googly stuff like a millionaire; Clarrie bowls it like a miser."

Mailey tossed up his spin with all the blandness in the world; his full tosses were like a generous sort of fattening diet — before the killing and the roasting! Mailey did his mischief by daylight. Grimmett goes to work with a dark lantern; his boots are rubbered. Mailey's wickets were like a practised and jolly angler's "catch", Grimmett's wickets are definitely "swag".

When he goes off the field after he has had seven for 57, I can see the bag he is carrying over his shoulder. He is the greatest right-handed spin bowler of our period. The comparison with Mailey was employed not to stress resemblance but difference; Grimmett is less a "googly" than a leg-break bowler.

He uses the "wrong" one sparsely; he is content to thrive on the ball which breaks away and leaves the bat; that is the best of all balls.

A straight ball, wickedly masked, is Grimmett's foil to the leg-break. He makes a virtue of a low arm; his flight keeps so close to the earth that only a batsman quick of feet can jump to the pitch of it. And then he must be aware of Oldfield, the most gentlemanly of wicket-keepers, who stumps you with courtesy; as he does not make a noise to the umpire, but almost bows you from the wicket. Or is he like a perfect dentist who says when your heart is in your mouth: "It's all over; I've already got it out; here it is". To play forward to Grimmett, to miss and then to find yourself stumped by Oldfield — why it is like an operation under anaesthetic.

Moments come to all of us when we are uplifted beyond the ordinary; we become touched with grace for a while; we become vessels of inspiration. Felicity descended on Grimmett at Trent Bridge in June, 1930, on the first day of a Test match. I have never seen cleverer bowling on a good wicket against great players. Hammond was batting; he made two of his own great forcing off-side hits, off the back foot. These strokes told us that Hammond was in form. Grimmett bowled him a straight ball which sped sinfully from the beautiful turf. Hammond lbw to Grimmett.

Next came Woolley. Left-handed batsmen love leg-spin bowlers; the break turns the ball inwards to the middle of the bat.

But Grimmett did not send a leg-break to Woolley; he sent the "googly", whipping away. Woolley's forward strike was seduced by the fulsome length. Woolley was stumped by Oldfield. A few minutes afterwards Grimmett drew Hendren a yard out of his crease like a mesmerist; then having got Hendren where he wanted him, not far enough down the pitch but yet too far, he bowled him. Grimmett will remember in his old age how he spun and "floated" the ball that day; by the chimney corner he will babble of the way he turned a batsman's smooth lawn into a "sticky" dog. By sheer craftsmanship he overthrew three great batsmen; nothing to intimidate, no brute force (as George Lohmann called fast bowling of sorts); nothing but a slow spinning ball bowled by a little man with an arm as low as my grandfather's. The first sight of Grimmett bowling arouses mild laughter. His action recalls the ancient round-arm worthies or it recalls cricket on the sands with a walking stick for the wicket and a father of six playing for the first time in years. A few steps, a shuffle, and Grimmett's arm seems to creak. But watch his wrist and fingers; they are sinuous and beautiful. The wrist twirls and swivels; the fingers seem to adore and caress the ball, with the touch of a parent. Grimmett's fingers are always light and tactile; when he passes the salt at dinner he imparts the " 'fluence".

He is, I believe, a signwriter by profession. Can't you see his right wrist at work, sweeping the brush along the ornamentation?

Can't you imagine the fingers intimately putting the finishing flick to a full-stop? Or can't you see the skeleton key at work, turning the lock, finding the way through the bolted door of Sutcliffe's bat? He is, as I say, a master of surreptitious arts. His countenance expresses no joy when he confounds his opponents. But I imagine that long after close of play, as he lies in bed and thinks about it, he laughs far into the night. That apparent half-volley which Walters tried to drive; that obvious longhop that Hendren tried to hook. Confidence tricks! — O my lungs and liver, the wickedness of the world.

He seldom gets a man out caught in the deep field. That is an open and brazen way to rifle the English house. Better by far a swift catch at first slip or at the wicket; best of all lbw! — nobody knows anything about it away from the scene of the burglary. He is a great character, not only a great bowler. Sometimes he fancies himself as a batsman. He thrusts his left foot across and drives. Or he waits for it and cuts elegantly. Occasionally he plays and sees his stumps all awry. Then, and only then, does he wear his heart on his sleeve.

Everybody cherishes private ambitions; we all wish to be what we are not. Dan Leno sighed to play Hamlet; Henry Irving himself best when he sat on his top hat and pretended to be a Jingle in a farce derived from "Pickwick".

Grimmett made fifty in a Test match at Nottingham in June; perhaps in his old age he will not remember Trent Bridge for his great bowling of 1930 but for his preposterously stylish and first-class half-century of 1934. The rest of the world will dwell forever on his spin, learned in Australia, where a slow bowler must do his own work and not depend on nature and friendly wickets.

For my part I shall think of him always as I saw him at Worcester in May, taking the county's last wicket and winning the game. A catch was missed from him, and in the same over another lofty chance was skied near cover. Grimmett would trust nobody but Grimmett this time: he ran after the ball himself, and when he caught it he put it in his pocket and glided from the field, concealed entirely amongst ten other victorious Australians.

On the 1934 tour Clarrie had his trusty little Midget camera. It produced for him some excellent pictures and he always received a fair price for his efforts. In those days there was not a camera at every portal; no all-prying eye of the television. There were good photographs to be taken and Clarrie normally confined his shots to cricket, though he loved England with its old stone houses, thatch and cobbled laneways. In 1926, his first tour, Clarrie had been fascinated when he visited Faringdon, in Berkshire, the village of his ancestry where Thomas Grimmett, a mason, had owned a quarry.

In 1934 the Australians met up with King George V again, as they had in 1930, this time at Windsor Castle. Again the cameras were out in force and again the King obliged, expressing the wish that he might receive another album of photographs like that the "boys" gave him in 1930.

On the day of that presentation, Clarrie brought a cricket ball along with his Ensign Midget camera. He demonstrated the various angles of spin to the King.

"No wonder they call you the old fox, Clarrie," said the King, "you never forget."

Bill O'Reilly came to the Grimmett house at Firle whenever he was in town with the New South Wales team. When Clarrie's son Vic was young, he pictured big Bill as a friendly man with a penchant for devouring Lizzy's onion sandwiches. The former was true, but the onion sandwiches? "No," declared Bill.

The 1935–36 South African tour was Bill and Clarrie's most memorable as a team for they not only decimated the opposition as they had in England in 1934, but the trip was also a thoroughly enjoyable one. Grimmett took 44 wickets at 14 runs apiece, a record which stands to this day for an Australian in Test matches. Clarrie made an interesting and telling observation about the state of the nation. "The South Africans [whites] will have nothing to do with the native races because their experience has made them believe that the native must be kept under. We saw a great deal of the native life and found how complicated is the colour problem. The natives outnumber the whites by four to one and do all the manual work."

Clarrie also found the rarified atmosphere in Johannesburg (2000 metres above sea level) played havoc with his bowling. "At this altitude the ball travelled differently through the air and along the ground and it was impossible to flight the ball as well as in the heavier atmosphere at sea level." The second Test at Johannesburg saw Grimmett take 3/29 off 15 overs and 3/111 off 58 overs in a drawn encounter. O'Reilly took a match haul of 5/145 off 55.5 overs.

It was during that match, where Grimmett and O'Reilly failed to slam the lid tight on the Springbok Test coffin, that the Tiger introduced the old Fox to the "pleasures of drinking the amber fluid". Until that Christmas Day in Johannesburg, 1935, Grimmett had been strictly teetotal, but it was hot. O'Reilly and McCabe, Darling and Fingleton were enjoying an icy-cold beer. Clarrie stunned his mates by accepting the O'Reilly offer. He drank and he liked, and whenever Bill visited Adelaide after World War II when bayonets and hand grenades were replaced with bats and balls, the old spin pair would adjourn to the Members' Bar for a cold beer. Vic Richardson was ever popular. As a leader he had the unique ability to be one of the boys, yet he commanded total respect. Richardson was unafraid to do what he thought was best for the side, even if he provoked an argument. Tiger O'Reilly was in a rare mood of indifference, going through the motions, so Vic took him out of the attack. He ignored Tiger, even during the lunch break and again on the field, before bringing him back at the perfect psychological moment.

An Australian Rules player of note, Richardson had observed the effectiveness of the coaching ploy of not allowing the player to handle a football during an entire training session, then in the game watching those men almost obsessed in their desire to win possession. O'Reilly claimed 27 wickets in the South African series to complement Clarrie's haul of 44. They operated together in just 15 Tests before they were separated in 1936–37, taking 169 wickets at 21.16, a joint average of 11.2 wickets per match.

Richardson was the man Clarrie credits for bringing in two short-legs for O'Reilly. He had a steeply-bouncing Bosey (wrong 'un) which often had batsmen fending the ball off at chest height. O'Reilly bowled with the wind. He was quite quick through the air, about Derek Underwood's pace, and it proved impossible for most batsmen to get down the wicket to drive him.

In South Africa Dudley Nourse with a brilliant 231 at Johannesburg tamed the Tiger and the Fox, O'Reilly and Grimmett. In that match Stan McCabe blasted an unconquered 189 as Australia raced towards inevitable victory, but the fielding side appealed successfully that McCabe's powerful cuts and drives were endangering the fieldsmen in the failing light. The Australians were amazed and quite irate, for the side was hitting runs at hurricane rate, needing just 125 runs with eight wickets in hand.

Ten minutes after the umpires led the players from the field a heavy storm washed out any chance of a resumption. Clarrie reckoned McCabe's batting was extraordinary. "It was one of the greatest displays of batting I have seen. His stroke play was fascinating. A classic effort." The old Fox was once bowling to McCabe in Adelaide. He loved to keep Stan at bay, knowing the strokemaker was ever ready to charge down the track to drive. O'Reilly was at the non-striker's end. Ball after ball Grimmett bowled to contain the anxious McCabe. Then came a quiet plea, "Please toss one up, Grum?" The Fox smiled and O'Reilly roared.

Clarrie rarely bowled in the nets to his colleagues on tour. He would practise all right, but he liked to bowl in an empty net, his idea being that batsmen in the nets rarely play as they would in a game and he would also have to bowl against them when they returned to Australia and resumed battle against him in interstate competition.

Darling told me Clarrie hardly ever batted in the nets during the 1934 tour of England or in South Africa, for it might interfere with his golf swing. Clarrie played many rounds of golf in South Africa.

The side turned out to play baseball in Johannesburg to raise funds for the H.B. "Jock" Cameron Memorial Fund. Jock died suddenly after the 1935 South African tour of England.

Originally there was to be a cricket match, but because of the monotony of their Test victories, the Australians jumped at the chance to play baseball. Six of their number, including Grimmett and Richardson, had played the game. They played Transvaal, the home of baseball in South Africa.

"We wore our boots and caps and the Wanderers lent us their uniforms," Clarrie said. "When I saw our opponents warming up I thought we were in for a bad time, but in addition to six of us having played baseball, we all possessed a good eye and were in splendid physical condition."

The Australian baseball nine comprised: Ben Barnett, Ernie

McCormick, Leo O'Brien, Len Darling, Bill Brown, Jack Fingleton, Stan McCabe, Vic Richardson and Grimmett. When the game appeared safe, Bert Oldfield and O'Reilly came in as substitutes. Clarried described the game:

> Neither side scored for a couple of innings and then Transvaal got two runs. In our fourth, with bases full, I managed to hit safely and, before the innings had ended, we got seven runs. In their last innings a Transvaal batter hit high and hard. It seemed certain to go for a homer. The ball flew towards me at left field. I put up my gloved hand to prepare to catch it, but found I couldn't raise my arm above my shoulder…so I reached up with my bare right hand and caught it!

The catch brought the house down and then Darling hit a home run with bases loaded to ensure victory, 12–5. A week later, Clarrie realised why he had trouble raising his left arm. He had sustained a broken rib!

There were lighter moments. In Durban there was a function for the players. Clarrie sat next to a pretty woman who answered his casual question as to her knowledge of cricket with, "Oh, yes, I know all about a maiden over".

"That's fine," Clarrie said, "And what is a maiden over?"

"It's his first!"

During the match against Transvaal in Johannesburg, Langton faced O'Reilly and promptly hit him over the square leg pavilion. Clarrie could hardly contain his mirth and next ball Langton repeated the dose. Bill was furious. Clarrie was still chuckling over his spin twin's bad treatment when he bowled to Langton, only to suffer the same fate as O'Reilly. As the ball disappeared for a third time, McCormick sidled up to Grimmett and said, "Now we start on the coloureds". That was the origin of the story which has been retold down the years. In Cape Town in 1970 Mike Proctor hit yours truly for five successive sixes and Doug Walters is credited with having said, "Right, that's got rid of the reds, now we start on the coloureds". The McCormick story is true, the Walters story is apocryphal.

Grimmett and O'Reilly played for the last time together in a Test match in Durban, the game beginning on 28 February, 1936.

Again Australia dominated, with Grimmett finishing his Test career on the same triumphant note as he had begun, taking bags of wickets. He took 7/100 off 45 overs in the first innings and 6/73 off 48 in the second. O'Reilly bowled 37 fruitless overs in the first innings, conceding 59 runs, but took the only four wickets Grimmett left him for 47 off 40.1 overs in the second innings.

As a pair of bowlers they were wonderful, as good as any pair in history. The pity of their spin partnership was that Grimmett missed the 1938 tour of England. O'Reilly called it the "shameful omission".

It was an odd liaison, for they were direct opposites: Grimmett quiet in the extreme, wheeling away diligently, almost blending with the scenery and O'Reilly, burly, robust and bellowing like a bull. He snorted and ranted, what hair he had was red and it often stood out like an Irish revolt. Together they formed the perfect spin bowling partnership.

11 INDIA

The Wicket Fox was not about to crawl into his den and hibernate. Clarrie wrote about the 1938 tourists, wishing he was there, and hinting rather strongly that the bowling lacked potency and no-one could deny that, but he was itching for some action. It was one of the longest winters he had known. Not only had he been left behind on what would (and should) have been his fourth tour of England; Clarrie also had to endure the taunts about the Australian team — poor old Bill O'Reilly. He must have torn what little red hair he had left out by the roots, for he was in the position of having to carry the Australian bowling line-up, miserably weakened by the absence of Grimmett. The Tiger didn't need stirring at any time, but during this 1938 series he *was* the attack! His workload went along these lines: 56 overs 3/164 in the drawn Nottingham first Test; 37 overs 4/93 and 29 overs 2/53 in the drawn second Test at Lord's; 34.1 overs 5/66 and 21.5 overs 5/56 when he bowled Australia to a famous victory at Leeds; the third Test was abandoned without a ball being bowled and then came the fifth Test at Kennington Oval. O'Reilly toiled for hours, bowling 85 overs for a return of 3/178 in the match where twenty-two-year-old Len Hutton hit 364, the then world record Test score, in 13 hours and 17 minutes. There was many a time when the Tiger yearned for the stealth and cunning of his friend the Fox.

While England churned out 7 declared 903, the Fox sat at home in Firle, tending his garden, and when the Adelaide winter rain abated he played tennis with friends.

The temptation was there to tell the cricket world, "I told you so", but somehow he didn't have to do that; everyone knew. The Fox envied his friend the Tiger because O'Reilly was in England in the thick of the battle he so enjoyed. He also felt sorry for Bill, because the two of them, bowling in tandem, would not have allowed any batsman, even the immensely-gifted Hutton, to hit such a massive score on any wicket, at any time.

Right in the heart of the winter, Clarrie received an interesting letter from H. Roy Gollan, the Australian National Travel Association's representative in India. It seemed His Highness the Rajah of Rath wanted the Fox to travel to India to become his personal cricket coach:

> The proposal is that you will be in India approximately from the middle of September until the end of November. His Highness is prepared to pay a reasonable fee and all expenses but he leaves it to you to suggest the amount of fee.

That letter, dated July 4, 1938, was followed by another bearing the date 10 August, 1938, confirming the deal. Clarrie had written to the Rajah on 27 July, 1938. There was an exchange of cables; the important one for the Fox was the cable which read: "Offer two thousand including fee and return fare."

> I hope this offer will suit you... Your services are required as a cricket coach to me and my brother who is an excellent cricketer... ' usually we play some first-class [cricket] at Bombay and elsewhere and we have a very good team. These matches are not of any representative character and I hope, therefore, you will have no objection in playing in some of these. Most of the time you will be required to be with us, but whenever there would be any chance you would be able to do some sight-seeing, and I will arrange all that for you.
>
> I am expecting a reply from you any day; and as soon as I will learn from you, I will send you the required money.

Clarrie gladly accepted the offer. Two thousand pounds was a veritable fortune in 1938. Such a fat fee, over and above the cost of the voyage to India, plus board and lodging in the sub-continent, meant one thing: Clarrie wasn't about to refuse such a chance. Quite apart from his coaching of the Royals of Jath, Clarrie took under his wing a young, enthusiastic all-rounder, Vijay Hazare. On 22 February 1939, months after Clarrie had returned to Australia, Vijay wrote with relish: "Of course I played on behalf of the Central India XI in which, I am glad to inform you, I scored 138 not out and captured 6/57. Again quadrangular matches were played at Surat and I was invited

to play on behalf of 'Rest'. I made 66 and took 5/45 and 3/18."
Hazare was destined to become an idol for millions of Indian
fans and one of the great players in world cricket.

Born in 1915, Hazare played 239 first-class matches in a
distinguished career which saw him hit 18,754 runs at an average of 58.06 with 46 centuries, his highest being the 316 not out
he hit for Maharashtra v. Baroda at Poona in 1939–1940. As with
his mentor, Clarrie Grimmett, Hazare had a liking for playing
against Yorkshire. Clarrie took 10/37 against Yorkshire in 1930
and Hazare hit an unconquered 244 against them at Bramall
Lane in 1946. Two of Hazare's six Test hundreds were against
Australia in the one match; significantly at Adelaide in January,
1948. Hazare said of his double in a recent article for *The Telegraph* in Calcutta:

> Although I was the first to score a Test hundred on successive days,
> I also became the first to do so and finish on the losing side. But I
> had the greatest satisfaction of playing those two knocks in the
> presence of my mentor, Clarrie Grimmett, who had coached me
> thoroughly in 1938 and had held high hopes for me.
>
> An ideal coach, Grimmett did not change my rather unorthodox
> grip or my unusual stance but bowling with a tennis ball from a
> shorter distance helped me tighten my defence and execute all
> strokes.

During Hazare's time in Adelaide, Grimmett invited him to
his Firle home, "Dundula", for dinner. There they spoke animat-
edly about the old days, some ten years before, when Clarrie
had coached in India. Then in a moment of seriousness, Clarrie
stood at the dinner table and raised his glass and toasted Hazare,
the man of the moment: "Vijay, a toast. You have made me a
proud man today."

Indian cricketers have perhaps more of a bond with the
cricket tradition than any other people of the cricket-playing
nations. Maybe it is because their ancient land is steeped in rich
history. There is a certain mystique about India which Clarrie
found to his liking. The Indian people exude a gentleness which
belies the national character. Manners and gentleness in some
quarters can be misconstrued as weakness.

Clarrie knew better. Hazare, a young man who had just hit
hundreds (116 and 145) in the Adelaide Test match, and who had

also clean bowled the Don (Bradman b Hazare 201), was sitting at the Grimmett dinner table with a humble dignity that moved his mentor to deliver the words Hazare yearned to hear. They were words from the heart of the great bowler, a compliment Hazare would always cherish.

In that Adelaide Test, Neil Harvey's debut, Ray Lindwall claimed his best Test figures (7/38) while Hazare stood alone; tall and handsomely impressive in the Adelaide sunshine. Clarrie took the opportunity of expressing his admiration for Hazare's skill in his comments in the *Melbourne Sun* newspaper.

Clarrie wrote it as he saw it, displaying on paper the attributes which made him a great bowler; an unwavering command of a neat line and length. His old partner in spin, Bill O'Reilly, had advised Clarrie about the sort of fee he should command to write for English newspapers when he was approached to cover the Wally Hammond 1946–47 Test tour of Australia. In a letter, dated 6 August, 1946, O'Reilly wrote:

> Dear Grum,
> So far as English offers are concerned I have just replied to a cable from London, inquiring as to my terms for doing the Tests, to say that I am prepared — at great personal sacrifice I might warn you — to accept £1500 plus reasonable expenses. I do not feel prepared to take less. All the boys have landed figures about that dimension and I reckon that you should not ask for less. If you expect to do anything for Australian papers you must impress on the English mob that you are prepared to sell them only English or British rights. If you don't do that you'll find them cabling your stuff back through AAP. I hope you land something decent old boy. It's time we did get something out of the sweat and toil of the past.
>
> With every personal good wish.
> Bill O'Reilly.

Clarrie wrote for the *Melbourne Sun* for a number of years. He did not possess O'Reilly's great command of English; however, wielding the pen did enable the pair to catch up more often. Bill would often join Clarrie in a beer. They talked old times, reliving the old battles, the Fox and the Tiger happy together in peace or war. The Hazare Test brought O'Reilly from Sydney with the *Sydney Morning Herald* and Clarrie was there.

O'Reilly's knees prevented him from continuing in the game. It was a pity. Clarrie had hoped his spinning mate might go on and prove once more what a force he could be in world cricket. The alternatives to O'Reilly were the gentle off-spin of Ian Johnson and flighty leg-breaker Colin McCool. Neither was a world-beater, but Johnson trapped Hazare (116) with his top-spinner in his haul of 4/64 off 23.1 clever overs and McCool took 1/102 off 28 overs, only once beating the forward defensive stroke with a genuinely spun leg-break, which defeated Vinoo Mankad's bat to hit the top of off-stump.

The first Test Australia played after the war years was against New Zealand on the Basin Reserve, Wellington, in March 1946. O'Reilly cut through the poor Kiwi batting line-up like a hurricane in a cornfield, taking 5/14 and 3/19. In just two days Australia had defeated New Zealand. However, Bill decided to call it a day; hang up the boots and take to the pen. While Bill and Clarrie watched the Adelaide Test where Hazare batted so brilliantly, they knew that only leaden-footed batsmen could be mesmerised by Johnson's style of bowling. He wasn't a vicious spinner. He tossed it up and got it to curve, but apart from Hazare, the Indians seemed bolted to their creases. In the Sydney Test of 1946–47, Johnson bowled 30.1 overs into the Randwick breeze and took 6/42, beating the likes of Hutton (39), Ikin (60), Yardley (25), Smith (4), Evans (5) and Bedser (14).

Clarrie thought McCool had potential, but the combined skills of Johnson, McCool and the left-hand unorthodox spinner George Tribe were no match for O'Reilly, the bowler many claim to be even better than the legendary Sydney Barnes, whom many good judges have rated to be the greatest bowler in Test history.

Coaching always held a high place in Clarrie's life. He loved to impart the wealth of knowledge he had gleaned from a lifetime in the game. Hazare's success was a great thrill for Clarrie, and Hazare's acknowledgment of Grimmett's help was greatly appreciated.

Hazare said: "Let me note here that this little success of mine in the cricket sphere is entirely due to your valuable instructions which I will never forget, at least in this life. I will also be thankful to you if you will in future, as in the past, kindly help me by giving necessary instructions."

In his 22 February, 1939 letter to Clarrie, Hazare started: "I carefully read also the *Times* of India in which your cricket activities are described and I believe strongly that you are in good form at present. Are you playing tennis at present? I have also taken to tennis as the cricket season is over now. I remember tennis which we played together at Jath and your words, "play ceriously [sic]'."

The contrast between the stunning beauty and almost indescribable poverty in the ancient land of India cannot but make a lasting impression on the mind of the sensitive, thinking person. Clarrie loved his time in India. He noted the classic and undying beauty of the Taj Mahal; that world-renowned heavenly edifice of marble, hewn so grandly as if by the hand of God himself. Clarrie reckoned that half the battle to see the good and great in this ancient land was to have a good bearer, as he later recalled:

> My bearer was Goanese. He had previously travelled the country in the services of Hobbs and Sutcliffe and this in itself was a great help and comfort to me.
>
> Travelling by train is a novel experience. All windows and doors are fitted with bolts and on this first journey of mine I did not know that it is wise to ensure that everything is secured before one retires.
>
> Next morning my bearer knocked on the door with some tea for me. Having received no response he tried the handle and opened the door. He was concerned to find the door unlocked and warned me never to leave it open again. Strangely enough, a fortnight later, in exactly the same place, a young European girl was murdered and robbed and her body thrown from the train as it passed over a bridge. An Indian was being tried for her murder the very day I left the country to return home.

Clarrie was fascinated by the Indian's method of washing themselves at railway stations and their clothes in the streams and riverbanks, the clothes being soaked and beaten on the rocks until they were clean.

> On my first visit to Jath torrential rain had turned rivers into vast floodplains. The roads were often swollen, making it almost impossible for a motor vehicle to cross the small *nallas* or small rivers.

Often teams of oxen would be required to be hitched to our vehicle and we would be hauled across from one side of the *nalla* to the other. On such occasions a good photograph was to be had, but, as usually is the case when you really need it, I did not have my camera with me.

Grimmett's photography was legendary within the Australian and South Australian teams. He loved taking movies or still pictures. He took them by the hundreds. In the village of Jath, Clarrie revelled in the social life. He played tennis each morning with the sari-clad Ranee of Jawhar, a sister of His Highness the Rajah of Jath.

"She plays a good game," he said. "Although she played in a sari she covered the court very quickly." There was little to do after a morning's tennis. Not, that is, until the late afternoon when the cricket would be played, practice or a match. Clarrie, however, enjoyed the social part of his time at Jath best of all. He revelled in the dinners he was invited to have in the company of His Highness and various officials.

War clouds were again threatening Europe. This time the German threat was ever more sinister. On 12 August, 1938 Germany mobilised its forces. Three days later, Neville Chamberlain visited Hitler for crisis talks in Britain. The Jewish pogroms began in Germany in November. Chamberlain talked of "peace in our time" but those with their feet on the ground suspected and mistrusted the Nazis. A greater visionary, Winston Churchill, protested against Chamberlain. Winston knew war was inevitable.

Politics was never Clarrie's cup of tea. He kept abreast of world and local events, but he had seen enough of "cricket politics" not to become involved. He feared a new world war, but his battlefield was the sun-drenched green sward, where bats, not bayonets, faced leather balls bowled, not hand grenades hurled. Grimmett arrived back in Adelaide in plenty of time to take his place in South Australia's first Sheffield Shield match of the 1938–39 summer. He was keen to show the world that he had lost none of his rare skill, although he was only nine days short of his forty-seventh birthday when the match against New South Wales began on the Adelaide Oval.

Bradman hit 143 and Jack Badcock an unbeaten 271 as South

Australia rattled up 8 declared 600. Clarrie took 7/116 in the New South Wales first innings and South Australia won the match easily, by an innings and 55 runs. Victoria amassed 499 a few days after Clarrie had celebrated yet another birthday on Christmas Day, 1938, by snaring 6/33 to demolish Queensland: it was his favourite Christmas dinner. Lindsay Hassett hit an unbeaten 211 for the Vics and Clarrie, batting for South Australia, tore a muscle in his leg. He was quick to allay any thought that the injury was due to his age. "It all happened so easily and I have never been feeling so fit in my life," he said.

"In the last over before tea yesterday I square cut a ball and ran two. I regained my crease easily enough, but in pulling up, propped one leg and felt the muscle go. My boot sprig must have caught in the ground. So here I am in hospital and I was so fit that I did not even feel tired after a full Sunday afternoon's tennis, capped by three sets of singles." Clarrie spoke from his bed at Epworth Hospital in Melbourne, surrounded by a bevy of pretty nurses. When informed that the Victorian second innings was going badly, he was in no way interested in the Victorians who were out and their scores.

"Who got the wickets?" Clarrie asked with an urgency which implied that he would not be too taken to hear that Frank Ward, the leg-spinner who went to England in his stead that year, had taken even one of the four wickets to fall.

Clarrie returned to the MCG later in the game to stay at the wicket for 93 minutes, collecting 34 invaluable runs to add to Bradman's 107 and Dick Whittington's even 100. Yet it all was not quite enough. South Australia scored 488, eleven runs shy of the Victorian first innings 499.

When Britain declared war on Germany on 3 September 1939, Clarrie was preparing for what was destined to be one of his last first-class summers. He continued to hunt for wickets, as great a predator as ever. Against Victoria at Adelaide he grabbed 5/118 to help South Australia win outright; he took 6/122 to help beat New South Wales by 7 wickets and his forty-eighth birthday saw him again gobble up the Queenslanders with 6/124. South Australia won the Sheffield Shield for the sixth time in 1938–39, Clarrie getting 27 wickets at 20.85. Bradman dominated with the bat and Jack Badcock began well with an impressive 271 not out. Next summer, Grimmett created a record with 63 wickets at an average of 23.15; seven times he bagged five or more wickets in an innings. Again he dominated with the ball as Bradman reigned supreme as the king of batsmen. His last Shield match was on his beloved SCG. He took 6/118 and 5/111. It was a fitting finale at the SCG, despite the fact that New South Wales won the match, O'Reilly getting 6/77 in the South Australian first innings and Cec Pepper 5/49 in the second innings. It was then almost fifteen years to the day when *Sydney Mail* photographer Herbert Fishwick captured perfectly the ball which crashed through the defences of Frank Woolley. It was Grimmett's first Test wicket, Woolley b Grimmett 47. He would always cherish that famous picture.

Clarrie was appointed State cricket coach in 1939, a post he held until 1946. He was a State selector from 1940–42. The war was hurting. Young men in their thousands joined the services. Among them was Clarrie and Lizzy's only son, Victor. How Clarrie prayed for Vic to return home safely. He remembered his son sitting on his knee as he sketched for him. How, only hours before the Adelaide Bodyline Test match, there was the world's best slow leg-spinner on his hands and knees on his Firle home tennis court. Praying? No, Vic and Clarrie were working at a feverish rate, spreading newspaper, then spraying the area with a hose to keep the paper from blowing in the wind. It was the biggest Grimmett family coverup in their history. A plague of locusts had hit Adelaide; there were millions of insects with an insatiable appetite for anything green. Grass was high on their menu. The locusts proved more damaging than Larwood and Voce at their vicious best. Clarrie and son beat the locusts and saved most of the grass on the court, which was always so lovingly tended by the old Fox.

When the time came for Vic to be posted overseas with the Air Force, Clarrie presented him with his cherished little Midget camera. It meant a great deal to Vic and he pledged he would do everything in his power to bring it home in one piece. Vic took his Midget everywhere, even on dangerous bombing missions over German-occupied Europe. Sometimes the flak was terrific, as Vic struggled to control his cumbersome Lancaster

Bomber and prevent it from tumbling into an uncontrollable spin.

Fear was a pilot's constant companion. Flight Officer Victor Grimmett was awarded the Distinguish Flying Cross for his heroism. The citation reads: "Flying Officer Grimmett has completed numerous operations against the enemy in the course of which he invariably displayed the utmost fortitude, courage and devotion to duty". Flight was a Grimmett strong point.

On 6 June, 1945, SACA secretary Bill Jeanes wrote to Clarrie, saying in part: "The president and Committee ask me to convey to you their most cordial congratulations and to request that you will pass their sentiments along to Victor. We appreciate how delighted you and Mrs Grimmett have been at receiving such splendid news, and we express the hope that the early termination of the war will permit the return of your son to his home in good health." During the war, Clarrie was involved in district cricket until 1942, the year in which the armed forces used the Adelaide Oval for a brief period, when the SACA committee decided to abandon district matches in favour of a "pool" cricket scheme in which players available were pooled into teams led by appointed captains in a series of round-robin matches or against services teams. The first summer of "pool" matches ended with Clarrie Grimmett's team winning eight matches of its allocated fourteen, with five lost and one a tie. The other teams were led by Ron Sharpe, Cecil Starr and Ron Hammence.

During the dark days of World War II, Grimmett had a chance meeting in Sydney with Neville Cardus, the English cricket writer. Cardus spent the entire war living in Sydney, writing and waiting for the hostilities to end so cricket could re-commence.

"Why, it's not you...the old Fox. Dear Clarrie. How terrible the devastation in Europe...some of the great building and works of art crushed in this terrible war," lamented Cardus.

"Oh, yes, Neville, I'm very sad about it...you see I've developed this new ball and I won't be able to test it in top company. Blast the war!"

Clarrie had quit his South Australian coaching job to become a cricket writer in 1946. He covered the 1946–47 England tour of Australia. When in Perth, he turned up at the nets and bowled to Wally Hammond and co., he still had a great command of line and length.

Down the years Clarrie continued to write and to coach and to spin yarns of the old days. He played golf twice, sometimes three times a week and attended all the SACA functions, delighting in the company of old friends, renewing acquaintances. Vic Grimmett believes one of his father's lessons helped him to concentrate and therefore survive during dangerous wartime bombing raids. When Vic was aged fifteen Clarrie offered his son his entire stamp collection. It was a large collection and quite valuable. But there was a catch. Clarrie challenged Vic to a game of table tennis. However, this was to be no ordinary game. "Vic, you get one chance and one chance only. I'll stand one side of the net, you the other. The idea is that you can have the entire stamp collection if *we* can keep the ball in play 500 times across the net without a mistake. If there is a mistake before the 500, the deal is off." Vic eyed his father. He loved him, although he could never understand why Clarrie would never go to his school (Rostrevor College) and watch him play cricket. He bowled leg-breaks. Yet his father always came to the sports day. Clarrie often wore a gold shield, the prize he won in 1908 as the Wellington YMCA one hundred-yards champion. He had always felt that by attending Vic's cricket matches he would have placed undue pressure on this budding school leg-spinner. Vic took up the table-tennis challenge. Clarrie wasn't giving the stamps away; he knew this test of concentration and hand-eye coordination he had set Vic would be tough on his son. They got there, and Clarrie was glad to hand over the stamps, but Vic knew that one slip and his chance would have been gone forever. It was to be a more deadly test at the controls of the Lancaster Bomber.

Throughout his career Clarrie was not particularly religious, although he would always drive Lizzie to Mass on Sunday, before settling down to coaching budding cricketers on his Firle backyard pitch. Religion had played a dastardly role in dividing his family. A number of his Test mates, including O'Reilly, McCabe and Fingleton, were Catholics, and Clarrie joined them at church of a Sunday on tour, but gradually he eased himself away from the church. His passion was cricket.

He entertained such notables as Alan Kippax, Bill O'Reilly, Lindsay Hassett, Arthur Mailey, Jack Gregory, Monty Noble, Herbie Collins and the young Don Bradman; tennis identities such as Harry Hopman and Jack Crawford and old mates such as Bill Stirling, the amateur billiard player Bert Hearndeen, Jim Keo (Kensington Cricket Club) and the well-known bookmaker Bob Dugan.

There was always a display of spinning when a visiting touring side came to the Grimmett house. Clarrie entertained his guests by spinning a table-tennis ball and getting them to pick its direction of turn. They had to nominate. Few could do so consistently; some guessed correctly. All were fascinated. Clarrie would toss the ball in the air. It was spun hard. He would hit it over the net and before his partner could return the ball it would land and spin back to Clarrie's side of the net. There the Wicket Fox chuckled and grinned. It was all trick and treat.

When Vic was in his teens he yearned to be a radio announcer. He rigged up turntables and jack points, so a microphone could be connected. There was volume control and with expert use of the controls, Vic, or his father, could present concerts, playing Jack Davey records along with music and the odd announcement. When one of Clarrie's friends arrived, Vic's dad would wink and Vic would divert the attention of the guest. Clarrie would dart into Vic's room, fiddle with the controls and broadcast a message in the most perfectly-diguised authoritative voice: "Car thieves have stolen a 1927 Rover from the Firle area. The car, registration SA…[Clarrie's guest immediately noticed the make and registration] has been found abandoned in the city. Its tyres have been…"

The guest would rush outside the front door and then slump in relief against the brick pillar which supported the front verandah. His car was safe. Almost immediately Vic and his father would turn up behind the guest, roaring with laughter.

Always tinkering with gadgets, Clarrie, according to his son, Vic, was a master of improvisation. Nothing was too difficult. Once he cut and fashioned a key from a solid length of brass, rather than go and have a key re-cast. Lizzy and Clarrie spent most of their time inside in the kitchen. Lizzy was an inside person. She rarely ventured into the garden and whenever

TELEGRAMS:
LORD'S GROUND LONDON
TELEPHONE NOS.:
PAVILION   ..   ..   LORDS 1611-3
TENNIS COURT..   ..   LORDS 1288
TAVERN ..   ..   ..   LORDS 1724-5
WORKS DEPT. ..   ..CUNNINGHAM 6855

PROSPECTS OF PLAY ··CUNNINGHAM 6011

Marylebone Cricket Club

Lord's Ground,

London, N.W.8

EOC/DMC.

4th July, 1960.

My dear Mr Grimmett.

It is the wish of the M.C.C. Committee to invite a certain
number of overseas cricketers and administrators to become
Honorary Life Members of the Club, as a token of our appreciation
of the high service they have rendered to the game.

It is with real pleasure that I write on behalf of the
Committee to convey this invitation to you: we should be very
happy to think of you as a member of our Club.

I enclose a copy of Rule XI A of the Rules of the Club,
governing this particular form of Life Membership, and I would
be grateful if you would let me know as soon as you can if you
are willing to accept.

Yours sincerely,

H.J. Altham

President, M.C.C.

C.V. Grimmett, Esq.

MCC life membership invitation

people came to the front door it meant the verandah had to be
cleaned; she kept that Firle front verandah like a new pin. Both
Vic and Clarrie were strongly encouraged to use the back door.
When the back door key went missing, it placed great pressure
on Clarrie to finish crafting the brass rapidly for Lizzy did not
relish the thought of people despoiling her scrubbed verandah.

There were always alcohol and cigarettes in the house; Clarrie
normally kept them as offerings to guests. In his later years,
while tea remained his constant drink, he enjoyed a cold beer
on a hot summer's day and in winter he liked a glass of claret.
Often a player would be presented with a sterling silver ciga-
rette or cigar box. Invariably these gifts were filled to capacity
with the "merchandise". Clarrie never bet, although I wonder

whether he might have done so in a Ladbroke's tent with odds afoot on how many wickets Grimmett might take in a particular session.

12 STRATEGY

Clarrie Grimmett was fascinating to watch. He took just a few jaunty steps, made a pretty shuffle and a seemingly square motion of the arm that sometimes appeared to creak. As his right arm moved upwards before that final downswing and over, his left hand met his right, as if to conceal for one last fleeting moment his spin grip. His front leg "collapsed" in a way which would have been fatal for an orthodox spinner (who must be high and drive over a braced front leg). The crouch at delivery tended to make Grimmett's arm appear lower than it usually was. His action was the sort often seen on the sands at a beach when an elderly gentleman bowled to his grandson.

Clarrie didn't mind batsmen thinking his arm was too low and that he could not deceive them in flight. He was the cleverest and most devious of all the slow leg-breakers. Clarrie glided to the crease, yet his delivery was potent, full of venom. He devised a hundred plans for any one outing. If five or more came off he was in for a good day. Clarrie usually had a good day. In 1964 Neville Cardus confessed that it was the Australian writer, Ray Robinson, who had coined the famous passage, "Mailey bowls leg-spin like a millionaire, Grimmett like a miser".

Bill O'Reilly was still in short pants when he sat on the SCG hill and saw Mailey clean bowl Victorian batsman Les Keating with a ball which bounced twice before hitting the stumps.

"I distinctly remember Keating, nose knee high, using his bat more in the way of a scythe as he tried unsuccessfully to deal with the second bounce. Mailey's philosophy allowed him to regard that delivery as a good ball — it got a wicket. Grimmett's reaction would have been contemptuous, as mine was, even though I was still in short pants and sitting on the Hill," said O'Reilly.

Don Bradman played fleetingly against Mailey and the leg-spinner defeated him at least once. Sir Donald wrote to the author recently in glowing terms about Grimmett's bowling.

> Arthur Mailey spun the ball more [than Grimmett] — so did Fleet-wood-Smith and both of them bowled a better wrong 'un, but they also bowled many loose balls. I think Mailey's Bosey was the hardest of all to pick. Clarrie's wrong 'un was, in fact, easy to see. He telegraphed it and bowled very few of them. His stock in trade was the leg-spinner with just enough turn on it, plus really good top-spin delivery and a good flipper (which he cultivated late in life). I saw Clarrie in one match take the ball after some light rain when the ball was greasy and hard to hold yet he reeled off five maidens without a loose ball. His control was remarkable. That is the problem with young leg-break bowlers — it takes years to develop such control and in the meantime they are too expensive and get discarded.
>
> I always classified Clarrie Grimmett as the best of the genuine slow leg-spinners and what made him the best in my opinion, was his accuracy.

As he grew older Clarrie became intolerant of bowling to a batsman in the nets. He preferred to bowl to a spot, a handkerchief or similar mark, on a good length. A fellow player was there to toss the balls back. Perhaps that inclination evolved from those years of patient training, alone in his backyard pitch at Prahran with his faithful dog, Joe, doing the "foxing". Clarrie reckoned, with justification, that most batsmen tend to play differently in the nets. They attempt shots they would not play in the middle. The Grimmett idea of bowling alone in the nets may have displeased some people.

Accuracy was the key to Grimmett's extraordinary success. He built his bowling plan around the leg-break and the top-spinner. Variations of pace were vital. That his Bosey was easy to pick did not matter a fig to Grimmett. He reckoned his leg-break was also easy to pick; the job of the batsman was to negotiate each ball. There was no magic attached to Clarrie's thinking. Subtle changes of pace, spinning the ball hard, and pinpoint control were the cornerstones of Grimmett's wicket plan. Young leg-spinners these days tend to lose heart if their direction of turn is easily detected.

Batsmen might pick it, but can they play it? *That* is the crucial test. Clarrie delved in subtle changes of pace. His greatest and only fear was coming up against the batsman who *consistently* picked those changes of pace.

That happened on occasion; it was done by Macartney in Sydney, by the young Bradman at Adelaide and by Hammond in Australia in 1928–29, but generally Clarrie's clever flight deceived them all most of the time. With his change of pace, his arm speed would be the same, yet the slower ball would merely be released at a point fractionally before the release of his stock ball. The quicker one would be released slightly ahead of the point of release for his stock delivery. Variations also in the height of the arm were important, but Clarrie realised very early on that there were many variations available for the leg-spinner even when bowling the stock ball.

His top-spinner was a devil of a ball. It looked innocent enough, but upon pitching, the enormous over-spin imparted caused the ball to dip and fairly scream off the pitch at an alarming speed. I have already described how Grimmett, early in 1926, had watched Tommy Andrews heading for the pavilion, and showing incoming batsman Alan Kippax the amount of turn Clarrie had achieved in dismissing him. So Clarrie gave Kippax what he least expected first up — the top-spinner, when Kippax was looking for a big turning leggie.

The Grimmett strategy was to provide batsmen with virtually no options to score unless they took a risk. With a player such as McCabe, who loved to get down the wicket, Clarrie forced him back, giving him nothing to drive, until he had him within his psychological grasp. Then he would lure him forward with a ball that wasn't quite there for the drive.

This strategy is not confined to the slow spinner. I've seen the same ploy, albeit at a much faster pace, work for pacemen Dennis Lillee. Lillee would force a batsman onto the back foot, until the player's first movement was back and across before he delivered the ball. Then when he produced his well-pitched out-swinger, the batsman would only be fractionally forward, given that his first movement was always back and across. It made his out-swinger more effective. The great fast bowlers have used this strategy for years. It still works.

In Grimmett's case, he did not have the pace effectively to have the batsman moving back and across before he delivered, but he did lull the batsman into thinking about back foot play. Then he would produce the leg-break of fuller length, luring the man forward, often to his doom. With such a strategy, his quicker deliveries were designed to drive the man back. Then the fuller delivery suddenly became a more lethal ball...

Rarely did Grimmett do a Mailey and toss the ball high into the air. Never did he do so against the top-order players, but occasionally he did so against the tailenders. Here Clarrie indulged himself, having fun at their expense.

He would toss high and spin hard, the poor lower-order batsmen getting tangled up with bat and pads, bumbling about until the inevitable attempted slog produced an easy stumping chance or skied catch to cover or mid-off.

Where Mailey would think nothing of deliberately bowling a juicy full-toss, Clarrie would have been horrified. Once in 1926 he shuddered when Mailey clean bowled Hobbs with a full-toss. Then in 1934 Neville Cardus mentioned to Grimmett that he had never seen Clarrie bowl a full-toss; "I don't think you could bowl one if you tried".

Clarrie said nothing but a smile, ever so faint, flickered momentarily across that leathery face. Weeks later Leslie Ames, the England keeper, was holding up proceedings with Grimmett and O'Reilly bowling their hearts out as Australia went all-out for victory. Ames defended like a Boycott, with the utmost care and watchfulness. Then it happened. Clarrie wheeled up the fattest, gorgeous full-toss to leg a ball which was so tempting it was wicked. Ames hit out gaily and picked out Bill Brown at long leg. Heavy rain prevented the spinners from finishing the job, with England six down and five hours to play.

However, Clarrie made a point of finding Cardus, as he was preparing his article that night for the *Manchester Guardian*. "I showed you how I could bowl a full-toss this morning, didn't I? And you said I couldn't?" Clarrie was beside himself, his whole frame shaking as he chuckled. The ball which got Ames could not have delighted him more than if he had watched it swerve towards leg-stump and then spin viciously away to take the top of off-stump.

Once in Adelaide Clarrie had taken two quick New South Wales wickets before lunch. Bradman was still there at lunch and, unhappily for South Australia, he was still there at 5.30 p.m. Grimmett had toiled all day, bowling impressively, but Bradman's bat was, on this day, showing greater magic than Grimmett's spin.

South Australian captain Vic Richardson came up to Grimmett, saying, "Well bowled — now put on your sweater, there's a breeze getting up." Clarrie wouldn't lie down. "Are you taking me off? — just as I was working out my plan."

Whether a spinner is bowling at the nets in the backyard or in the middle of a Test match at Sydney or Lord's, he must bowl to a plan. Clarrie planned and schemed like no other. Of course, he had his failures. Not all of his plans worked, but only a small percentage of his schemes needed to bear fruit for him to achieve unrivalled success. In his Test debut Clarrie bowled very few Boseys. This was all part of his plan.

His first over to the gifted left-hander Frank Woolley saw Clarrie totally ignore the bowling of the Bosey, even though it might have been potentially more dangerous for the tall left-hander, as its spin would have the ball leaving the bat. However, Clarrie reckoned that he would swerve the ball away from the left-hander, open up the gap between bat and pad, and spin the ball back through the gate to bowl him. It worked to perfection.

Yet at Nottingham in 1930 Grimmett was bowling a spell which many, including Cardus, believed was the perfection of leg-spin artistry. He sent Hammond back with his devil of a top-spinner, lbw for 8, in the wake of the Hobbs-Sutcliffe opening partnership of 53 which was broken when Sutcliffe fell to Fairfax for 29.

The tall Kent left-hander Woolley, looking for all the world like a Grenadier guard, strode to the crease. Straight-backed and handsome, Woolley was compelled forward and out of his crease by an incurving Bosey. It hummed as it spun its way towards Woolley, although it could have been a dirge, as Woolley stretched forward, mesmerised, and missed the big turning wrong 'un. Bert Oldfield had the bails off in a flash.

The SACA medical officer Dr Donald Beard, a tall and kindly ex-fast bowler who served with distinction tending the sick, the maimed and the dying on distant battlefields in Korea and Vietnam, described batting against Grimmett in the 1940s. "I played well forward, was beaten and given out lbw to a ball which Clarrie said was 'half as fast through the air and twice as fast off the pitch'."

It was a part of the Grimmett strategy to have the umpires on side, it was vital for that close lbw decision to go his way. Clarrie loved to kid to the umpires. In grade matches, and interstate games, the old Fox would have the umps eating out of his hand as they watched closely for the ball he nominated: a big turning leg-break on middle and leg; a top spinner, the flipper, a Bosey.... In a grade match in Adelaide in 1944 Clarrie nominated three leg-breaks turning away just outside off, then the "fatal top-spinner" to trap him lbw. The umpire was so excited he roared an lbw appeal the very instant the ball crashed into the pads of the beaten batsman and little Clarrie turned and raised his finger: "That, Mr Umpire is out, lbw!"

Bowling, to Grimmett, was the ultimate study. He searched for a better way to deceive batsmen. At the age of 76 he was working on the "wrong" wrong 'un, but the wrist was turned so far round that the ball actually came from the crooked wrist as a leg-break. Clarrie could bowl it, but only over a distance of roughly ten metres. O'Reilly maintained that there are still mysteries to be unlocked for the bowler who experiments.

In 1934 O'Reilly bowled what he thought to be a wrong 'un and the ball turned appreciably from the leg, thus beating Bert Oldfield after it careered past the bemused batsman and scuttled away for four byes. "If only I could have cultivated that ball," Bill lamented. "Next ball did the same. Alas, it never happened again."

I recall an off-break of mine spinning prodigiously the other way at Leeds in 1972. Rodney Marsh, like Oldfield, moved one way and the ball took the opposite direction, with a resulting four byes. Ray Illingworth was batting. He peered up from under his England cap and smiled. It happened again, twice. Perhaps Illy put those two extraordinary balls down to Fusereum, the disease which allegedly took the green out of the grass on a particular area just twenty-two metres long. The rest of the ground was lush green. But that's another story. O'Reilly's wrong wrong 'un in 1934 and Grimmett's experiments in 1967 might mean that the greatest spin mysteries are yet to come.

The finger flick spinner, Jack Iverson, burst onto the scene in 1949–50. During World War II, Jack entertained his army team-mates in a tent in New Guinea, spinning a table-tennis ball. He flicked the ball with his middle finger, in much the same manner a boy would flick the top of a Coke bottle, sending it in a spin like some ancient frisbee. He held the ball between his thumb and his bent middle finger. By changing the position of his thumb he could deliver a leg-break, off-break or wrong 'un with almost no change of action.

With all the star bowlers away in South Africa, Iverson took our domestic cricket by storm. He spun his way to 46 wickets at an average of 16.60 for Victoria, and at the end of that summer he toured New Zealand with an Australian XI. Iverson played for Victoria against South Australia in Adelaide for the first time in December, 1949. Clarrie couldn't contain himself. He rushed to the Adelaide Oval nets the day prior to the Shield match and watched the Victorians train.

"I wanted to see first hand the type of spin he [Iverson] used," Clarrie once told me. "Iverson told me how he practised spin-ning a ball onto a ledge. How history repeats itself. I did exactly the same with a tennis ball onto a verandah." Grimmett said his interest in Iverson was heightened because the way the big Victorian spun the ball was along the same lines as Clarrie's experiments back in Wellington before World War I.

"Actually the [Iverson] method of spinning he used was the one by which I bowled my first Bosey with a tennis ball, except that I used the third finger instead of the middle one," Grimmett explained. "When I came to use a cricket ball, I found that my finger was not strong enough to spin the heavier ball. As a result I did not persist with it and eventually mastered the more commonly known type of Bosey." However, it was the Iverson type of delivery which caused Clarrie to develop his famous flipper.

"While I couldn't achieve over-spin with the finger flick method, I developed a closely related type of ball which I spun by holding the ball between thumb and middle finger. The spin was applied in the same way that is often used to click the fingers to attract attention," remembered Clarrie.

Iverson didn't last long in the game. He was well into his thirties when he burst onto the scene. The burly Victorian played against Freddie Brown's Englishmen in 1950–51, taking 21 wickets at an average of 15.23, with his 6/27 in Sydney being his best effort. He was a freak of a bowler, but he didn't have the background of a bowler who had survived the highs and lows of the craft. Iverson couldn't take a hiding. Keith Miller and Arthur Morris decided to attack him when they played for New South Wales against Victoria; however, at the Brisbane practice before the Brisbane Test that 1950–51 Test summer, skipper Lindsay Hassett refused to allow Iverson to bowl to either Miller or Morris.

"What's this, Lindsay, an Australian team practice or New South Wales versus Victoria?" Miller and Morris chided. Hassett, a happy little man, but as shrewd as any to have worn the green baggy cap, smiled. Later that year, in the wake of Iverson's extraordinary success in Test matches, the day came when Victoria's Iverson was about to bowl to New South Wales' Miller. Miller stood half a metre outside the leg-stump when Iverson bowled. Morris did the same. Grimmett would have licked his lips in anticipation of easy prey, but Iverson, instead of sticking to his line, did not know where to bowl. Morris got 182 and Iverson was thrashed unmercifully. Iverson then quit the game.

Some said he trod on a ball and injured his ankle, but others leaned towards the story that Iverson walked into the VCA office in Melbourne and declared himself unavailable. Either way, he never played big cricket again. It was a pity. Clarrie saw in Iverson a part of himself. Had his fingers been strong enough, Grimmett may have been the first of the finger-flick brigade. Years later, Johnny Gleeson took on a similar role to Iverson. Gleeson flicked the ball with his finger in much the same manner as Iverson, and strangely, he was a better bowler on a seamer's wicket than on a real turner. His Test captain, Bill Lawry, liked Gleeson's style because he kept the runs at a minimum. A shrewd man, Gleeson took 93 Test wickets at 36.20 in 30 Tests. Some of the England players in Illingworth's 1970–71 touring side Down Under could not "read" Gleeson's deliveries.

Came the fourth Test in Sydney and opener John Edrich rushed down the wicket to greet his partner Geoff Boycott. "I say, Boycs, I can now say with certainty that I know which way Gleeson's spinning…every time." Boycott raised his left eyebrow. "Yep, I worked 'im out a month ago during the second Test in Perth. Now don't tell any other booger!"

One of the attributes Clarrie saw in Gleeson's cricket was that the New South Wales finger flick merchant made the most of the mystery associated with his craft. Gleeson bowled a regulation off-break, flat and easy to play. He also had the finger flick leg-break, which, at first glance, appeared to be an off-break.

After watching a couple of deliveries he was easy to pick. He also had a wrong 'un which was easy to pick. But the crafty and best spinners know that picking it is one thing; the batsman's biggest task is to play the ball, whether he picks which direction it is going to spin or not. However, Gleeson made the most of the media discussion of his bowling; it sounded as if he were as difficult to fathom as the Indian rope trick. Gleeson played his part to perfection. I remember the South Africans in 1970 having trouble against Gleeson, but though they couldn't pick his spin, the likes of Graeme Pollock and Barry Richards flayed the Australians, including Gleeson.

Grimmett's genius was that he not only trumped up the mystery with relish; he also bowled with the unerring skill of a living legend. Therein lies the difference. Clarrie made such a study of the game that he wrote numerous coaching articles in various newspapers and magazines. He didn't merely devote his piece to bowling. He was adamant that the bowler must be the most aggressive man in the cricket team. "A bowler must live, think and practise aggression. Even in exploitation and run-saving the bowler who employs negative tactics to keep runs down is wasting time," Clarrie maintained.

Oh, that first-class captains throughout the world could put such commonsense to work. Attack is the only method by which a bowler can survive, be the need positive or negative — wicket-taker or run-saver.

Clarrie reckoned a bowler could, if he had the training behind him, be both tight and attacking at the same time. It did not make sense to him that a bowler needed to give runs away in the

Mailey way for him to be labelled an attacking bowler. To become a good bowler, Grimmett believed it was necessary to have full command of his approach. It had to be "mechanical", in that he should not have to think about it. It had to come naturally. "There must be no stutter in your run," he said to students. He continued:

> It [the run] must be practised until it is smooth and regular. The right foot in the last stride must be parallel to the bowling crease. Thus the bowler presents his left side to the batsman. By his parallel right foot and his left side to the batsman the bowler automatically cultivates body swing.
>
> To approach the bowling crease square on has the effect of slowing the ball off the wicket. Scientists will tell us that a ball will always come off the wicket at a slower pace than the pace it travels in the air beforehand.
>
> However, if you assume a square on body action at delivery the ball will come off the wicket more slowly than it would if you have a nice side-on action.

Clarrie was perfectly correct when he stressed the need for a smooth, rhythmic approach. Rhythm means a great deal to the slow man who seeks momentum, zip off the pitch and the path towards disguising subtle changes of pace.

The little spin wizard believed that a bowler should practise his approach to the wicket by going through the motion of bowling without a ball. "It is akin to swinging a golf stick before attempting to hit the ball. Swing through all the motions until they become second nature."

Classical actions of Dennis Lillee, Richard Hadlee and Kapil Dev immediately come to mind among the faster brigade; Richie Benaud, of the spinners I have seen at close quarters, and films of Clarrie Grimmett and Bill O'Reilly, have made a huge impression upon me. They all possessed rhythm and balance, great skill and stamina. They all had fabulous follow throughs: vigour and vitality, which in O'Reilly's case tended to belie his awkward gait. The great opener Sid Barnes made it universally known in 1938 that he could easily pick the Grimmett "mystery" ball, the flipper.

"For twelve years I practised this ball before I bowled it in a match. Let that be an example to a youngster! It proved to be my greatest ball. I called it my 'flipper'. I had to perfect it before allowing the batsman to sample it," Clarrie said. "Barnes had been talking a lot about his success in picking the 'flipper', but as far as I could remember I had never bowled it to him." (Then came that match in 1940, the day ten-year-old Richie Benaud saw Grimmett bowl.)

Clarrie went on: "The New South Wales batsman came in and I was in a bit of a state, wondering and doubting the wisdom of using the flipper, not in any way my confidence to pitch it exactly as I intended. I was keen to show Sid up. As I went back to bowl I was tossing up whether to test him [Sid Barnes] out. As I ran up to the wicket I thought I would, so over went the flipper. It cut through and left Barnes right in front lbw. Chipperfield came in next so I turned it on him and he too went lbw."

Little Richie Benaud never forgot those deliveries. He developed the flipper after it had been passed down the chain of leg spinners, from Cec Pepper, to Dooland, to Benaud.

Clarrie found that when he bowled the flipper he could not disguise a loud clicking noise. So he would click the fingers of his left hand every ball, so that when his flipper did arrive it did not matter; the batsman could not be alerted because the clicking noise was always present.

"Guile is vital, so too the rhythmic approach and follow through so that you continue your action on and through so your body moves to the left, off the wicket and not obstructing the umpire's view. Zip is important. The ball that comes slowly off the wicket will never dismiss class batsmen. The ball must fizz if success is to be won among the best players."

Since Grimmett and O'Reilly, Australia has had a number of good leg-spinners. Benaud stands head and shoulders above the pack. He was self-made, much like Grimmett, practising assiduously and with a scheming brain.

Dooland was good, so too Pepper, but they played most of their best cricket in England. Left-hand orthodox spinner George Tribe was the best of his type, with Johnny Martin and Lindsay Kline having their moments, along with the big turning, but erratic David Sincock. Colin McCool and Doug Ring were competent leg-breakers, but neither blossomed in Test cricket. The finger flickers, Iverson and Gleeson, created enormous interest, with Iverson startling the Englishmen in 1950–51 and Gleeson proving economical, if not a match winner. Kerry O'Keeffe, Terry Jenner and Peter Sleep all did well in Sheffield Shield cricket but, apart from O'Keeffe, failed to impress on the Test arena. In his time the Sri Lankan-born Malcolm Franke was the best leg-spinner about, but Franke, who served Queensland well, was never rewarded with a Test cap.

Jim Higgs was a throwback to the big turning Mailey type and he did well, taking 66 wickets in 22 Tests, although his fielding was a big minus and Trevor Hohns performed with credit on the 1989 England tour, although he rarely turned his leg-break. Like Keith Stackpole, for whom Prime Minister Sir Robert Menzies arranged coaching lessons from Grimmett in 1964, Hohns had a good top-spinner. It was the leg-break which was missing. New South Wales leg-spinner Bob Holland had to wait his chance. He stayed long enough to win a Test match against the West Indies in Sydney, but away from the SCG "turner" he was noticeably less effective in big games.

Grimmett regarded Lindsay Hassett as one of the greatest batsman he had bowled against. Grimmett described why:

> Bradman was a relentless, run-making machine, but I never minded bowling to him, because good length spin bowling always worried him. It was a flaw in his batting.
>
> I have had great opportunity to study him [Bradman] and had opposing captains discovered what I did, that he was not comfortable against good length spin bowling, they would have turned it on him more frequently than they did the fast or medium attack.
>
> Hassett's footwork was almost perfect. He used his feet magnificently in any duel with bat and ball. In addition, he was a great fighter.

Grimmett's admiration for Hassett might also have been influenced by the diminutive Victorian's century in each innings for Victoria against a New South Wales attack, which included the great O'Reilly.

Hassett told me recently of his first encounter with the wily Grimmett. "The first ball was a gift, a leg-break wide down the leg side and I immediately swept him to the square leg boundary. He pegged me for a few deliveries, then slipped in a ball which skidded on straight and I was out lbw." Lindsay reckoned the old Fox was a real terror for any batsman who had not faced him before. Hassett said he later played in matches and from the non-striker's end watched horrified as newchum batsmen made the same mistake he had made first up against Clarrie's wiles.

Grimmett put Charlie Macartney next to Hassett:

> Macartney's ability to recover himself was astounding. I remember once beating him by luring him down the wicket. Realising his mistake, he danced back and cut the ball to the fence. Only a great batsman could do that.
>
> The little West Indian, George Hedley, was a magnificent player, the best on-side batsman against whom I bowled.
>
> So clever was Jack Hobbs' footwork, he made a good length ball a full-toss and Patsy Hendren was a tiger.
>
> One never quite had his measure; Alan Kippax was almost perfect in his footwork and execution of strokes and Wally Hammond was a brilliant off-side player, although I could restrict him when attacking his middle and leg stumps.
>
> Bradman not only had problems with me; Hedley Verity [the England left-arm orthodox spinner] and Bill O'Reilly too made him guess badly many times.

I wrote to Clarrie Grimmett in 1965, with the thought of making the two-day train journey from Perth to Adelaide in order to receive tuition in spin from the master.

However, initially I was disappointed for Grimmett wrote back and said the weather was too wet and he suggested we postpone my trip for a while. I agreed, albeit reluctantly. He may well have been testing my patience. If I didn't have patience I was not worth the trouble. Finally in April, 1967 I made the trip.

I ventured on to Lizzy's polished front porch and knocked on the door, the same door that had opened to greet the young Don Bradman, Bill Ponsford, Jack Crawford, Lindsay Hassett and a host of others who could easily slip into the pages of *Wisden*.

"You must be Ashley? Ah, Clarrie's in the back yard. You'll find him round the back," Mrs Grimmett smiled. I heard a sawing sound and looked up in time to catch sight of the little man of spin springing from the overhanging branch of a pepper tree. He greeted me with a broad grin and a firm handshake. Then it was straight down to business.

"Let's look at your batting." Clarrie had a ball in a stocking suspended from the newly-sawn branch of the pepper tree. He swung the ball and I played a couple of forward strokes; the old Fox seemed pleased. He had watered and rolled his Firle backyard pitch. It appeared a good track. He indicated that he now wanted me to bowl to him. He took up his stance at the wicket and I measured out my run. Grimmett wore no gloves. My first ball landed right on the spot, just outside the line of the off-stump and it turned in to meet the middle of Clarrie's Jack Hobbs' Autograph bat. My second delivery landed in much the same place and again the seventy-six-year-old Grimmett played the perfect forward defence. I was pleased that bowling in the presence of the great man did not hinder my accuracy. Clarrie looked up and indicated that we should talk. We met in mid-pitch.

"Now Ashley, I've seen you shape with the bat and I've seen, for now, enough of your bowling. My advice is that you give up bowling and become a batsman!" I was still suffering from shock when Clarrie volunteered: "I could play you blindfolded." Immediately I produced a handkerchief, which Clarrie placed about his eyes.

The little man chuckled and again took up his stance. My third ball of that session landed spot on, again turning in from the line of off-stump and again meeting the middle of Clarrie's Jack Hobbs' bat. I was either very accurate or very predictable or both. The old man could hardly contain his glee. He then softened his approach and explained that the predictability of my bowling; the same trajectory and pace made it all too easy.

Clarrie used the analogy of a person standing on a bridge overlooking a motorway. It was dark. There was a car approaching. "You can see the lights of the car," Clarrie said. "Do you think you would be able to tell how fast the car was going?"

I mumbled something in the affirmative, hoping I was on the right track, when Clarrie said, "Of course, yes! But if you were so ill-advised, as to be standing in the middle of the freeway — now please don't try this — say, in a manhole with your head at the level of the approaching lights, it would be difficult to know how fast that car was going. Right?" (Looking down, it is possible to judge the speed perfectly. But when the object is travelling towards you at just above eye-level, judging the speed is difficult.)

Clarrie's comments were designed to illustrate that a spinner operating at a trajectory above eye-level was far more difficult to play than one bowling a "flat" delivery.

"If the batsman can look down on the ball he will know immediately if the ball is overpitched or slightly short," Clarrie said. "Your trajectory must be just above the level of the eyes most of the time. That makes a batsman's judgment of length difficult." The Grimmett lesson in flight was the best cricket lesson of my career.

Two years later in India I was bowling to the opposing captain, the Nawab of Pataudi, who was picking up my length easily. If it was fractionally short, Pataudi would be in position straight away to hit off the back foot. If anything was remotely full, he was onto it in a flash. It was on 29 November, 1969 at Feroz Shah Kotla, Delhi that I decided to experiment in the middle of a Test match. I thought of Clarrie and the lesson in flight. I knew my bowling was too flat. The batsman was controlling events: he was looking down on my "flat" deliveries. I tossed one a little higher, just above eye-level; Pataudi was at sea. He struggled for two or three deliveries, then offered Ian Chappell an easy catch at forward short leg; via an edge onto the bat, the ball ballooning to offer an easy chance.

Johnny Moyes' book *A Century of Cricketers* helped me learn about great spinners of Australia.

I had learned about the likes of Grimmett and O'Reilly long before I met them and about Mailey and Hordern. I wish Moyes had devoted more space to his subjects, especially Grimmett. While the book dealt largely with statistics, Moyes avoided bringing to light Grimmett's 127 bags of five wickets in big matches, yet he made a feast of Don Bradman's 117 centuries in 234 matches. Perhaps he wasn't aware of Grimmett's figures.

In Autralia's list of talented leg-spinners only three — Grimmett, O'Reilly and Benaud — have taken 100 Test wickets or more. Grimmett was the first Test bowler to reach 200 Test wickets and he finished with 216 wickets in 37 matches. O'Reilly took 141 wickets in 27 Tests and Benaud captured 248 wickets in 63 Tests.

Among the off-spinners, Hugh Trumble won the most Test wickets; 141 in 32 games; Ashley Mallett, 132 in 38; Bruce Yardley 126 in 36; Ian Johnson 109 in 45; C.T.B. Turner 101 in 16 and George Giffen 103 in 31.

It was always my ambition to take 100 Test wickets and I aimed to reach that goal in 20 Tests; my target was five wickets per match. I didn't quite attain that strike record, but I came close. How does that compare with Grimmett, O'Reilly and Benaud?

Comparing wickets in Tests

Player	State	No. of Tests to reach 100 wickets
C.T.B. Turner	NSW	16
C.V. Grimmett	SA	17
W.J. O'Reilly	NSW	20
A.A. Mallett	SA	23
R. Benaud	NSW	32

When I came into Test cricket, spin bowling was a force in the scheme of things. It helped to balance an attack. There were the pacemen and the spinners. If there was a medium pacer he had to be very good, or he would be cast aside as "cannon fodder". The Dennis Lillee-Jeff Thomson partnership, which began with the demolition of England Down Under in 1974–75, changed cricket thinking. Spinners became the lowly serfs to the fast bowler landlords, made to scramble for the scraps of a bowl just before lunch or tea, or perhaps to rest one of the fast men.

Clarrie Grimmett would have understood. He played under Edgar Mayne. So I got my 100 Test wickets in 23 Tests, a strike rate almost in league with Lillee, who took 22 Tests to notch his first 100. But while Lillee grabbed in excess of 100 in his next 15 Tests, I came up with a paltry 32.

The experience of having tasted success as a strike bowler, then having to adapt to survive as a negative run-stopper has given me a valuable insight into the business of coaching spinners. I can identify with the highest of the craft and the great frustration many spinners experience today from playing a bit part on the Test stage.

When South Australia was batting on the Adelaide Oval and we sat in the Members Stand in the special players' area in the shade of the George Giffen Stand, we always knew when C.V. Grimmett was present. The instant a grey felt hat glided past our position (we couldn't see under the hat for there was a partition in the way) the South Australian players awaiting their turn to bat would say in good cheer: "Morning Clarrie!"

In his prime Grimmett only reached a height of 160 centimetres and as he meandered into his eighties the little bloke was decidedly hunched and he seemed to have shrunk. Sadly, few of the South Australians who greeted Clarrie on those occasions realised just how great a bowler he had been.

Behind that lined and toughened countenance was a keen sense of humour. When I knew him he wore a perpetual grin, and he wasn't afraid to try out his humour to defuse a situation. Once a garage man in Firle presented Clarrie with a hefty bill for the repair of his lawn mower. The bill came attached to a rather testy note, along the lines of pay up or else — Clarrie sent the bill back to the garage man and attached his reply to it: "I am glad to attend to this account. Please find my bill enclosed. I have deducted the amount of the mower repair bill from my account for having coached your son on my backyard pitch every Sunday morning for the past four years! [Signed] C.V. Grimmett."

Clarrie sold insurance in the latter days of his working life. Immediately his old South Australian team-mate, Homesdale "Slinger" Nitschke heard about Grimmett's new profession he announced: "Put me down for a million!" As the years passed Clarrie would revel in the comradeship at the Commercial Travellers' Club in Adelaide. There he would chat about the old days with the likes of Cec Starr and Nitschke.

One day, late in the 1960s, Clarrie got chatting to the young Ian Chappell, then a sales representative with W.D. and H.O. Wills and starting to make a name for himself as a cricketer. Leaning over to catch the Chappell ear, he said: "Ian, I must say you will have to watch your running. I think you should back up more…"

"Well, Clarrie, Sir Donald [Bradman] says my problem at the moment is that I back up too far," Chappell said.

Clarrie scratched his chin and thought for a moment.

"That's it then, Ian. I think you run too slowly." Another Grimmett victim; Chappell comprehensively stumped.

Grimmett was one of the first Australians to snap up a gleaming new Holden when Lawrence Hartnett came up with his uniquely Australian-designed car. He sold his Vauxhall, the vehicle which replaced the Rover, and cared for his Holden as if it were his 1930 Test cap. I recall Clarrie driving off to golf in that car. It was 1967, the car then nineteen years old, yet the old Fox had it preened to perfection. In that car he devised a method to run the green lights; a green light at every intersection. It was a game he played on every outing to town. The city fathers changed the sequence of the lights to try and outwit the Fox, but he altered his strategy to suit.

Golf was a Grimmett passion. Clarrie and Oscar Klemich, owner of the National Paper Bag Company and an old family friend, used to venture regularly to Freeman's Paddock in Firle to hit a bucket of golf balls into the distance. There with Oscar's daughter, Elaine, Vic Grimmett was armed with Clarrie's old baseball glove. His reward for catching a drive was to be able to down the glove, pick up his golf stick and belt the ball back from where it came. Clarrie taught Klemich how to play golf. The pair also played tennis regularly, either at Oscar's St Peter's home or at the Grimmett court in Firle.

On 11 December, 1985, Vic Grimmett hit a hole in one at the eleventh at Marino, a course south of Adelaide. That very day Vic was sifting through some of his father's things when he came across one of Clarrie's golf trophies: "Presented to C.V. Grimmett for a hole-in-one, 8th hole, Glenelg Golf Course, June 6, 1939". Clarrie played golf until he was eighty. Only failing eyesight preventing him playing on.

Lizzy Grimmett died on September 23, 1968. For years there had been a cloud over Clarrie's age and whether he was much older than he admitted. But it was Lizzy who really stumped Clarrie. When they married that day on 1 November, 1919 in Victoria, Lizzy was, in fact, thirty-seven years of age, not thirty as she wrote in the marriage register.

Vic and Louie Grimmett had two children, Helen and Brenton. Brenton was the apple of his grandfather's eye. A left-arm orthodox spinner, Brenton probably conjured up visions for his grandfather of becoming another Wilfred Rhodes or Bert Ironmonger. Whenever his grandson got a bag of wickets in a school match Clarrie would give him a piece of his rich cricket collection; a ball, a stump, a cherished cap.

Three years after Lizzy's death, Clarrie remarried. He chose Gwen Montgomery Beeton, an old family friend. Gwen and Clarrie wed on 28 May, 1971. He was in his eightieth year. Clarrie severed ties with "Dundula", his beloved home at Firle. Too many memories. He began his new married life in a house at 16 Orient Road, Kensington. The name of the street suggested intrigue, befitting the mysterious Grimmett.

EPILOGUE

Clarrie Grimmett died peacefully in May, 1980. He was eighty-eight. Hundreds of his friends and old cricket comrades made the journey to Adelaide's Centennial Park Cemetery to pay their last respects. Bill O'Reilly and Jack Fingleton flew in from Sydney. His old South Australia and Test team-mate Tim Wall was there; so too Clarence "Nip" Pellew, a survivor from the Herbie Collins 1919 AIF team, the ex-Victorian and Test left-hander Len Darling, Sir Donald Bradman and a host of the moderns, many of whom had come under the old Fox's influence as a coach or a valued friend or both.

Stories abounded. We heard how Clarrie had strict rules when coaching the Adelaide Cricket Club, once chaining a batsman's left leg to a peg to prevent him from stepping away against the quick bowlers. Some bordered on the apocryphal, but not the story of this man's struggle to win recognition. Clarrie Grimmett earned his place in cricket fame.

Rain poured down on the chapel roof; eyes glistened and I stood and remembered the help the old man had given me. He was honesty itself, blunt and forthright. At his cricketing zenith, Clarrie was compounded of tea, leather, patience and subtlety. At seventy-six he had zest and bounce; he was remarkably agile, so much like Bradman when he reached that age. I've read Clarrie's books on getting wickets and how to trick the batsman, but often he tells how he dismissed a certain batsman, without letting on how he planned his demise.

Thomas Edison would not be getting his message of electricity across to a student if he wrote, "The bulb lit up when I flicked the switch". Trying to fathom the depth of Clarrie's spinning knowledge and the strategy he used against different types of players under varying conditions was a mission impossible for those limited to reading Clarrie's books.

Grimmett's strategy largely remained a mystery. In the quest to become a better bowler, the young student could learn a great deal from talking to Clarrie or attending one of his coaching sessions. Even when Clarrie was well into his seventies he religiously coached on that manicured turf pitch in his Firle backyard. A few years after his death, the northern entrance at Adelaide Oval was named the Clarrie Grimmett Gates. A large stone rests just inside the entrance and upon it are placed a couple of plaques. On one is the Grimmett action, his profile frozen in bronze. The other details the Grimmett bowling record. These permanent tributes to the memory of Clarrie Grimmett are just a pitch length or two from the old pepper tree where Clarrie used to park the Rover. The old tree still stands tall at the northern entrance.

The minister summed up and as the coffin slowly descended, O'Reilly reached for a handkerchief. Bill O'Reilly, in the cricketing sense, understood Clarrie better than anyone. He revered the man and he loved him as a brother.

Clarrie would have been with his mates in spirit. Perhaps at that very moment he was working on a new mystery ball, one to bowl many of the great batsmen who have already taken up their stance on the heavenly turf.

Under the green baggy penthouse of his cap, those blue eyes twinkled with amusement. Besides he had some unfinished business with Victor Trumper.

BOWLING CAREER IN FIGURES

Overall Figures

In Tests

Matches	Balls	Wkts	Ave.	5-wkt inns	10-wkt match	Best
37	5231	216	24.21	21	7	7/40

First man to reach 200 wickets in Tests

First-class

Matches	Balls	Wkts	Ave.	5-wkt inns	10-wkt match	Best
248	31740	1424	22.28	127	33	10/37

Career batting

Tests — 557 runs at 13.92 (highest score 50)
Career — 4720 runs at 17.67 (highest score 71*)
*denotes not out

Catches

Tests — 17
Career — 139

C.V. Grimmett in first-class cricket

Year	Where	For	Against	Venue	Dates		Bowling
1911–12	NZ	Well	Auck	Well	Feb 23-26	0/68	4/48
1912–13	NZ	Well	Auck	Auck	Jan 1, 2, 3	1/57	0/8
1913–14	NZ	Well	Cantby	C. Ch	Jan 1, 2, 3	2/73	3/55
	NZ	Well	Otago	Dun.	Jan 9-12	3/54	1/17
	NZ	Well	Auck	Well.	Jan 29-31	1/26	1/44
	NZ	Well	H. Bay	Hast.	Feb 6, 7.	3/94	2/61
	NZ	Well	Aust XI	Well	Feb 13-16	0/19	0/24
	NZ	Well	Aust XI	Well	Mar 20, 21	0/31	—
	NZ	Well	Reese XI	Well	Apr 10-12	1/0	—
1918–19	Aus	Vic	NSW	Syd	Jan 25-28	—	0/34
1920–21	Aus	Vic	MCC	Melb	Feb 4-8	1/10	0/6
1921–22	Aus	Vic	Tas	Lcn	Feb 14-16	4/89	2/72
1922–23	Aus	Vic	MCC	Melb	Nov 17-20	1/43	1/7
1923–24	Aus	Vic	S. Aust	Adel	Feb 15-20	1/12	8/86
1924–25	Aus	Aus XI	NSW	Syd	Oct 17-20	3/138	—
	Aus	SA	Vic	Adel	Oct 31-Nov 6	5/97	4/170
	Aus	SA	MCC	Adel	Nov 7-11	4/87	1/2
	Aus	SA	Vic	Melb	Nov 21-27	5/97	0/43
	Aus	SA	NSW	Syd	Nov 28-Dec 2	5/137	—
	Aus	Aus XI	MCC	Bris	Dec 4-8	4/176	—
	Aus	SA	NSW	Adel	Jan 9-14	3/43	6/103
	Aus	Aust	England	Syd	Feb 27 Mar 4	5-45	6/37
	Aus	SA	MCC	Adel	Mar 13-16	1/40	7/85
1925–26	Aus	SA	WA	Adel	Oct 30-Nov 2	5/60	5/62
	Aus	SA	Vic	Adel	Nov 13-18	5/95	1/60
	Aus	SA	WA	Adel	Nov 21-23	6/76	4/57
	Aus	Rest	Aust XI	Syd	Dec 4-8	2/65	5/91
	Aus	SA	NSW	Adel	Dec 18-22	0/174	—
	Aus	SA	NZ	Adel	Dec 26-29	3/130	1/35
	Aus	SA	Vic	Melb	Jan 1-9	2/61	2/192
	Aus	SA	NSW	Syd	Jan 11-16	4/192	6/202
	Aus	SA	Qld	Bris	Jan 23-26	3/77	2/77
	Aus	Aus XI	WA	Perth	Mar 12-15	3/88	—

Year	Where	For	Against	Venue	Dates	Bowling	
1926	Eng	Aust	Leics	Leics	May 3, 4	2/26	0/9
	Eng	Aust	Surrey	Oval	May 8-11	1/72	—
	Eng	Aust	Comb Uni	Camb	May 19-21	0/25	6/28
	Eng	Aust	Oxf. Uni	Oxford	May 22-25	1/27	2/30
	Eng	Aust	Middlesex	Lord's	May 29-Jne 1	2/92	—
	Eng	Aust	Yorkshire	Brad.	June 5-8	6/87	0/3
	Eng	Aust	Yorkshire	Sheff.	June 16-18	—	—
	Eng	Aust	Derby	Chest.	June 23, 24	4/53	1/24
	Eng	Aust	Northants	North.	June 30 July 2	2/50	5/28
	Eng	Aust	Notts	Notts	July 3-6	0/23	1/18
	Eng	Aust	Worcs	Worcs	July 7, 8	4/2	4/31
	Eng	Aust	England	Leeds	July 10-12	5/88	2/59
	Eng	Aust	Lancs	Livrpl	July 14-16	0/40	—
	Eng	Aust	England	Man.	July 24-27	1/85	—
	Eng	Aust	Surrey	Oval	July 28-30	4/30	—
	Eng	Aust	Glam	Swans.	Jly 31-Aug 3	4/56	4/45
	Eng	Aust	Gloucs	Chelt.	Aug 7-10	7/67	4/59
	Eng	Aust	England	Oval	Aug 14-18	2/74	3/108
	Eng	Aust	Somerset	Tntn	Aug 21-24	5/64	3/85
1926	Eng	Aust	Kent	Cant	Aug 25-27	1/55	3/56
		Aust	Sussex	Brgtn	Aug 28-31	4/63	4/42
		Aust	Eng. XI	Folks.	Sept 1-3	1/33	—
		Aust	Thntn XI	Scarb.	Sept 8-10	5/68	1/36
		Aust	Eng. XI	B. Pool	Sept 11-14	1/26	—
1926-27	Aust	SA	Vic	Adel	Dec 3-8	2/110	1/107
		SA	NSW	Adel	Dec 17-22	4/110	1/123
		SA	Qld	Adel	Dec 25-28	2/72	5/107
		SA	Vic	Melb	Jan 1-6	4/101	5/180
		SA	NSW	Syd	Jan 8-12	4/70	2/50
1927-28	Aust	SA	Vic	Adel	Dec 2-6	3/175	—
		SA	NSW	Adel	Dec 16-21	3/160	8/57
		SA	Qld	Adel	Dec 23-27	5/85	5/101
		SA	Vic	Melb	Dec 30-Jan 3	5/170	—
		SA	NSW	Syd	Jan 6-10	2/106	4/137
		SA	Qld	Bris	Jan 14-18	4/62	3/98
1927-28	NZ	Aust	Well	Well	Feb 17-20	3/65	4/94
		Aust	Otago	Dun.	Feb 24-27	6/23	—
		Aust	Canter.	C. Ch	Mar 2-5	6/128	7/115
		Aust	Auck	Auck	Mar 9-12	2/79	7/92
		Aust	NZ XI	Auck	Mar 24-27	3/85	0/15
		Aust	NZ XI	Dun.	Mar 31-Apr 3	6/47	3/52

Year	Where	For	Against	Venue	Dates	Bowling	
1928–29	Aust	Aus XI	Rest	Melb	Oct 19-22	3/29	4/125
		SA	MCC	Adel	Oct 26-30	6/109	1/22
		SA	Vic	Melb	Nov 9-13	3/99	1/109
		Aust	England	Bris	Nov 30-Dec 5	3/167	6/131
		Aust	England	Syd	Dec 14-20	2/191	—
		Aust	England	Melb	Dec 29-Jan 5	2/114	2/96
		SA	NSW	Adel	Jan 11_16	3/128	3/105
		SA	MCC	Adel	Jan 25-29	4/174	0/88
		Aust	England	Adel	Feb 1-8	5/102	1/117
		SA	Qld	Bris	Feb 22-26	2/49	5/49
		SA	NSW	Syd	Mar 1-6	4/112	5/116
		Aust	England	Melb	Mar 8-16	0/40	2/66
		Aus XI	MCC	Perth	Mar 21-23	4/94	—
1929–30	Aust	SA	MCC	Adel	Nov 8-12	6/61	3/136
		Ryder	Woodfull	Syd	Dec 6-11	3/68	7/173
		SA	NSW	Adel	Dec 19-24	3/91	7/136
		SA	Qld	Adel	Dec 25-30	6/146	2/68
		SA	Vic	Melb	Jan 1-6	1/135	2/80
		SA	NSW	Syd	Jan 9-13	4/163	—
		SA	Qld	Bris	Jan 17-21	4/83	4/98
		SA	WA	Adel	Jan 31-Feb 3	0/67	6/50
		SA	Vic	Adel	Feb 14-17	5/55	5/155
		Aus XI	Tas	Hbt	Mar 13-15	5/30	1/20
		Aus XI	WA	Perth	Mar 21-24	6/75	2/53
1930	Eng	Aust	Worcs	Worcs	Apr 30-May 2	4/38	5/46
		Aust	Leics	Leics	May 3-6	7/46	—
		Aust	Essex	Lytn	May 7-9	2/17	3/57
		Aust	Yorkshire	Sheff	May 10-13	10/37	—

Year	Where	For	Against	Venue	Dates	Bowling	
1930	Eng	Aust	Lancs	Lvrpl	May 14-16	6/57	2/71
		Aust	MCC	Lord's	May 17-20	0/78	—
		Aust	Surrey	Oval	May 24-27	—	—
		Aust	Oxford U.	Oxford	May 28-30	5/48	2/31
		Aust	Hamps	Sthamp.	May 31-June 3	7/39	7/56
		Aust	Middlesex	Lord's	June 4-6	3/36	3/81
		Aust	England	Notts	June 13-17	5/107	5/94
		Aust	Surrey	Oval	June 18-20	6/24	1/35
		Aust	England	Lord's	June 27-Jul1	2/105	6/167
		Aust	Yorkshire	Brad.	July 2-4	6/75	5/58
		Aust	England	Leeds	July 11-15	5/135	1/33
		Aust	Scotland	Edin.	July 16-18	2/42	—
		Aust	England	Man.	July 25-29	0/59	—
		Aust	Somerset	Tntn	July 30-31	3/38	7/33
		Aust	Glamorgan	Swans.	Aug 2-5	4/34	4/69
		Aust	Warwicks	Birm	Aug 6-8	0/14	—
		Aust	England	Oval	Aug 16-22	4/135	1/90
		Aust	Gloucs	Bristol	Aug 23-26	3/28	2/83
		Aust	Kent	Cant.	Aug 27-29	4/80	—
		Aust	Sussex	Brgtn	Aug 30-Sep2	2/115	—
		Aust	Eng XI	Folkes.	Sep 3-5	0/35	—
		Aust	Eng XI	Scarb.	Sep 10-12	0/1	—
1930-31	Aust	Aus XI	The Rest	Melb	Nov 14-18	5/89	0/32
		SA	W. Indies	Adel	Dec 5-8	4/71	5/43
		Aust	W. Indies	Adel	Dec 12-16	7/87	4/96
		SA	NSW	Adel	Dec 18-22	5/180	—
		SA	Qld	Adel	Dec 25-26	4/23	5/31
		Aust	W. Indies	Syd	Jan 1-5	4/54	1/9
		Aust	W. Indies	Bris	Jan 16-20	4/95	5/49
		SA	W. Indies	Adel	Feb 7-11	5/144	3/93
		Aust	W. Indies	Melb	Feb 13-14	2/46	2/10
		SA	Vic	Adel	Feb 20-24	4/105	1/13
		Aust	W. Indies	Syd	Feb 27-Mar 4	3/100	1/47

Year	Where	For	Against	Venue	Dates		Bowling
1931–32	Aust	SA	S. Africa	Adel	Oct 30-Nov 3	6/50	2/82
		SA	Vic	Adel	Nov 13-17	5/93	2/32
		Aust	S. Africa	Bris	Nov 27-Dec 3	2/49	1/45
		Aust	S. Africa	Syd	Dec 18-21	4/28	4/44
		SA	Qld	Adel	Dec 25-29	2/68	4/70
		Aust	S. Africa	Melb	Dec 31-Jan 6	2/100	6/92
		SA	S. Africa	Adel	Jan 22-26	6/155	1/45
		Aust	S. Africa	Adel	Jan29-Feb2	7/116	7/83
		Aust	S. Africa	Melb	Feb 12-15	—	—
		SA	Vic	Melb	March 4-8	3/118	—
		SA	Qld	Bris	Mar 12-16	3/14	5/44
		SA	NSW	Sydney	Mar 19-22	1/75	4/32
1932–33	Aust	SA	MCC	Adel	Nov 4-8	4/176	—
		SA	Vic	Adel	Nov 25-29	5/161	1/13
		Aust	England	Syd	Dec 2-7	1/118	—
		SA	NSW	Adel	Dec 16-20	4/138	2/41
		SA	Qld	Adel	Dec 23-26	6/55	1/31
		Aust	England	Melb	Dec 30-Jan 3	1/21	0/17
		Aust	England	Adel	Jan 13-19	2/94	1/74
1932–33	Aust	SA	Qld	Bris	Jan 27-31	6/49	7/86
		SA	NSW	Syd	Feb 3-6	0/47	2/84
		SA	Vic	Melb	Feb 10-13	6/109	3/52
		SA	MCC	Adel	Mar 10-14	3/124	0/85
1933–34	Aust	SA	Vic	Adel	Nov 3-7	7/80	0/122
		Rich	Wood	Melb	Nov 17-22	2/108	
		SA	NSW	Adel	Dec 15-18	2/17	5/103
		SA	Qld	Adel	Dec 22-26	5/58	6/134
		SA	Vic	Melb	Dec 29-Jan 2	1/76	4/52
		SA	NSW	Syd	Jan 5-9	3/75	0/34
		SA	Qld	Bris	Jan 12-16	5/132	1/45
		SA	WA	Adel	Feb 10-13	4/45	3/38
		SA	WA	Adel	March 3-5	7/57	2/33
		Aust XI	Tas	Lcn	Mar 10-13	2/96	2/46
		Aust XI	WA	Perth	Mar 23-26	5/90	

Year	Where	For	Against	Venue	Dates	Bowling	
1934	Eng	Aust	Worcs	Worcs	May 2-4	5/53	5/27
		Aust	Cmbdge	Camb	May 9-11	9/74	0/17
		Aust	MCC	Lord's	May 12-15	1/81	4/90
		Aust	Essex	Chelms	May 16-18	3/80	5/54
		Aust	Ox. Uni	Oxford	May 19-21	—	7/109
		Aust	Mdsex	Lord's	May 26-28	3/80	5/27
		Aust	Surrey	Oval	May 30-June 1	3/113	1/16
		Aust	Lancs	Manch	June 2-5	1/57	—
		Aust	Eng	Notts	June 8-12	5/81	3/39
		Aust	Gent	Lord's	June 16-19	4/76	4/71
		Aust	Eng	Lord's	June 22-25	1/102	—
		Aust	Surrey	Oval	June 30-Jul3	4/64	5/33
		Aust	Eng	Manc	July 6-10	1/122	0/28
		Aust	York	Sheff	July 14-17	4/113	0/30
		Aust	Eng	Leeds	July 20-24	4/57	3/72
		Aust	Gloucs	Bristol	Aug 1-3	0/44	—
		Aust	Warw	Birm	Aug 8-10	5/76	—
		Aust	Notts	Notts	Aug 11-14	4/70	3/35
		Aust	Eng	Oval	Aug 18-22	3/103	5/64
		Aust	Kent	Cntby	Aug 29-31	—	—
		Aust	Eng XI	Folkes	Sept 1-4	0/1	—
1934–35	Aust	Wood	Rich	Melb	Nov 16-20	5/64	4/108
		SA	NSW	Syd	Nov 23-27	4/124	—
		SA	Qld	Bris	Nov 30-Dec 4	6/138	5/94
		SA	NSW	Adel	Dec 14-18	4/140	7/90
		SA	Qld	Adel	Dec 22-26	9/180	7/109
		SA	Vic	Melb	Dec 29-Jan 2	0/0	—
		SA	Vic	Adel	Feb 15-19	4/70	3/98
1935–36	S.Africa	Aust	Natal	Durb	Nov 23-26	7/83	2/52
		Aust	W. Prov	C. Town	Nov 30-Dec 3	2/47	3/36
		Aust	Trans	Joburg	Dec 7-10	6/57	3/60
		Aust	S. Afr	Durban	Dec 14-18	2/48	3/83
		Aust	S. Afr	Joburg	Dec 24-28	3/29	3/111
		Aust	S. Afr	C. Town	Jan 1-4	5/32	5/56
		Aust	E.P.	Pt Eliz	Jan 7-8	3/33	3/25
1935–36	S. Africa	Aust	OFS	Bloemf.	Jan 18-20	5/35	5/67
		Aust	Trans	Joburg	Jan 25-27	2/58	3/56
		Aust	S. Afr	Joburg	Feb 15-17	3/70	7/40
		Aust	Natal	Durban	Feb 22-25	4/111	—
		Aust	S. Afr	Durban	Feb 28-Mar 3	7/100	6/73

Year	Where	For	Against	Venue	Dates	Bowling	
1936–37	Aust	Rich	Brad	Syd	Oct 9-13	4/146	3/82
		Comb XI	MCC	Perth	Oct 22-24	1/137	1/13
		SA	MCC	Adel	Oct 30-Nov 3	2/62	0/26
		SA	Vic	Melb	Nov 13-17	1/112	1/85
		SA	NSW	Adel	Dec 18-22	6/64	2/81
		SA	Qld	Adel	Dec 25-29	3/89	2/71
		Comb XI	MCC	Hobart	Jan 15-18	2/114	1/31
		SA	MCC	Adel	Jan 22-26	4/77	—
		SA	Qld	Bris	Feb 12-15	4/18	1/35
		SA	NSW	Syd	Feb 19-23	3/77	4/71
		SA	Vic	Adel	Mar 12-15	3/52	—
1937–38	Aust	SA	NZ	Adel	Nov 5-8	3/21	—
		Benefit	DGB	Adel	Nov 26-30	3/39	—
		SA	NSW	Adel	Dec 17-21	5/103	4/51
		SA	Qld	Melb	Dec 25-29	2/11	2/107
		SA	Vic	Bris	Dec 31-Jan4	6/95	1/62
		SA	Qld	Syd	Jan 8-12	3/42	1/28
		SA	NSW	Perth	Jan 15-19	2/50	1/52
		SA	Vic	Perth	Feb 4-8	3/56	0/29
		Rigg XI	McCabe	Syd	Feb 18-19	3/56	2/43
1938–39	Aust	SA	NSW	Syd	Dec 16-20	7/116	4/59
		SA	Qld	Melb	Dec 24-28	6/33	3/96
		SA	Vic	Adel	Dec 30-Jan 3	0/98	—
		SA	NSW	Melb	Jan 14-18	4/53	2/51
		SA	Vic	Adel	Feb 24-28	1/57	—
1939–40	Aust	SA	Vic	Adel	Nov 17-21	3/67	5/118
		SA	NSW	Adel	Dec 15-18	3/102	6/122
		SA	Qld	Adel	Dec 22-26	4/71	6/124
		SA	Vic	Melb	Dec 29-Jan2	2/136	2/78
		SA	Qld	Bris	Jan 6-10	4/52	3/116
		SA	NSW	Syd	Jan 13-17	6/118	5/111
		SA	WA	Perth	Feb 10-13	3/94	0/26
		SA	WA	Perth	Feb 16-19	5/67	6/57
		Rest	NSW	Syd	Mar 8-11	5/65	5/130
1940–41	Aust	SA	NSW	Syd	Dec 6-9	1/83	1/32
		SA	Vic	Melb	Dec 13-17	7/114	1/36
		SA	Vic	Adel	Dec 25-28	3/54	4/75
		McCabe	Brad	Melb	Jan 1-4	3/100	4/46
		SA	NSW	Adel	Feb 21-24	1/128	—

Career summary

Team	Matches	Runs	Wkts	Ave.	5wkt/i	10wkt/m	b/b
Wellington	9	679	22	30.86	—	—	4/48
Victoria	5	453	18	25.16	1	—	8/86
South Aust	105	16566	668	24.79	62	16	9/180
Australia	37	5231	216	24.21	21	7	7/40
Rep. teams in Australia	21	2860	114	25.08	9	2	7/173
Rep. teams on tour	71	5951	386	15.41	34	8	10/37
Totals	248	31740	1424	22.28	127	33	10/37

Season by season

Season		M.	I.	No.	Runs	HS	Ave.	100s	50s	C.	St.	Runs	Wkts	Ave.	5wkts/ 10wkts
1911-12	NZ	1	2	—	3	2	1.50	—	—	2	—	116	4	29.00	— —
1912-13	NZ	1	2	—	53	28	26.50	—	—	—	—	65	1	65.00	— —
1913-14	NZ	7	13	1	185	33*	.15.41	—	—	5	—	498	17	29.29	— —
1918-19	Aust	1	2	—	7	7	3.50	—	—	1	—	34	—	—	— —
1920-21	Aust	1	2	2	34	31*	—	—	—	—	—	110	1	110.00	— —
1922–22	Aust	1	1	—	23	23	23.00	—	—	2	—	161	6	26.83	— —
1922-23	Aust	1	2	1	23	18*	23.00	—	—	—	—	50	2	25.00	— —
1923-24	Aust	1	1	—	3	3	3.00	—	—	2	—	98	9	10.89	1 —
1924-25	Aust	9	15	1	232	49	16.57	—	—	6	—	1300	59	22.03	7 1
1925-26	Aust	10	15	1	368	57	26.29	—	1	10	—	1794	59	30.41	6 3
1926	Eng	24	21	2	263	41	13.84	—	—	17	—	1857	105	17.68	7 1
1926-27	Aust	5	9	2	204	48	29.14	—	—	4	—	1030	30	34.33	2 —
1927-28	Aust	6	10	3	300	61*	42.86	—	3	2	—	1151	42	27.40	4 2
1927-28	NZ	6	6	1	136	59	27.20	—	1	4	—	795	47	16.91	5 1
1928-29	Aust	13	20	5	335	71*	22.33	—	1	9	—	2432	71	34.25	5 —
1929-30	Aust	11	17	2	289	53	19.27	—	1	8	—	1943	82	23.69	9 3
1930	Eng	26	23	3	237	50	11.85	—	1	12	—	2427	144	16.85	15 5
1930-31	Aust	11	14	1	258	54	19.85	—	2	5	—	1417	74	19.14	7 1
1931-32	Aust	12	19	4	253	63*	16.87	—	1	8	—	1535	77	19.93	7 1
1932-33	Aust	11	20	4	196	36	12.25	—	—	2	—	1577	55	28.67	5 1
1933-34	Aust	11	15	5	208	30	20.80	—	—	1	—	1441	66	21.83	7 1
1934	Eng	21	20	3	255	39	15.00	—	—	8	—	2159	109	19.80	10 1
1934-35	Aust	7	10	3	115	35	16.43	—	—	5	—	1215	58	20.94	6 3
1935-36	SAF	12	11	2	125	30*	13.89	—	—	6	—	1362	92	14.80	9 4
1936-37	Aust	11	15	2	151	33	11.62	—	—	3	—	1443	48	30.06	1 —
1937-38	Aust	9	14	2	131	46	10.92	—	—	8	—	845	41	20.60	2 —
1938-39	Aust	5	3	1	69	35	34.50	—	—	1	—	563	27	20.85	2 1
1939-40	Aust	9	11	3	108	27	16.00	—	—	8	—	1654	73	22.65	9 4
1940-41	Aust	5	8	—	156	67	19.50	—	1	1	—	668	25	26.72	1 —
Totals		248	321	54	4720	71*	17.67	—	12	140	—	31740	1424	22.28	127 33

Sheffield Shield Cricket — the top bowlers

Player	matches	Wickets	Average
C.V. Grimmett	79	513	25.29
G.F. Lawson	103	367	23.82
T.M. Alderman	89	366	23.74
J.R. Thomson	84	355	24.20
A.A. Mallett	77	344	23.76
D.K. Lillee	75	338	23.92
G.A.R. Lock	63	302	23.87

N.B. C.V. Grimmett played one Sheffield Shield match for Victoria, taking nine wickets, the balance (504) he captured when playing for South Australia. D.K. Lillee took 15 wickets for Tasmania, the rest (323) for Western Australia. In all of his 105 matches for South Australia (from 1924–25 to 1940–41) Clarrie Grimmett took 668 wickets. He leads George Giffen (419) and Ashley Mallett (390) in the State list of highest wicket-takers. (Adelaide-based statistician Geoff Sando provided much of the C.V. Grimmett bowling record.)

Grimmett's club performances in Sydney, Melbourne and Adelaide are as remarkable as his figures in first-class cricket. He captured five wickets or more an over on one hundred occasions, with his 9/49 for Kensington against Glenelg (the other man was run out) in 1933–34 being his best effort in any one innings. However, in 1943–44 he took 9/55 for Kensington against a combined East Torrens and Glenelg eleven. The war years saw sides amalgamate. During World War II, which robbed cricket of many experienced and up-and-coming cricketers, Clarrie, with people such as Ron Sharp and Cecil Starr, kept the spirit of cricket going in Adelaide. They arranged mid-week matches, coached youngsters and generally fostered and promoted the game.

Clarrie must have known the war had literally closed the chapter on his great career, for he was in his mid-fifties when hostilities ended, yet his last year in district cricket, with

Kensington in 1944–45, Clarrie bagged 64 wickets at 11.21, with six bags of five wickets or more; 6/33 (v University): 6/89 (v Sturt); 5/37 (v West Torrens); 5/46 (v Prospect); 7/43 (v East Torrens-Glenelg) and 8/86 (v University).

Grimmett's bowling and batting record in Adelaide club cricket

Season		I.	No.	Runs	HS	Ave.	100s	R.	Wkts	Ave.	5wkt/I	10wkt/M	BB
1924-25	Adel	8	1	121	41*	17.28	—	722	44	16.40	5	1	7/119
1925-26		6	—	66	24	11.00	—	348	27	12.88	3	—	7/84
1926-27		7	—	131	43	18.71	—	675	39	17.30	5	2	7/102
1927-28	Colts	7	4	233	105*	77.66	1	258	19	13.57	3	—	6/57
1928-29	Kensn	3	1	16	8*	8.00	—	117	9	13.00	1	—	7/62
1929-30		8	3	165	56*	33.00	—	500	31	16.12	3	—	7/83
1930-31		2	—	8	8	4.00	—	262	15	17.46	2	—	6/41
1931-32		3	—	25	14	8.33	—	99	7	14.14	1	—	6/90
1933-34		6	1	38	15	7.60	—	427	39	10.94	4	—	9/49
1934-35		6	—	72	24	12.00	—	371	32	11.59	4	—	8/37
1935-36		2	—	35	31	17.50	—	132	11	12.00	1	—	8/51
1936-37		.5	—	90	41	18.00	—	313	18	17.38	2	—	6/86
1937-38		8	2	60	25	10.00	—	567	47	12.06	6	1	8/59
1938-39		1	—	12	12	12.00	—	187	14	13.35	1	—	6/68
1939-40	Colts	10	1	223	56	24.77	—	364	18	20.22	2	—	5/25
1940-41	Kensn	8	1	99	35*	14.14	—	547	34	16.08	3	1	7/46
1941-42		11	1	146	50	14.60	—	462	.36	12.83	2	1	7/45
1943-44		16	5	172	46*	15.63	—	712	75	9.49	7	—	9/55
1944-45		11	5	115	27*	19.16	—	718	64	11.21	6	—	8/86
Totals		128	25	1827	105*	17.73	1	778	579	13.44	61	6	9/49

* Not out

GRIMMETT (after Longfellow's "Hiawatha")

Then the little Clarrie Grimmett
Learned of ev'ry ball its turnings,
Learned their ways and all their twisitings —
How they swerved and dropped and scuttled,
How they broke and swung and floated,
Learned the leg-break and the off-break,
And the straight-break and the wrong-un,
Ev'rything there was in bowling
Till he knew that he could treat them
Just as if each were a yo-yo,
(Gentle and submissive yo-yo),
And he had the batsmen guessing
As he crept towards the wicket,
Crept towards the bowler's wicket,
And they found him devastating,
For they never guessed correctly.

Arthur Mailey

The five wicket (or more) hauls by Grimmett in club cricket in Adelaide, Sydney and Melbourne

1914-15 (2)

7/32}
5/33}   Sydney v Redfern (Sydney CG)

1915-16 (5)

6/98   Sydney v Wn Subs (Pratten Park)
6/73   Sydney v Middle Hbr (Rushcutters Bay)
8/60}
6/55}   Sydney v Balmain (Rushcutters Bay)
5/72   Sydney v Middle Hbr (Sydney CG)

1916-17 (1)

6/57   Sydney v Petersham (Sydney CG)

1917-18 (4)

5/36}
5/24}   Sth Melb v St Kilda (St Kilda)
5/76   Sth Melb v Richmond (South Melb)
5/32   Sth Melb v Fitzroy (South Melb)

1918-19 (2)

6/21   Sth Melb v University (South Melb)
7/41   Sth Melb v Prahran (South Melb)

1919-20 (4)

7/84   Sth Melb v Melbourne (South Melb)
5/96   Sth Melb v Essendon (South Melb)
5/68}
6/27}   Sth Melb v East Melb (South Melb)

1920-21 (5)

8/111   Prahran v Fitzroy (Fitzroy)
7/59   Prahran v Carlton (Toorak Park, Prahran)
6/61   Prahan v Melbourne (Melb CG)
7/54   Prahran v St Kilda (Prahran)
6/98   Prahran v Melbourne (Prahran)

1921-22 (4)

5/72	Prahran v HEM (Glenferrie)
7/53	Prahran v University (Prahran)
5/37	Prahran v Richmond (Richmond)
8/60	Prahran v Fitzroy (Fitzroy)

1924-25 (5)

5/104	Adel v Sturt (Unley)
5/44}	
6/51}	Adel v North Adel (Adelaide)
6/37	Adel v East Torrs (Norwood)
7/119	Adel v West Torrs (Thebarton)

1925-26 (3)

7/84	Adel v Colts (Adelaide)
6/62	Adel v Glenelg (Glenelg)
5/80	Adel v University (University)

1926-27 (5)

6/110	Adel v Sturt (Unley)
5/129	Adel v East Torrs (Norwood)
6/65	Adel v Colts (Adelaide)
6/46}	
7/102}	Adel v University (University)

1922-23 (8)

5/52	Prahran v Sth Melb (South Melb)
7/43	Prahran v Melbourne (Melbourne)
8/82	Prahran v St Kilda (Prahran)
6/109	Prahran v Nth Melb (North Melb)
8/50	Prahran v Collingwood (Prahran)
7/100	Prahran v Fitzroy (Fitzroy)
7/38	Prahran v Fitzroy (Prahran)
5/65	Prahran v Nth Melb (Prahran)

1923-24 (8)

5/23	Prahran v Sth Melb (Prahran)
6/68	Prahran v Essendon (Essendon)
6/70	Prahran v Carlton (Prahran)
6/97	Prahran v Melbourne (Prahran)
5/39}	
5/54}	Prahran v Fitzroy (Prahran)
5/68	Prahran v St Kilda (St Kilda)

6/76   Prahran v Collingwood (Collingwood)

1927-28 (3)
5/53   Colts v East Torrs (Norwood)
6/64   Colts v Glenelg (Adelaide)
6/57   Colts v North Adel (Prospect)

1928-29 (1)
7/62   Kenan v University (University)

1929-30 (3)
6/84   Kensn v Prospect (Kensington)
7/83   Kensn v Glenelg (Kensington)
5/66   Kensn v East Torrs (Kensington)

1930-31 (2)
5/93   Kensn v Prospect (Kensington)
6/41   Kensn v Port Adel (Kensington)

1931-32 (1)
6/90   Kensn v Colts (Adelaide)

1933-34 (4)
7/55   Kensn v West Torrs (Kensington)
6/87   Kensn v Sturt (Unley)
6/36   Kensn v Colts (Kensington)
9/49   Kensn v Glenelg (Kensington)
         (the other man was run out)

1934-35 (4)
8/37   Kensn v Sturt (Kensington)
6/53   kensn v East Torrs (Kensington)
7/64   Kensn v Prospect (Kensington)
6/42   Kensn v Sturt (Unley)

1935-36 (1)
8/51   Kensn v Colts (Adelaide)

1936-37 (2)
6/86   Kensn v Port Adel (Alberton)
5/69   Kensn v Adelaide (Kensington)

1937-38 (6)

6/105	Kensn v Adelaide (Kensington)
6/84	Kensn v West Torrs (Kensington)
8/62	Kensn v Glenelg (Kensington)
8/66	Kensn v East Torrs (Norwood)
5/91	Kensn v Glenelg (Glenelg)
8/59	Kensn v Colts (Unley)

1938-39 (1)

6/68	Kensn v Port Adel (Kensington)

1939-40 (2)

5/49	Colts v Glenelg (Glenelg)
5/25	Colts v University (University)

Hat-trick

Adelaide v Sturt (Unley) 1924-25 (on debut)

1940-41 (3)

5/50	Kensn v Port Adel (Alberton)
7/46}	
5/41}	Kensn v Port Adel (Kensington)

1941-42 (2)

7/45}	
5/47}	Kensn v Prospect (Prospect)

1943-44 (7)

6/37	Kensn v West Torrs (Adel No 2)
9/65	Kensn v University (Adelaide)
7/50	Kensn v ET-Glen (Norwood)
5/41	Kensn v Adelaide (Norwood)
6/60	Kensn v West Torrs (Adelaide No 2)
5/31	Kensn v University (Norwood)
9/55	Kensn v ET-Glen (Norwood)

1944-45 (6)

6/33	Kensn v University (University)
6/89	Kensn v Sturt (Unley)
5/37	Kensn v West Torrs (Thebarton)
5/46	Kensn v Prospect (Adelaide)
7/43	Kensn v ET-Glen (Glenelg)
8/86	Kensn v University (University)

INDEX